BAR INTERNATIONAL SERIES 3077 (I) | 2022

Sylloge of *Defixiones* from the Roman West

A comprehensive collection of curse tablets from the fourth century BCE to the fifth century CE

Volume I

CELIA SÁNCHEZ NATALÍAS

BAR
PUBLISHING

Published in 2022 by
BAR Publishing, Oxford

BAR International Series 3077 (I)

Sylloge of Defixiones from the Roman West, Volume I

ISBN 978 1 4073 5931 1 Volume I (paperback)
ISBN 978 1 4073 5932 8 Volume II (paperback)
ISBN 978 1 4073 1532 4 (Set of both volumes) paperback
ISBN 978 1 4073 5382 1 (Set of both volumes) e-format

DOI https://doi.org/10.30861/9781407315324

A catalogue record for this book is available from the British Library.

COVER IMAGE *Numen from SD 118 (drawing: Celia Sánchez Natalías).*

BAR
PUBLISHING

BAR titles are available from:

BAR Publishing
122 Banbury Rd, Oxford, OX2 7BP, UK
EMAIL info@barpublishing.com
PHONE +44 (0)1865 310431
FAX +44 (0)1865 316916
www.barpublishing.com

Of Related Interest

Nuove epigrafi greche da Halaesa Archonidea
Dati inediti sulle Tabulae Halaesinae e su una città della Sicilia tardo-ellenistica
Emiliano Arena

Oxford, BAR Publishing, 2020   BAR International Series **3017**

Blame it on the Gender
Identities and transgressions in Antiquity
Edited by Maria Cristina de la Escosura Balbás, Elena Duce Pastor, Patricia González Gutiérrez, María del Mar Rodríguez Alcocer and David Serrano Lozano

Oxford, BAR Publishing, 2020   BAR International Series **3005**

Paleoetnología de la Hispania Céltica, Tomo I y Tomo II
Etnoarqueología, etnohistoria y folklore
Pedro R. Moya-Maleno

Oxford, BAR Publishing, 2020   BAR International Series **2996**

Le c.d. gammadiae nelle catacombe cristiane di Roma
Censimento, confronti ed ipotesi interpretative
Cristina Cumbo

Oxford, BAR Publishing, 2019   BAR International Series **2947**

Roles for Men and Women in Roman Epigraphic Culture and Beyond
Gender, social identity and cultural practice in private Latin inscriptions and the literary record
Peter Keegan

Oxford, BAR Publishing, 2014   BAR International Series **2626**

The Archaeology of Gender, Love and Sexuality in Pompeii
Lourdes Conde Feitosa

Oxford, BAR Publishing, 2013   BAR International Series **2533**

Lifting the Veil: a New Study of the Sheela-Na-Gigs of Britain and Ireland
Theresa C. Oakley

Oxford, BAR Publishing, 2009   BAR British Series **495**

For more information, or to purchase these titles, please visit **www.barpublishing.com**

A Bonfilio, mi padre,
a quien recuerdo cada día.

To Bonfilio, my father,
whom I miss every day.

1949–2020

Va, pensiero, sull'ali dorate;
va, ti posa sui clivi, sui colli,
ove olezzano tepide e molli
l'aure dolci del suolo natal!
(Nabucco, G. Verdi.)

Λ . I . Ɇ . Ç . Ļ

SOCIETAS INTERNATIONALIS EPIGRAPHIAE GRAECAE ET LATINAE

GRUPO HIBERUS
GOBIERNO DE ARAGÓN

I would like to thank the Ministerio Español de Ciencia, Innovación y Universidades for funding the research project (with reference number RTI2018-098339-J-I00) that allowed me to finish this volume.

Acknowledgements

I have been lucky to count on the contribution of many people, who have greatly helped me finish these volumes. The first incarnation came to light in June 2013 as a PhD dissertation, after six years filled with blood, sweat and tears. During this time, my research was carried out under the umbrella of the Grupo Hiberus, and more specifically, as part of three research projects on Ancient Magic led by Francisco Marco Simón (University of Zaragoza). I am extremely grateful to him and to Attilio Mastrocinque (University of Verona) for supervising my research as well as their outstanding dedication and patience. In addition, I am also thankful to many other colleagues and friends who have helped me improve the following pages over these years. Among them, special thanks are owed to Francisco Beltrán Lloris, Gabriella Bevilacqua, Alfredo Buonopane, Richard Gordon, Chris Faraone, Miguel Ángel Rodríguez Horrillo and Roger Tomlin.

I also owe my deep gratitude to all those who have been cheering and helping me along at the different institutions where I have been lucky enough to work or research (the Universities of Zaragoza, Verona, Oxford, Padua, Basque Country, Complutense of Madrid, Heidelberg, Yale and Chicago, together with the Escuela Española de Historia y Arqueología at Rome, the Hardt Fondation and The Center for Epigraphical and Palaeographical Studies at The Ohio State University). Sincere thanks also go out to all the curators and personnel of the museums and laboratories that I have visited to carry out the (not-so-morbid) 'autopsies' of many curse tablets (located in Madrid, Ampurias, Barcelona, Tarragona, Sagunto, Cuenca, Cordoba, Seville, Cadiz, Nantes, Verona, Este, Cremona, Florence, Bologna, Reggio Emilia, Perugia, Rome, Naples, Pompeii, Budapest, Bad Kreuznach, Worms, Mainz, London and Bath).

I am very thankful to my friends who helped with the completion of this volume through their precious time and company. Last, but not least, I am extremely grateful to my family for their unconditional love and support and to my ancestors for providing me with possibilities that they could never have dreamt of. As I have talked about with my deeply missed father, I feel very lucky for having had the opportunity of benefiting from lifelong learning, especially when one of my great grandparents, Amado, was illiterate his whole life, and one of my grandfathers, Bonfilio, only learned to write and read in prison (1939 was not the best year for democrats and leftists here in Hispania). It is thanks to their effort and hard work that I have had the chance to continue with my studies, without 'liquidizing' my brain, as Anuncia, one of my grandmothers, had feared.

In addition, not only I, but also the reader, should be extremely grateful to my husband Ben A. Jerue (Universidad San Jorge), who translated this volume from Spanish to English, posed insightful questions and left pesky comments, which definitely improved this book, all of which he did without asking me for a divorce. Together with Ben, the love of my life, I owe gratitude to Toil & Trouble for giving me the best deadline ever to finish this project.

Zaragoza, 18 November 2020*

---

* This book was last proofread in April 2022, after many virtual trips back and forth between Zaragoza and Oxford. Any mistake remains my responsibility (and should be blamed on my tired eyes). I thank Ruth Fisher and Lisa Eaton from BAR Publisher and eVC-Tech team for all their efforts and patience to make this happen.

Contents

VOLUME I

VOLUME II

List of Figures

List of Tables

I. Prolegomena

1

A Brief History of Previous Scholarship[*]

Despite the fact that traditional historiography long spurned the study of 'aggressive magic' and branded it as an aspect of Graeco-Roman culture that was unworthy of serious study, *defixiones* have nevertheless attracted a good deal of scholarly attention when compared to other facets of ancient magic. While some scholars have identified the origin of the modern study of *defixiones* with the publication of isolated Greek tablets that appeared in 1796 and 1813,[1] we can look even further back to 1737, when the priest and scholar A.F. Gori published the second volume of his *Museum Etruscum exhibens insignia veterum Etruscorum Monumenta*, in which he included an Etruscan *defixio* from Volterra.[2] During the nineteenth century and especially from 1840 onwards, the discovery of new tablets precipitated the publication of a large number of isolated studies.[3] It was not until later, and in conjunction with a series of groundbreaking archaeological discoveries in Cnidus and Cyprus, that these artefacts increasingly came to capture the scholarly imagination. Nevertheless, the publications of these corpora by C.T. Newton and L. Macdonald respectively,[4] only gave a taste of what was to come.

The systematic investigation of ancient cursing practices, however, did not reach maturity until the very end of the nineteenth century and beginning of the twentieth, when three monumental corpora of *defixiones* edited by R. Wünsch and A. Audollent appeared. In the first, Wünsch studied and edited 220 curse tablets from Attica, which were published in 1897 as part of *Inscriptiones Graecae* [III, 3], where the author also provided the briefest of treatments of the other Greek and Latin curses that were known at that time.[5]

Just one year later, Wünsch published a collection of the 48 so-called 'Sethian' *defixiones* from Rome, discovered in a columbarium near Porta San Sebastiano, which are largely written in Greek (cf. Wünsch 1898). Six years later, in 1904, Audollent published the third magisterial collection of curses, his *Defixionum tabellae quotquot innotuerunt tam in graecis Orientis quam in totius Occidentis partibus praeter atticas in 'Corpore Inscriptionum Atticarum' editas* (*DT* for short), in which he collected and edited 305 *defixiones*, the majority of which were written in Greek and Latin, though he included curses in Oscan, Etruscan, Iberian and Phoenician.

Thus, with the appearance of Wünsch's and especially Audollent's volumes, the study of *defixiones* was forever transformed from being an occasional curiosity to an established and coherent corpus of inscriptions. This work proved to be the foundation for twentieth-century scholarship, which included the publication of numerous new finds as well as various studies that dealt with particular aspects of the *defixiones*. Among the latter are the linguistically focused work of M. Jeanneret[6] and that of M. Besnier,[7] who sought to improve the published readings of the *defixiones* that had been edited between 1904 and 1920.

In the 1960s, two compilations were published that deserve special attention: the first, published by E. García Ruiz in 1967, is largely focused on linguistic questions and examines 100 curses;[8] in the second, H. Solin published an edition of a new *defixio* from Ostia (cf. **53**) with an appendix containing a list of 38 tablets published between 1920 and 1968.[9]

The number of publications dealing with individual *defixiones* continued to grow, thus leading to the need for a more systematic approach to the study of curse tablets. In an attempt to address the growing problem, Solin and D.R. Jordan announced in print their intention to compile a new authoritative corpus of *defixiones*. Nevertheless, this work never came to fruition,[10] perhaps because of the

---

[*] In the following pages, bold numbers refer to curse tablet entries. For ancient sources, abbreviations follow A. Spawforth and S. Hornblower (eds), *Oxford Classical Dictionary*[4] (Oxford 2012).
[1] Preisendanz (1930: 119–20) has argued that the first study of *defixiones* should be placed in 1796 when Ignarra published a discussion of a tablet found in Italy. Jordan (1990: 440), however, has rejected the identification of this item as a curse and hence dated the beginning of modern research on the topic to 1813, when Åkerblad published a Greek *defixio* discovered in a grave near Athens. Either way, and as the following discussion shows, the systematic study of the phenomenon did not begin until later.
[2] Gori 1737: 404. Cf. **87**.
[3] The original publication of the following tablets belongs to this period: **1–4, 56, 61, 69–70, 85, 92–93, 150–55, 461, 520**, etc.
[4] The 14 tablets from Cnidus, all written in Greek, were still folded or rolled when found in the temenos of the sanctuary of Demeter. Several of them were written by women who had been robbed. For a discussion, see Newton 1863: 382f.; 719–45; Gager 1992: no. 89; Faraone 2011. The Cyprian *defixiones* were found in what appears to have been a common grave. The published texts from Cyprus (only 22 of 260!) mostly belong to the group of juridical *defixiones*. In these texts, Greek and Oriental deities are invoked in order to silence those who planned to testify against the *defigens* in court; for a discussion, see Macdonald 1891; Gager 1992: nos 45–46; Wilburn 2013: 169–218.
[5] Cf. Wünsch 1897. Currently, J. Curbera is re-editing this corpus; for a preliminary notice, see Curbera 2012.

[6] See Jeanneret 1916 and 1917. In both articles, he carried out a comparative study of 125 curse tablets (specifically, the 103 Latin *defixiones* collected by Audollent in his corpus as well as another 22 items that were mostly published between 1904 and 1917).
[7] See Besnier 1920, where the author compiled the Latin *defixiones* that Audollent had not included in *DT* (specifically those published by Olivieri in 1899) as well as all curses published between 1904 and 1920. This tallied up to a total of 61 additional texts. Some of these tablets were identified as *defixiones*, though subsequent work has shown that in fact they were not (e.g., the lead labels *CIL* XI, 6722, no. 1, 3–12, 14 and 17, which I examined in the year 2010 at the Museo Archeologico Nazionale dell'Umbria, concluding that they were not curse tablets).
[8] Cf. García Ruiz 1967.
[9] See Solin 1968: 23–31, where 44 Latin *defixiones*, three Greek curse tablets (nos. 40 and 44–45) and two *phylaktéria* (nos 3 and 43) are collected and arranged by provenance.
[10] See the note published by Susini 1973: 139.

sheer number of new discoveries during the last third of the twentieth century. In 1979, just six years after these scholars announced their ambitious project, two large and extremely important caches of *defixiones* were discovered in the British sanctuaries of Sulis Minerva (Aquae Sulis/Bath) and Mercury (Uley), where 130 and 140 curses were found, respectively. These two finds alone drastically increased the project that Solin and Jordan had intended to undertake. Fortunately, R.S.O. Tomlin has dedicated years to the study and publication of these large and important collections.[11] Only four years after Tomlin's masterful edition of the curses from Aquae Sulis/Bath, J.G. Gager edited a book containing an interesting selection of mostly Greek curses, which brought the topic to a wider audience.[12]

But happily this was not the end, since then extraordinary discoveries continued: in 1999, excavators unearthed two more large caches of *defixiones* at both the sanctuary of Isis and Magna Mater (Mogontiacum/Mainz) and the fountain of Anna Perenna (Rome), both of which have been edited by J. Blänsdorf.[13] Though smaller than the British collections, these two discoveries have proven exceedingly important.

These large discoveries have undoubtedly revolutionized and reinvigorated the study of *defixiones*, which have been the object of various studies and research projects since 2000. Notable scholarship includes the work of J. Tremel, who has studied agonistic curses, E. Eidinow, who has focused on Attic *defixiones* from a psychological perspective, and S. Sichet, who has collected the curses from North Africa and studied them in conjunction with the particular magical practices of their social and geographical context.[14]

B. Mees has analysed (though not always exercising an appropriate level of caution) the Celtic and Gaulish curses from Britain and Gaul, while F. Murano's masterful study has greatly improved our understanding of the Oscan curses.[15] In a study of nearly 400 tablets, A. Kropp has provided a more global perspective on ancient cursing practices, paying attention to the language employed in Latin *defixiones*, with a special interest in pragmatics.[16] In a different vein, G. Németh has published 86 sketches that Audollent made while editing the North African tablets for *DT*.[17] These sketches, which are housed in the regional archive of Puy-de-Dôme, had previously been unpublished and unedited. Accordingly, Németh's work has revealed a wealth of new details concerning the layout and iconography of these curses. Most recently, A. Alvar has published a study of the magical practices employed by slaves in the Roman world, while D. Urbanová has recently written a monograph on Latin *defixiones*, which seeks to distinguish the so-called 'prayers for justice' in a compilation of 309 curse tablets.[18]

This brings us to the present sylloge, which follows in Audollent's footsteps and collects 535 *defixiones* written in Latin, Oscan, Etruscan, Gaulish and Celtic from the Roman West. Traditionally, much of the scholarly effort has been dedicated to the study of the formulae and linguistics of the tablets. Nevertheless, in the present volume, these inscriptions are studied with a particular emphasis placed on the *defixiones*' archaeological and cultural contexts. Far from being monolithic, the practice of writing curse tablets changed and evolved over a millennium in the area that would become the Roman West. Recognizing this fluidity, this book aims to be a trustworthy source for scholars interested in the topic, offering not only an overview of the phenomenon but also an updated and reliable collection of texts.[19] With this purpose in mind, and unlike the majority of scholars working on *defixiones* after Audollent, I have directly examined the texts whenever possible while compiling this sylloge. Luckily, most curse tablets that were discovered long ago remain legible,[20] and in many cases an autopsy (i.e., an in-person examination) has yielded new results that can improve our readings and understandings of the corpus.[21] To conclude, the ambition of this sylloge is not to be just another compilation of texts, but rather a tool that clearly presents the evidence and is capable of generating further interest in this fascinating topic.

---

[11] For Bath, see Tomlin's masterful edition (1988a). Of the 140 tablets from Uley, which are generally in worse condition, see Tomlin's brief publication (1993a) as well as the individual editions of various curses which are annually published in the journal *Britannia* (for references, cf. **355–73**). Currently, Tomlin is preparing a monograph dedicated to the curses from Uley.

[12] Cf. Gager 1992. The curse tablets, which are translated into English (no original Greek or Latin), are organized by content and accompanied by a brief commentary with relevant bibliography. The only 'downside' of the volume is that the editor focuses disproportionately on Greek texts, giving short shrift to Latin curses.

[13] For the Mainz collection, see the magisterial edition of Blänsdorf 2012a. For the fountain of Anna Perenna (in general), see Piranomonte 2002 and 2015. Several of the curses have already been published by Blänsdorf in various publications (for references, cf. **19–47**). The whole collection is the subject of a forthcoming monograph.

[14] Tremel 2004 provides a collection of 100 tablets, which were written in both Greek and Latin and were mostly directed against charioteers, gladiators and *venatores*); Eidinow 2007 examines a corpus of 170 Greek curse tablets and compares them with the oracular questions and responses from the Dodona oracle; Sichet 2000: 865–939 collects 120 tablets written in Greek and Latin from North Africa.

[15] Mees 2009 chapters 1–6 focuses on the Gaulish and Celtic inscriptions (both curses and other types of inscriptions); for the Oscan curse tablets, see Murano 2013.

[16] See Kropp 2008. Her catalogue lists 578 tablets, 391 of which are subject to linguistic analysis.

[17] See Németh 2013, which includes neither a reading nor transcription of the texts.

[18] See Alvar 2017 and Urbanová 2018 (which is an English translation of the original in Czech, published in 2014).

[19] Although the sylloge does not include curses published after summer 2018, new scholarly discussions of previously published texts have been included in the commentary and bibliography. For a fuller explanation of the inclusion criteria for the sylloge, see the Note to reader under section II.

[20] *Contra* Urbanová 2018: 13.

[21] For the tablets that I have examined personally, not only have many readings of some texts been improved, but autopsy has also provided new important details about the curse's layout or iconography. Furthermore, this meticulous process has allowed me to discover that certain artefacts that have previously been classified as *defixiones* have actually been misidentified. Just to mention some examples, in addition to the lead tags included in Besnier 1920: nos 40–50 and 52 (cf. note 7), see also another label currently housed in Florence. The text, considered by Besnier 1920: no. 52, Kropp 2008: dfx 1.1.1/2 and Urbanová 2018: no. 2 as a *defixio*, is actually a label of an *officina plumbaria*, whose text reads: *M(arci) Ponti Secundi oficina plum(baria)* (cf. Paolucci 1994: 106–07, *contra* Gordon 2019b: 423).

2

A Definition

According to Philoxenus, the Latin lexeme *defixio*, derived from the verb *defigere,* is equivalent to the Greek κατάδεσμος.[22] Both of these terms refer to a popular practice in Antiquity, namely, cursing. Documented in the epigraphic and literary records,[23] these two terms allude to a magico-religious practice in which an unfortunate individual inescapably became the victim of a spell (see Figure 2.1).

In 1985, D.R. Jordan provided the most widely accepted definition of a *defixio*: '*Defixiones*, more commonly known as curse tablets, are inscribed pieces of lead, usually in the form of small, thin sheets, intended to influence, by supernatural means, the actions or welfare of persons or animals against their will.'[24] Jordan's definition can be further refined to stress that the true essence of a *defixio* is found neither in the material used[25] nor in the inscribed message, but rather in its harmful nature and desire to manipulate. Every curse is born from rancour, envy, anger, fear, desire, love or desperation and seeks to accomplish what a *defigens* (the person who writes or commissions a curse tablet) cannot do through the available means, due to a lack of knowledge, power or economic/legal resources.[26] A curse, then, is a strategy for obtaining 'individual justice', which was illegal in Rome and feared throughout ancient societies. Indeed, Pliny captures the widespread fear of being cursed when pointing out that *defigi quidem diris precationibus nemo non metuit,* that is 'there is no one who is not afraid of being enchanted with malevolent prayers'.[27]

Within epigraphical discourse and debate, *defixiones* have traditionally been considered a subset of 'private' epigraphy. This category is meant to describe inscriptions that were written by private individuals with an ephemeral purpose in mind and were destined for a small audience (e.g., wax tablets, graffiti or texts on *instrumentum domesticum*). Accordingly, the survival of such texts is the happy result of their being inscribed on non-perishable materials that happened to be preserved almost by accident.[28] There are numerous factors that have led to *defixiones* being categorized as a sort of 'private' epigraphy. First off, these texts are certainly hard to classify as 'public', since cursing was an illegal act from at least the time of the *XII Tables* (VIII, 1a, 1c and 4, cf. section I.9.2 below). As a result, these texts were rather secretive as can be seen in several of their common features: not only were the texts themselves at times designed to be inscrutable through the use of coding devices, but they were also deposited in hidden places away from public view that were widely believed to help in their activation (e.g., graves, wells or sanctuaries). In addition, the intended 'readers' of these texts were certainly not a wide human audience, but rather were the deities invoked.

Up to this point, *defixiones* appear to conform to the category of 'private' epigraphy. That said, we ought to nuance this view and consider one final and fundamental aspect of curse tablets, that is, their 'expiration' date. While private texts are characterized by having ephemeral messages, we can say that the opposite is the case with the messages contained in *defixiones*. As is the case with public epigraphy, curse tablets were intended to last in time and have an enduring impact: during the process of manufacture, which included a performative ritual, the practitioners would 'activate' the spells contained in the tablet. Once activated, these texts were believed to have a nearly inexhaustible agency and to establish a lasting bond between spell and victim that, on certain occasions, could

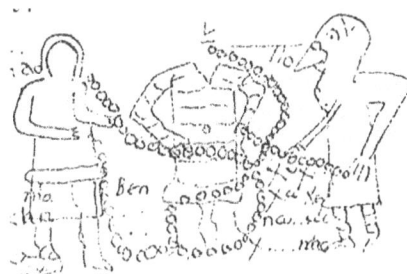

Figure 2.1. Two *daemones* shackling a charioteer (From *SV 29*).

---

[22] Philoxenus, *Glosas,* Lat II, 40.

[23] Among the literary sources, we find Pl. (*Resp.,* 364b; cf. n. 27) as well as some passages from the *PGM*, such as IV, 336 (παρακατατίθεμαι ὑμῖν τοῦτον τὸν κατάδεσμον, θεοῖς χθονίοις...: 'I entrust this binding spell to you, chthonic gods...' [translation by E.N. O'Neil, *apud* Betz 1992²]). *Defixio* in the ablative (*cum defictcsione*) has been recently attested in a curse tablet against thieves from Abusina/Eining (Raetia) dated to the first century CE (see Blänsdorf 2019, no. 1). For just a few of the examples of the verb *defigere* in the tablets, see **105** (l. 8: *defigo illos quo pereant*), **345** (l. 4: *Tacita deficta*), **338** (A, l. 1ff: *T(itus) Egnatius Tyran(n)us defic<t>us est*), etc.

[24] Jordan 1985a: 151. For a general definition of curse tablet, see also Bailliot 2010: 71f.; Martin 2010: 9–11; Edmonds 2019: 53–64; Eidinow 2019: 351f.; Watson 2019: 57–63.

[25] As the author himself pointed out in 2001: 6.

[26] In this volume, the terms *defigens*, principal, practitioner, author, *scriptor* ('writer') are used interchangeably to refer to the person who was writing the curse tablet.

[27] Pliny, *HN* XXVIII, 19 (translated by Bailliot 2019: 190, n. 79). As is well known, this fear affected not only the lower classes but also elites. The widespread nature of this fear is affirmed through examples of 'famous victims' of aggressive magic, such as Germanicus (Tac., *Ann.* II, 69 and Dio Cassius LVII, 18; see section I.6.5 and n. 323–24), the orator Libanius (Libanius, *Orat.* I, 249; cf. section I.6.5 and n. 325), or the doctor Theodorus of Cyprus (see Sophronius, *Narratio*, LV; see section I.6.5 and n. 327). To these, we must add the victims of φαρμακεία or *venenum* that are documented in a series of inscriptions collected by Graf (2007).

[28] Here I follow the definition of Beltrán Lloris 2014a: 89.

not be broken until a conflict was settled to the *defigens*' satisfaction.[29] The use of a particular materials and deposit context that were isolated or difficult to access ought to be analysed in light of a *defixio*'s lasting nature: such media and locations were chosen to prevent a spell from being deactivated.[30] Given these considerations about the nature and purpose of curse tablets, the traditional binary distinction between public and private epigraphy does not properly capture the social and magical-religious characteristics of *defixiones*.

Traditionally, the spread of *defixiones* has been closely associated with the processes of territorial expansion and 'Romanization'.[31] This view of a practice simply spreading and being adopted by new populations, however, can be misleading: curse tablets, which were in use for more than a millennium in a wide geographical area, should be seen as a 'living' magical-religious technology, which developed and evolved alongside many other aspects of ancient life. In this regard, we should heed to words of Owen Davies, who has claimed, 'artefacts have life histories that need to be considered and contextualized in order to understand better their meaning, and the societies that employed them, at any point in time.'[32] While Davies wrote these words to describe domestic magical practices in modernity, his description is completely suitable for understanding the different ways that curses were used in different ancient contexts. Indeed, *defixiones* were adopted and adapted by different provincial societies, whose unique characteristics are reflected in their language,[33] onomastics,[34] the deities invoked,[35] their manipulation[36] and depositional contexts.[37] All of this precludes us from understanding the use of *defixiones* as a monolithic practice that was passively taken up by new groups and populations. In fact, it is possible to distinguish extraordinarily rich and meaningful regional variations across the Roman West, not to mention the observable changes in the same geographical region over time.

Another fundamental question is who exactly wrote these texts? While a passage from Plato tantalizingly refers to 'beggar-priests and prophets' and suggests that there were magical professionals already in classical Athens,[38] in the

Roman West there is no evidence for such professionals writing curses until the second or third century CE in North Africa[39] and Late Antiquity in Italy and other provinces.[40] Until these later dates, *defixiones* (with rare exceptions) were written by aggrieved individuals with different levels of magical-religious *savoir faire*, thus attesting to what R. Gordon has defined as a type of 'vernacular' practice.[41] The archaeological record has provided good evidence of *defigentes* with different levels of knowledge and skills: one the one hand, some deposited pseudo-inscriptions (or even uninscribed texts) in specific contexts (thus demonstrating knowledge of the basic mechanics of how curse tablets worked),[42] while, on the other hand, archaeologists have uncovered quite elaborate (and at times almost literary) texts. On the whole, the palaeographical, linguistic and textual analysis of the vast majority of curse tablets demonstrates that writers not only knew the ABCs of cursing but also were sufficiently literate to write curses on their own behalf.[43] Obviously, in all of these cases (whether tablets were inscribed or not), we cannot forget that there was an important oral component of cursing as well as a ritual action. In most cases, these aspects have been lost to us, but other forms of evidence, such as the *PGM*, remind us of their centrality in cursing rituals.

With the exception of North Africa, where we can already detect the presence of magical professionals in the Imperial Age, in the rest of the Roman West there is no generalized evidence for their presence until Late Antiquity. In this period we can detect a new and updated version of this magical technology that originated in Graeco-Egyptian magical practices. At this point, there were authentic magical professionals who specialized in techniques (e.g., the use of *charaktêres*, iconography or *voces magicae*). In the same period, there is still evidence for individuals writing their own curses, though to a lesser extent than before.

---

[29] On this point, see section I.4.1. For the 'agency' of these texts, see Sánchez Natalías 2018: 10.

[30] The act of deposition was accompanied by the recitation of certain formulae that were intended to help preserve the curse, as we learn, for instance, from *PGM* VII, 453ff. On this, see section I.4.1, n. 98.

[31] On this controversial concept, see Beltrán Lloris 2017.

[32] Davies 2015: 394.

[33] Cf. section I.4.2.1.2.

[34] For just several examples, see those listed in section I.9.3, n. 576.

[35] Cf. section I.8.

[36] Specifically, see section I.5.

[37] See section I.6.

[38] On this point, Pl. (*Resp.*, 364b) provides the best known passage: Ἀγύρται δὲ καὶ μάντεις ἐπὶ πλουσίων θύρας ἰόντες πείθουσιν ὡς ἔστι παρὰ σφίσι δύναμις ἐκ θεῶν ποριζομένη θυσίαις τε καὶ ἐπῳδαῖς, εἴτε τι ἀδίκημά του γέγονεν αὐτοῦ ἢ προγόνων, ἀκεῖσθαι μεθ' ἡδονῶν τε καὶ ἑορτῶν, ἐάν τέ τινα ἐχθρὸν πημῆναι ἐθέλῃ, μετὰ σμικρῶν δαπανῶν ὁμοίως δίκαιον ἀδίκῳ βλάψει ἐπαγωγαῖς τισιν καὶ καταδέσμοις, τοὺς θεούς, ὥς φασιν, πείθοντές σφισιν ὑπηρετεῖν: 'Beggar-priests [*agurtaí*] and prophets [*manteis*] go to the doors of the rich and persuade them that they have the power, acquired from the gods by sacrifices [*thusiais*] and

incantations [*epôidais*], to cure with pleasures and festivals any wrong done by the man himself or his ancestors, and that they will harm an enemy, a just man or an unjust man alike, for a small fee, if a man wishes it, since they persuade the gods, as they say, to serve them, by certain charms [*epagôgais*] and bindings [*katadesmois*]' (tranlsated by Ogden 2002: no. 14).

[39] The existence of magical professional is supported by series of tablets, whose palaeography, iconography and/or use of *charaktêres* and *voces magicae* are identical. For some good examples, see *DT* 276–85 from Hadrumetum (Németh 2011 has identified a possible *officina magica*), *DT* 286–91 (all of which invoke the demon *Baitmo Arbitto*; cf. Gordon 2005), etc.

[40] See the *defixiones* and containers discovered in the fountain of Anna Perenna (cf. **19–47** and Faraone 2005).

[41] See Gordon 2019b. The model that he puts forth for 'vernacular' and professionally written curse tablets in Italy could easily be applied to the rest of the Roman West. On this differentiation between 'vernacular' and 'professional' texts, see also Faraone and Gordon 2019: 320.

[42] For instance, see the pseudo-inscriptions from Bath (cf. **317–21**) and the uninscribed caches from Roccagloriosa (cf. **76**), Rom (cf. **159**) or Uley (cf. **355**), which were found in the same context as inscribed curses.

[43] It is important to note that within the corpus from the sanctuary in Bath (where 120 curses have been discovered), only two tablets appear to have been written by the same author (see **300–01**), which attests to the existence of 119 known *scriptores* at the sanctuary.

3

Media[44]

3.1. Introduction

In 1933, Audollent passed judgement on the relative importance of the text of *defixiones* and their material characteristics, claiming that '[c]ertes l'aspect de ces modestes documents importe beaucoup moins que leur contenu. Il n'est cependant, en plus d'un cas, nullement négligeable' (1933a: 31). In line with Audollent's appraisal, scholarship has traditionally paid relatively little attention to the study of *defixiones* from a material point of view that takes the curse's media into account: the most recent large-scale discussion of curse tablets (Urbanová 2018), for instance, dedicates a scant page to the materiality of these artefacts.[45] Despite this general trend, a volume edited by G. Bevilacqua (2010) has sought to analyse the relationship between writing, media and magic in Antiquity and to consider a wide range of objects including some curses, most of which come from a Greek context.[46] In a parallel vein, a major concern of the present volume is to draw more attention to the material features of this corpus of curse tablets.

To analyse the materiality of the *defixiones* from the Roman West, we must draw a fundamental distinction between two different types of material and media. The first contains the *defixiones* that were inscribed on objects intentionally created for the purpose of writing (specific media), whereas the second consists of objects inscribed on re-appropriated objects that had originally been manufactured for a different purpose (non-specific media). There are subdivisions within each of these groups based on the various materials used and whether they were perishable or non-perishable.

3.2. Specific Media

This category includes all objects whose sole *raison d'être* was to serve as the surface on which a text was to be written. Within this category, practitioners used a range of materials that can be classified as either perishable or non-perishable (see Table 3.1).

Unsurprisingly, though there are a few rare exceptions, we know about the use of perishable materials through the literary record. Specifically, the *Greek Magical Papyri* (*PGM*) provide recommendations for materials like papyrus, which was seen as especially apt for writing erotic spells.[47] The papyrus to be employed ought to be hieratic (that is, of the best quality)[48] and new (not reused).[49] In a spell directed against an enemy or a woman, for instance, the *PGM* recommend the use of χάρτην ἱερατικὸν ἢ μολυβοῦν πέταλον (V, 304–5), that is, giving papyrus and lead as equally valid choices. Interestingly, these two materials are found together in an unparalleled curse tablet from Carthage (see Figure 3.1). In this instance, a sheet of lead was inscribed with four lines of Latin text and folded in such a way that the text would be exposed. Preserved within the folded tablet, archaeologists found a papyrus fragment, which, unfortunately, was so deteriorated that it could not be studied.[50]

When it comes to the use of non-perishable materials, we can create further subdivisions: those made of stone and those made of metal. Although the first category is never mentioned in the literary record, at least five examples have been preserved archaeologically. Two of them, which come from Braga (**146–7**) and date to the fourth or fifth century CE, were written on slate plaques. While we do not know the circumstances that led to these curses being written, we must note that slate was a commonly used material in Visigothic epigraphy and began to be used in throughout Hispania in Late Antiquity (cf. Velázquez 2004). The other two examples of curses inscribed on stone (see Figure 3.2) come from Pompeii (**72**)[51] and Emerita Augusta/Merida (**120**), the first on a piece of slate, the second on a piece of marble. Each curse betrays careful craftsmanship as well as a carefully arranged layout, and

---

[44] 'Medium' (pl. 'media') is an imperfect English translation for the Spanish word 'soporte' (Italian 'supporto', French 'support', German 'Textträger'), which is used to refer to the surface on which a text was inscribed.

[45] See *DT*, pp. XLVII–XLIX; Cesano 1961²: 1561–62; Preisendanz 1933: 3–4; Gager 1992: 3–4; Graf 1995: 129–31; Ogden 1999: 10–13; Kropp 2008: 80–82; Bailliot 2010: 76–77, Martin 2010: 15–17; Urbanová 2018: 36.

[46] See especially Bevilacqua 2010: 21–82, which includes several Latin *defixiones*, such as **3** and the curse from Thysdrus/El Jem (cf. Foucher 2000). For curse tablets from the Roman West, see Sánchez Natalías 2011b (where there is an earlier Spanish version of this section) and 2018 (for an in-depth study on the materiality of curses and the metaphorical connection between spell and medium).

[47] Currently, the *PGM* are the only preserved magical handbooks from Antiquity. Consequently, and despite their late chronology, they are taken as a frequent reference point throughout these prolegomena (and the scholarship more broadly). There is no doubt that these books circulated throughout Egypt, and it is quite probable that similar compendiums also circulated throughout the Roman West, where Graeco-Egyptian magical practices were considered to be especially effective. In this regard, we should not overlook a well-known passage from Dio Cassius (LXXV, 13) in which the historian claims that after his journey to Egypt in 199–200 CE Septimius Severus collected and brought home the secret books found in Egyptian temples. According to Mastrocinque (2019), the magical papyri which we can study today are probably substitutes of the older original texts. This would explain the Late-Antique dating of most papyri from the collection.

[48] *PGM* XI c, 1: εἰς ἱερατικὸν βιβλίον.

[49] *PGM* IV, 78; *PGM* VII, 940, etc.: χάρτην καθαρόν.

[50] Jordan 1996: 122. According to the editor (*per litt.*) 'the papyrus, folded inside the lead, had become frayed over the years, and when I saw it I didn't dare to try to touch it. I don't know whether the papyrus was inscribed'.

[51] This piece, which is still *in situ*, forms part of funerary monument 23 OS in the Porta Nocera necropolis (Pompeii).

Table 3.1. Materials used to make specific media

Perishable Materials		Non-perishable Materials	
Literary record	**Archaeological record**	**Literary record**	**Archaeological record**
Papyrus			Marble: **4**, **120**
Papyrus and lead	Papyrus and lead: Carthage		Slate: **72**, **146–47**
		Tin	Tin: **212**, **304**, **318**, **331**
		Copper	Copper: **30**, **31**, **45**
		Lead	Lead: **252**, **320**, **268**, *ex multis*

Figure 3.1. Curse tablet made of lead and papyrus (From Thysdrus/El Jem. Jordan 1996: 122).

Figure 3.2. Curse tablet on stone (From Emerita Augusta/ Merida [cf. 120]. Archivo Fotográfico MNAR, A. Osorio Calvo).

they belong to what Audollent called *defixiones* against slanderers and thieves. In both cases, the *defigens* opted for a material commonly used in monumental epigraphy. The choice of materials does not seem to have been influenced so much by ideas about the lasting nature of stone,[52] but rather by the unusual fact that these *defixiones* were meant to be displayed publicly (this is undeniable in the case of the Pompeiian curse).[53] Finally, a fifth example of a curse written on stone comes from Rome (cf. **4**). The text was inscribed on the back of the funerary altar of the child Junia Procula for two main reasons: first, in order not to be seen (although the back side was the only blank space available); second and more importantly, in order to invoke the deceased child to avenge the author of the curse. In addition, its composition in metre may suggest that the author was trying to hide the true nature of the inscription. Therefore, and by contrast with the inscriptions from Pompeii and Emerita Augusta/Merida, this text seems to have been written on the altar for practical reasons. In short, the use of stone is extremely uncommon and when it is used the choice of material can be explained in terms of practical considerations or as influenced by general trends in the current writing practices.

Turning to metal, the prominence of lead is undeniable. That said, there are also examples, attested both in the literary and archaeological records, of the use of tin and copper as the media for a curse. The *PGM*, for instance, recommend the use of tin sheets for *defixiones* intended to destroy chariots,[54] to be used as erotic curses[55] and even those meant to restrain a victim.[56] Metallurgic analysis of some curses from the sanctuary of Sulis Minerva in Aquae Sulis/Bath (Britannia) has shown that pure tin was

[52] Giorcelli Bersani 2004: 16 maintains, 'Si scrive perché lo scritto valga da quel momento in poi, in certi casi si scrive per l'eternità. L'incisione su un supporto duro e durevole come la pietra o il marmo, virtualmente eterno, fissava ancor di più il messaggio nella solidità della materia'. Likewise, Susini 1989: 278 affirms 'La scrittura su materiale durevole (...) quindi su superficie concettualmente eterne, comporta alcuni effetti sul pubblico (...): 1. la persuasione dell'importanza della scrittura (...); 2. di conseguenza, il senso di sicurezza che promana dal *monimentum* e dalla sua scrittura, proprio perché concettualmente imperituri...' For the idea that stone is eternal, also see Susini 1998: 105 and 108.
[53] Additionally, perhaps we should add an item from Remeseiros, which was inscribed on a piece of granite that has proven difficult to read and interpret (see the note in the introduction to Hispania in section II.2).

[54] *PGM* IV, 2212: ἐπὶ πλακὶ κασσιτερίνῃ.
[55] *PGM* VII, 459: ἐπὶ λάμνας κασσιτερίνης.
[56] *PGM* VII, 417: εἰς πέταλων κασσιτέρινον.

used in the creation of two curses (cf. **212** and **331**) and also formed more than 90 per cent of the alloys used to make another six tablets.[57] Unlike the instances from the *PGM*, the evidence does not suggest that the choice of tin was intentional in these British cases. As Tomlin has suggested (1988a: 82), tin and lead were both available and commonly used to produce other objects.

When it comes to copper, Saint Jerome mentioned the use of this metal (*aeris Cyprii lamina*) in a somewhat controversial passage dealing with an erotic spell.[58] Though the veracity of Jerome's account can certainly be called into question, it is beyond doubt that copper was at times used in the production of curse tablets, as has been confirmed by the discovery of three curses from the fountain of Anna Perenna in Rome (cf. **30**, **31** and **45**), which were both deposited inside a lamp, where they were inserted in the place where you would normally expect to find a wick. It is entirely within the realm of possibility that the practitioner chose this metal intentionally, since its colour could be seen as a reference to the lamp's flame.[59]

Leaving aside tin and copper, let's turn to lead, which was so commonly used in the production of curses that it came to be used as a metonymy for a curse tablet. As is well known, lead was one of the most commonly used materials for writing, since it was inexpensive, readily available and easy to inscribe. All these factors were instrumental in establishing lead as one of the main media for writing in Antiquity.[60] As F. Graf has argued,[61] once this metal was employed in the realm of magic, it was endowed with ritual significance and its properties were thought to guarantee its efficacy: associated with the malign star Saturn, lead was thought to bring misfortune and death (cf. Cesano 1961[2]: 1561). Like a corpse, this metal was considered cold and heavy.[62] According to Aristotle (Pliny

HN XI, 114, 275), saying that someone had a leaden hue was a not-so-ambiguous way of insinuating that death was quickly approaching.

Taking this series of connotations in account as well as the principle of persuasive analogy,[63] the *PGM* recommend that *defixiones* be made from lead taken from a pipe used for cold water[64] or one taken from a *frigidarium*[65] in order to symbolically 'freeze' a victim. In a similar vein, in a spell meant to restrain, it is specified that the lead has to be hammered while cold.[66] Another type of comparison based on the principle of persuasive analogy is laid out in two spells for subjugating victims, where the use of lead from a yoke is recommended,[67] since just as the yoke subjugates oxen, so too will the tablet subdue the *defigens*' enemies.

Metallurgic analyses have provided important data about the provenance and purity of lead used for cursing. L. Pintozzi's isotopic analysis of 11 tablets discovered in the circus of Carthage has shown that the metal used came from distant mines located in places like the Ural Mountains, Cyprus and the Iberian Peninsula.[68] At the present date, the only published study on the purity of lead used is abovementioned analysis of 75 of the 130 tablets from the sanctuary of Sulis Minerva in Bath.[69] In the case of these British curses, only 15 of the 75 *defixiones* were made from an alloy of more than 66 per cent lead.[70] The vast majority of tablets analysed were made from an alloy of tin and lead (or on several occasions, copper and lead) with varying proportions. This variation suggests that the alloys used for making these tablets were produced on a small scale, which is hardly surprising since the process was rather straightforward: once the alloy was made from the metals that can be smelted at low temperatures, it was cast either in a mould[71] or on a flat surface to make a larger sheet from which the tablet could be cut after the metal had cooled down. Any irregularities in the sheet were generally corrected by someone who would flatten

---

[57] Cf. **318**, **304**, **317**, **325**, **326** and **306**. For a discussion, see *Tab. Sulis* 7, 99, 101, 112–13, 120–21 and 126.

[58] Jerome, *vit. Hilar.* XI: *...et subter limen domus puellae portenta quaedam verborum et portentosas figuras sculptas in aeris Cyprii lamina defodit.* This has proven controversial due to both the veracity of the deeds (see Tomlin 1988a: 81, n. 2) as well as the interpretation of the phrase *aeris Cyprii lamina*, which some authors have taken as copper (Tomlin 1988a: 81 and Ogden 1999: 10), while others have seen it as bronze (Gager 1992: 261 and Ogden 2002: 230). Here I follow the first possibility, since Pliny refers to copper as *aes Cyprium* (e.g., *HN* XXXIII, 29–30 and *OLD s.v. aes*). In this way, the ambiguity of Latin *aes*, which can refer to either metal, is resolved through the qualifying adjective *Cyprius*. On this passage, see section I.6.5.2 and n. 326.

[59] In this regard, see the suggestive proposal of Mastrocinque 2007, who connects the flame to the victim's life as part of a larger ritual of symbolic homicide. Cf. also Sánchez Natalías 2018: 11.

[60] Poccetti 1999: 545–61; Graf 1995: 129; Ogden 1999: 11; Gordon 2015: 153–58.

[61] Graf 1995: 129–30: 'c'è stato chi ha affermato che in origine la scelta del piombo come supporto di questi testi fu determinata dalla natura morta e fredda di questo metallo. Ma si tratta di un'opinione ormai insostenibile... Fissare l'attenzione sul piombo e sulle sue qualità, e considerarlo come il materiale meglio adatto a far da supporto alle defissioni, sono sviluppi secondari, una ritualizzazione *a posteriori* di una pratica corrente'.

[62] All of these characteristics are reflected in the texts of several Greek curses, where the *defigens* asks that the victim be left cold as lead (see *DTA* 67, 105, 106 and 107) or that the victim's tongue be turned to lead (e.g., *DTA* 96 and 97). These metaphors, however, are not found in the

Latin curses, which employ different types of comparisons (see Sánchez Natalías 2018).

[63] Cf. Tambiah 1973: 212 and section I.4.3 for the formulae that follow this principle, according to which an aspect of the *actio magica* is compared with the victim of the spell.

[64] *PGM* VII, 397–98: μόλιβον ἀπὸ ψυχροφόρου σωλῆνος ποίησον λάμναν.

[65] *PGM* VII, 432: πλάκαν ἐς μολιβῆν ἀπὸ ψυχροφόρου τόπου.

[66] *PGM* XXXVI, 1–2: λάμναν μολιβῆν ψυχρήλατον.

[67] *PGM* VII, 925–26 and X, 36–37, respectively: λεπίδα μολιβῆν ἀπὸ ζυγοῦ μούλων... λάμναν <ἢ πέταλον μολιβοῦν ἀπὸ ἡμιόνων>.

[68] Pintozzi 1990: 113–33. The author argues that 'geologically, lead is unique in that the isotopic composition of each ore source varies markedly... When the ore is produced, the lead is separated from the parent isotopes which freezes the isotopic composition and leads to a fixed composition within a given deposit... By measuring the isotopic ratio of the ore sources and then comparing those to that of the final metal product, it is possible to determine the origin of a metal artifact' (Pintozzi 1990: 113–14).

[69] See *Tab. Sulis*, pp. 81–84.

[70] Some of these are uninscribed sheets of lead. Their inventory numbers are 690 (100%), 698 (100%), 487 (97.9%) and 20.002 (99.5) (see *Tab. Sulis*, p. 260). The following were inscribed: **252** (99.9%), **320** (99.9%), **268** (99.6%), **220** (98.3%), **218** (96.9%), **208** (90.5%), **279** (80.5%), **303** (73.9%), **266** (70.9%), **298** (67.4%) and **264** (67%).

[71] As was the case with **300–01** and perhaps **124**, the reverse of which contains mould markings in which the lead was flipped.

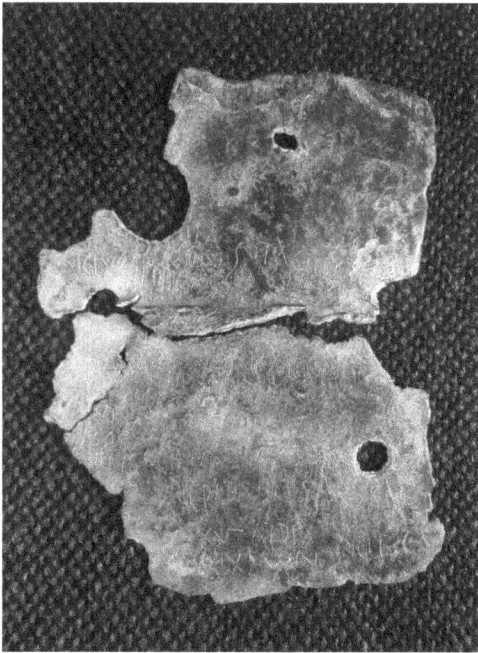

Figure 3.3. Different shapes of lead tablets: irregular (From unknown provenance [cf. 149]. Courtesy of P. Rothenhöfer).

Figure 3.5. Different shapes of lead tablets: disc (From Barchín del Hoyo [cf. 145], Museo de Cuenca).

Figure 3.4. Different shapes of lead tablets: *tabula cerata* (From Pompeii [cf. 71, author's photograph], Ministero dei Beni e delle Attività Culturali e del Turismo-Soprintendenza Pompei).

Figure 3.6. Different shapes of lead tablets: *tabula cum capitulo* (From Italica/Santiponce [cf. 127, author's photograph], Museo Arqueológico de Sevilla).

the sheet with a hammer.[72] The X-ray analysis of a *defixio* from Groß Gerau (Germania, cf. **482**) attests to another method of manufacture in which a small piece of lead was hammered into a sheet of the desired proportions to inscribe the curse.

When discussing the use of lead, it is always important to discuss the shapes into which it was formed. While most curses were inscribed on rectangular sheets, we cannot overlook the great diversity of shapes that *defixiones* could take, running the gamut from curses written on irregularly shaped scraps (see Figure 3.3) to those inscribed on carefully constructed sheets. In the latter group, there are curses that resemble *tabulae ceratae* (writing tablets, see Figure 3.4), are shaped like discs (see Figure 3.5) or

triangles,[73] resemble the outline of a foot,[74] or are *tabulae cum capitulo* (with a single handle, see Figure 3.6)[75] and even the well-known *tabulae ansatae* (with two handles, see Figure 3.7).[76] These last two forms deserve special attention, since they are frequently found in other forms of common writing. Texts inscribed on tablets with these shapes were originally made of wood before these same shapes were used for bronze inscriptions (e.g., for the display of public documents) and then lead ones (as demonstrated by the curses discussed here).[77]

---

[73] Such as **106**.
[74] Such as the erotic curse from Saguntum/Sagunto (cf. **140**).
[75] Such as the curses from Italica/Santiponce (cf. **127**) and Baelo Claudia/Bolonia (cf. **128**), in addition to the tablet from Arverni/Chamalières (cf. **163**), in which the text runs longitudinally.
[76] Such as **337**, **463**, **479** and **518**, among others.
[77] For *tabulae cum capitulo*, see Costabile and Licandro 2002: 25–34. For *tabulae ansatae*, see Cornell 1991: esp. 23–24.

---

[72] Clearly the case with **259**, **300** and **302**, among others.

0   10 cm

Figure 3.7. Different shapes of lead tablets: *tabula ansata* **(From Bodegraven [cf. 463], Museum Het Valkhof, Nijmegen [NL]).**

The *PGM* do not provide any rules or guidelines about the specific shape that tablets should take; instead, they only recommend that curses should be inscribed on sheets of whatever metal is most suitable for a particular spell. To refer to lead sheets and the forms that they can take, the *PGM* employ the following lexemes: λᾶμνα, πέταλον, πιττάκιον, πλάτυμμα, πλάξ and λεπίς.[78] In the texts of the *defixiones* themselves, the following Latin lexemes are used to refer to the physical object: *defixio, tabella, tabula, charta* and *plumbum*,[79] without providing any further specification about the tablet's shape. Given the silence of the *PGM* and the *defixiones* themselves about the possible shapes of curse tablets, it is reasonable to conclude that the choice was left to the practitioners, who were probably influenced by time and technical restraints (e.g., if they themselves made the tablets or had the help of a professional practitioner).

Finally, special attention must be paid to a series of containers from the fountain of Anna Perenna (see **24–27** and **35–36**) due to their exceptional nature.[80] These were made in sets that generally include three containers of various sizes so that they can be nested like Russian dolls. In seven cases, the smallest container of the group held a small human figure, which (with only one exception)[81] was placed upside-down so that the figure's head touched the bottom of the jar. In order to preserve each group of objects, the largest container was normally closed with a conical or flat lid, which was then either sealed with natural resins or bent along the lip so as to keep the object from being opened.

These nesting vessels have been included in the present volume since most of the innermost containers were used as the surface on which a curse was inscribed. Accordingly, on the curved surfaces of these objects, the *defigens* represented divine powers or the curses' victims, whose names were handed over to the deities invoked; furthermore, in the bottom of the innermost container belonging to **26**, we find a *defixio* inscribed on the round flat surface. The fact that the curses are found exclusively inscribed on the innermost of the three containers is clearly a sign that the practitioner sought to hide the written message (unlike curses written on lead sheets, these containers could obviously not be rolled up or folded).

M. Piranomonte has suggested that the Anna Perenna containers were reused inkwells or medicinal jars.[82] Her first suggestion should be rejected for various reasons: first, inkwells were not normally fashioned from lead; second, the lids do not have the extremely characteristic double or single opening for the *stilus*; third, inkwells were normally produced in pairs in a standard size, not in groups of three with different sizes. According to Piranomonte's second suggestion that the objects were originally medicinal jars, she was presumably referring to the ubiquitous *pyxis* (a small cylindrical container with a lid), which could

---

[78] Λᾶμνα is the most frequently used lexeme cf. *PGM* VII, 397–98; 459; X, 36–37; XXXVI, 1–2; 231 and LVIII, 6. Πέταλον appears in *PGM* V, 304–05; VII, 417 and X, 36–37. For πιττάκιον, cf. *PGM* IV, 2956 and XV, 9. For πλάτυμμα see *PGM* IV, 329 and 406–07, while πλάξ appears in *PGM* IV, 2212 and VII, 432. Finally, λεπίς (λεπ[ίδα μολιβῆν]), has been reconstructed in *PGM* LXXVIII, 3–4.

[79] *Defixio* is found (in ablative, *cum defictcsione*) in a curse tablet from Abusina/Eining (Raetia, cf. Blänsdorf 2019: no. 1); while *tabel(l)a* is found in **51** (A, l. 10 and B, l. 9); *tabula* in **494** (A, l. 1); *chârta* in **96** (A, ll. 1–2); *carta* in **484** (l. 11) and **367** (A, l. 1). *Plumbum* is used in **157** (A, l. 1) and **470** (l. 2), among others.

[80] When it comes to the containers and their respective contents, Piranomonte's numbers have not been completely consistent, but vary from 9 to 18, 21 or even 24 lead containers and from one to three terracotta containers with lead lids (compare Piranomonte 2005: 99 with 2006: 194, 2009: 257, 2010a: 204, 2010b: 23; 2012a: 167 and 2015: 79 and also Piranomonte and Marco Simón 2010: 8). Blänsdorf (2015b: 22), for his part, mentions the existence of 27 lead containers. It seems likely that the variation depends on the system used for counting the containers (i.e., whether they are counted individually or as sets of two or three). This has led to further confusion (see for instance, Urbanová 2018: 54). In any case, and given this inconsistency, it's best to follow the first notice about the group, published by Polakova and Rapinesi (2002: 40–45 and 48–52), who specify that the number of (sets of) containers is a total of ten, of which nine are in lead and one in ceramic (Polakova and Rapinesi 2002: 39). Since it has not been possible to consult the full and yet-to-be published catalogue of the materials from the *Fons Annae Perennae*,

the present study contains six of the nine lead containers (cf. **24–27** and **35–36**). The container with inv. no. 475541 has been excluded on the grounds that it was not inscribed, even though that it did have two *defixiones* inside (cf. **33** and **34**).

[81] The exception is the figurine found inside of **26** (see Polakova and Rapinesi 2002: 41 and 48).

[82] Piranomonte 2010b: 28–30.

Table 3.2. Non-specific media used for writing *defixiones*

Perishable materials		Non-perishable materials	
Literary record	**Archaeological record**	**Literary record**	**Archaeological record**
Hellebore leaf		Shells	mention in *DT* 234
Donkey hide		Magnetite	
Bat wings			Opus *sectile:* **57**
		Pot for smoked fish	
		Ceramic cup	Jar: **173**
		Unfired ceramics	Tegulae: El Jem (Foucher 2000)
			Ostrakon: **113**
			Cinerary urn: **16**
			Lamp: **3**
			Ceramic jar with lead lid: **526** and Rome (Polakova and Rapinesi 2002: 39, fig. 2).
			Tin disk: **223**
			Pewter plate: **235**

be made from a range of materials and could come in a variety of different sizes.[83] However, of all the sets from the fountain, only **24** presents a similar appearance to some *pyxides*, a fact that makes this argument inapplicable to the other containers from the fountain.[84]

It is more likely that the containers from Anna Perenna were created *ex professo* as an active part of the magical ritual and hence that they served a double function: first, to provide a place where the figurine representing the victim (always found in the innermost container) could be deposited; second as a surface on which a magical spell could be written. As Piranomonte has rightly pointed out,[85] the only archaeological discovery that parallels the sophisticated ritual carried out at Anna Perenna comes from the Kerameikon in Athens, where moulded lead figurines were placed inside inscribed miniature coffins that were also made of lead. But the Anna Perenna curses may also find a literary parallel of similar chronology. In a recipe from *PGM* XIII meant to keep a man from being cuckolded, the text recommends first moulding a crocodile out of earth, ink and myrrh and then placing it inside of a small lead cinerary urn (εἰς <σ>ορίον μολιβοῦν)[86] upon which the practitioner is then told to inscribe the proper cursing formula.

In addition to this parallel, a formal comparison of some of the Anna Perenna containers and certain types of lead cinerary urns dating to the Imperial Period provides intriguing results: the containers, with their ϲylindrical bodies and flat or conical lids, are striking similar.

Although the ritual described in *PGM* certainly did not have the same purpose as those from the Roman sanctuary, we can nevertheless establish a strong parallel between the two examples. Furthermore, if the Anna Perenna containers were truly miniature lead cinerary urns, these would have served the same function as the coffins from the Kerameikon: to bury the victim symbolically.

3.3. Non-specific media

This category contains all objects that were taken up and used in new or complementary ways to inscribe a curse. This includes non-manmade objects, such as shells or magnetite. Within this larger group, there are two large categories: perishable and non-perishable objects (see Table 3.2).

3.3.1. Perishable non-specific media

Within this group the *PGM* mention a range of suitable objects for aggressive-magical purposes that are not found outside of the literary record. Such objects include hellebore leaves (φύλ<λ>ων χαλπάσ(ου), cf. *PGM* XIX, b1) and a donkey hide (δέρμα ὄνου, cf. *PGM* XXXVI, 362), both of which were recommended for *agōgai* (erotic curses of attraction). Furthermore, we find recommendations for using the wings of a living bat (νυκτερίδαν ζῶσαν ἐπὶ τῆς δεξιᾶς πτέρυγος (...) ἐπὶ τῆς ἀριστερᾶς),[87] which were proposed for a curse to induce insomnia 'until she gives her consent'.

3.3.2. Non-perishable non-specific media

This is an extremely heterogeneous group in which we find objects ranging from shells, magnetite and pieces of metal to lamps, *tegulae* and *ostraka*.

---

[83] Hilgers 1969: 265–67, '*Pyxis*'. For a wider discussion, see Künzl 1982. For two bronze containers that come from Albalate de las Nogueras (Cuenca), see Fuentes Domínguez 1987: 259, fig. 7, no. 3 and 4 as well as fig. 8 no. 1 and 2.
[84] One of the containers (cf. **24**) resembles the inkwells published by Bilkei 1980: 89–90 tables III–IV, no. 22, 149 and especially 121. Likewise, it recalls the vessels recently found in a woman's tomb in *Aquincum* (see Lassányi 2008: 68, fig. 6).
[85] Piranomonte 2010a: 207 with useful bibliography in n. 51.
[86] *PGM* XIII, 322.

[87] *PGM* XII, 376–77. For another recipe to banish sleep that tells the practitioner to write a curse on bat wings, see *PGM* VII, 652.

To start with seashells (ὄστρακον ἀπὸ θαλάσσης),[88] the *PGM* contain four different curses (three being erotic) that are supposed to be written on this material with very particular inks that were certainly aimed to reinforce the power of the spell.[89] Another source for the use of seashells (with a clearly agonistic purpose) is found at *DT* 234, a curse tablet written against the charioteers and the horses of the blues and the greens. In ll. 6–7, the text states that the names of the enemy factions' horses have been written on seashells and then deposited alongside the *defixio* in a tomb. Unfortunately, the archaeological report of this nineteenth-century excavation does not record its findspot (for a discussion, see Faraone 2019: 170).

Drawing on the magical principle of persuasive analogy (*similia similibus*) and the well-known properties of magnetite (cf. Pliny, *HN* XXXVI, 127),[90] the *PGM* prescribe the use of this mineral (λίθον μάγνητα τὸν πνέοντα, cf. *PGM* IV, 1723–24) in erotic curses in order to attract the beloved. In its natural form, magnetite can be found in octahedral crystals, a shape which provides good surfaces for etching images and inscribing texts, which would then be accompanied by the recitation of a longer formula. As was the case with seashells, we only have literary evidence for the use of magnetite in the manufacture of *defixiones*.

Within the category of non-perishable media, there is a sizable group of ceramic objects. The use of this material is documented in both the literary and archaeological records. Accordingly, to those seeking to separate two lovers, the *PGM* recommend inscribing a curse on a pot for smoked fish (εἰς ταρίχου ὄστρακον, cf. *PGM* XII, 366) with a bronze stylus. This procedure would give rise to 'odiousness, enmity, just as Typhon and Osiris had'.[91] For those seeking to attract a lover, on the other hand, the *PGM* suggest using a ceramic cup (ποτήριον, cf. *PGM* VII, 643)[92] upon which the *defigens* ought to recite the spell seven times.

In a different love spell of attraction, the *defigens* is told to inscribe the curse on unfired clay (εἰς <ὄ>στρακον ὠμόν, cf. *PGM* XXXVI, 187).[93] In this case, the instructions found in the *PGM* appear to find direct parallels in the archaeological record: there are two erotic curses, from Maar (Gallia Belgica, cf. **173**) and from Thysdrus/El Jem (Byzacena, cf. Foucher 2000),[94] which were inscribed on a

Figure 3.8. Non-specific media: *tegula* **from Thysdrus/El Jem (From Foucher 2000: 58, fig. 1).**

small pitcher and a *tegula*, respectively, before the pieces were fired (see Figure 3.8).

In Italy, there are also examples of curses inscribed on fired ceramic. The first is a curse aimed to silence its victim found on an *ostrakon* from Neapolis/Terralba (cf. **113**). The other two extent Italian examples, from Rome (cf. **3** and **14**), were painted on a lamp and the lip of a cinerary urn, respectively (see the catalogue for images).

On a few rare occasions, ceramic objects have been found together with lead tablets. This is the case with the curse from Faviana/Mautern (Noricum, cf. **526**), where a *defixio* inscribed on a lead sheet was used as a 'lid' for a small ceramic jar, inside of which archaeologists found organic remains. There is a parallel case from the fountain of Anna Perenna (Rome), where excavators discovered a ceramic jar filled with the remains of bone and parchment. The vessel was covered with a lead sheet that apparently bears no inscription.[95]

In addition to the ceramic media, it is worth noting as well an unparalleled case from Fundi/Fondi (cf. **57**). The curse was painted as a *titulus pictus* on a reused *opus sectile* plaque made of marble. The choice of this media, which is certainly unparalleled, seems to be related both with the context in which the curse was finally deposited (i.e., an abandoned pool located in the so-called grotto of Tiberius) and with the content of the text. By the time the curse was composed, the cave still preserved the remains of its once luxurious decoration and was probably the place from which the practitioner took the object on which the curse was written, alluding to the destruction of the

---

[88] This same lexeme (ὄστρακον ἀπὸ θαλάσσης) appears at *PGM* IV, 2218, though the type of spell is not explicitly stated; VII, 300ᵃ (ὄστρακον θαλάσσιον); VII, 374 and VII, 467.

[89] For these inks, see *PGM* VII, 300ᵃ ff.; VII, 467 ff.; and IV, 2218 ff.

[90] According to Pliny, *trahitur namque magnete lapide, domitrixque illa rerum omnium materia ad inane nescio quid currit atque, ut propius venit, adsilit, tenetur amplexuque haeret.*

[91] Translated by R.F. Hock, *apud* Betz 1992.

[92] *PGM* VII, 643.

[93] *PGM* XXXVI, 187.

[94] In Sánchez Natalías 2011b: 86, I wrongly included a *tegula* from Wilhering (Raetia), whose text had traditionally been interpreted as a *defixio* (see Kropp 2008: no. 6.2/1 [with previous references], Urbanová 2018: no. 102). However, the re-reading of the text found in Thüry 2001 has made it clear that this is not a magical document.

[95] On this, see Polakova and Rapinesi 2002: 39 and 49. Jordan (1996: 115, n. 4), for his part, highlights the existence of cinerary urns with inscribed lead lids, which may provide an important Greek parallel.

Figure 3.9. Non-specific media: curse on a pewter plate from Aquae Sulis/Bath (cf. 235; The Roman Baths).

space in which the *defixio* was deposited. In addition, the content of the text was also related with this idea, since it aimed to destroy the house and spirit of two individuals through a series of comparisons based on famous passages of the Bible. Therefore, the choice of this medium was probably aimed to reinforce, through persuasive analogy, the purposes pursued in the curse.[96]

Finally, we must discuss the use of metal objects as non-specific media, for which all of our evidence comes from the archaeological record. There are two important curses from the sanctuary of Sulis Minerva (Aquae Sulis/Bath) which both list the names of cursed enemies. The first of these curses, **223**, was inscribed on a tin disc that was coated with bronze. The disc has a small protrusion that could have been used to attach some sort of cord, suggesting that it might have been a pendant. The second curse, **235**, was inscribed on a pewter plate, which was folded in two after the curse was inscribed (see Figure 3.9). In both cases, it appears that the media of the curses were everyday objects that were appropriated for writing a curse.[97] We are left to wonder whether these objects were chosen because they were typical offerings to the goddess (this would especially be the case with the plate) or because they were somehow connected to one or several of the curse's victims. Nevertheless, and given that both texts are just simple lists of names, neither hypothesis can be confirmed.

---

[96] See Alfayé 2019: 269 and in general, for magical practices among ruins.

[97] Discussing the tin disc, Mees (2009: 35) notes 'Its place of deposition and the metal was made of suggest that the Bath tablet was specifically created for the purpose of cursing (…) perhaps the pendant form of the first Celtic Bath find was supposed to suggest the magical quality of the item, if not, say, be a symbolic representation of an object which had been stolen from the curser.'

4

Inscribing the *Defixiones*

4.1. Introduction: the written and spoken word

In determined contexts and due to their performative value, speaking and writing were two actions that were thought to have a certain agency in Antiquity. This means that the contents of a verbal or written message could come to fruition in the physical world if a series of specific rules and procedures were adhered to.[98] Once the material on which a curse was to be inscribed was chosen, its content would be transmitted through two different modes of communication: the written and the spoken word. Accordingly, magical acts were performed on two separate but closely connected levels—even if today only one has been preserved. The important point that is easy to overlook due to the state of our evidence is that *defixiones* were both written and recited aloud.

The oral aspect of the *actio magica*, few traces of which have been preserved, was undoubtedly a fundamental part of any cursing ritual. As P. Poccetti has put it, oral recitation 'rappresentava il requisito essenziale per lo svolgimento e l'efficacia del rito magico' (2002: 16) and played a role both in the manufacture of a tablet as well as its deposition. Several recipes found in the *PGM* make this clear: after the inscribing of the tablet, practitioners are generally advised to recite various formulae that were designed to invoke (and urge on) the powers that were tasked with bringing the curse to fruition and also provided the *defigens* with the opportunity to reiterate his or her demands.[99] Here it is worth recalling the prohibitions enshrined in the *XII Tables* (dated to the mid-fifth century BCE), where cursing appears to have been conceived of as primarily an oral

endeavour. Consequently, we would be remiss to give the written part of magical acts more importance.[100]

Despite the inherent impossibility of preserving an oral utterance in the archaeological record, it is extremely likely, as the *PGM* clearly demonstrate and the *XII Tables* strongly suggest, that an oral recitation accompanied the deposition of the vast majority of *defixiones*. This is especially likely in the case of the non-inscribed tablets,[101] such as the tablets found by a metal detectorist near Lincolnshire, upon of which the likeness of the emperor Valens (from a coin) was impressed (see Figure 4.1). In a similar vein, it is logical to hypothesize that the pseudo-inscriptions found in the British sanctuaries in Aquae Sulis/Bath and Uley, which were inscribed by illiterate *defigentes* seeking to emulate the act of writing, were accompanied by oral cursing formulae that fleshed out the meaning and details of the inscribed 'texts'.[102]

What we know about the written portion of the ritual is, of course, more detailed, since in the majority of the cases this has been preserved. That said, and as is made clear in the catalogue, just because a text has been preserved does not mean it is legible, comprehensible or able to be deciphered. As various authors have pointed out, writing is a practice 'a cui la condizione esoterica in società non profondamente alfabetizzate conferisce poteri magici'.[103] These powers arise from the fact

Figure 4.1. *Defixio* from Lincolnshire (From: The Portable Antiquities Scheme).

---

[98] See Rodríguez Mayorgas 2010: 37, who explains in a discussion of orality: 'se le concede una fuerza creadora a la articulación sonora de las palabras, en especial de los nombres, como si tuvieran el poder de dar vida o de quitarla... Los ejemplos más elocuentes, sin duda, aparecen en la Biblia donde... Dios crea el mundo asignándole nombres'; for writing, see pp. 227–28. Likewise, Cardona 2009: 120 claims: 'Tutta la storia della scrittura ci mostra... come si sia sempre ritenuto possibile agire sul reale a partire dalla manipolazione dei simboli, e come anzi l'uomo sia giunto a nutrire un terrore sacro di quei simboli e del loro potere, quasi che, ormai tracciati, essi potessero da sé soli, e senza intervento di altri, scatenare la loro azione'.

[99] A good example can be found in *PGM* III, 30ff. (which recommends the recitation of formulae during the deposit of the tablets, which are to be placed inside of a ritually killed cat); *PGM* IV, 332ff. (which recommends reciting the formula written on the *defixio* and pronouncing others while depositing the tablet) and 1747ff. (which urges the reader to inscribe the formula and then recite it); 2235ff. (where the text is supposed to be recited after being written); *PGM* V, 319ff. (which recommends pronouncing a series of formulae, while piercing the tablet and a different series of formulae during the deposition); *PGM* VII, 453ff. (where the reader is told to recite a formula while depositing the tablet in order to increase the text's longevity); 474ff. (which tells the reader to recite a formula while depositing the curse); *PGM* XII, 366ff. (which says the recite the formula after inscribing the tablet); and finally, *PGM* LXXVIII, 4ff. (which recommends inscribing a figure while saying a specific name and then later reciting a formula to invoke the deity).

[100] See Poccetti's suggestive comparison of the Greek and Roman contexts (2002: 16–17, 2005 and 2015: 378–82); for the Hellenic world, see Faraone 1991a: 4–5. On this, see also section I.9.2.

[101] E.g., those from Saguntum (see the introduction to Hispania, in II.2) or Rauranum/Rom (see the commentary to **159**).

[102] See **317–21**, to which we could add **382** and **440**.

[103] Poccetti 2002: 15. Also see n. 98 above and Piccaluga 2010: 13–14, Graf 2015 and Chiarini 2019.

that through the act of writing the person named in the curse (i.e., the victim) along with his or her belongings, actions, life and destiny were thought to be irreversibly connected to the curse tablet and hence constrained by its spell. Writing was considered a dangerous practice for a spell's victim, as is made explicit in several formulae that establish a persuasive analogy between the victim and the act of writing.[104] Furthermore, guaranteeing the longevity of a curse was often one of the practitioners' main objectives:[105] *defigentes* could produce spells that would dog a victim *quoad vixerit*[106] or they could ask for its power to be renewed (*rediviva*)[107] in an attempt to perpetually prolong its power.

The *PGM*, for their part, allude to the act of writing a curse with the lexemes γράφω[108] and ἐγχαράσσω,[109] sometimes without any further specification. When it is specified that a curse should be inscribed on a lead sheet (except for rare exceptions), the *PGM* urge their readers to write their curses using a bronze stylus or nail.[110] When the curse is written on other materials, such as papyrus, seashells or the wings of a bat, however, the *PGM* recommend the use of ink, which is spread with a pen[111] and could be made of a wide range of ingredients (e.g., cinnabar,[112] myrrh[113] or even different types of blood[114]).

4.2. The act of inscription

As has been mentioned in the previous section, the *actio magica* was carried out on two levels that were tightly linked: the oral and written. Within the second category, the importance of the inscribed word is undeniable. In addition, other Graeco-Egyptian elements that were incised on the tablets played an extremely important role and were thought to have a close symbiotic relationship with the inscribed word. The most common of these elements include the deployment of iconography, *charaktêres* and certain *voces magicae* (such as palindromes, alphabetic sequences and *onómata barbariká*). Sometimes such elements are found in conjunction on a single tablet.[115]

That said, Table 4.1 clearly shows that the inclusion of such elements within the corpus of curses from the Roman West are actually quite rare. Provinces such as Africa or the Italian peninsula, which scholars have argued were more susceptible to the influence of Graeco-Egyptian magic,[116] stand out for an elevated use of such inscribed elements. Here, it is worth stressing that the use of such Graeco-Egyptian elements is also more common within a certain time frame: during the High Empire, these features are present in North African *defixiones*, though it was not until Late Antiquity that these new 'updates' to the technology of cursing reached the Italian Peninsula and other Mediterranean provinces. Furthermore, we should point out that the presence of these items has generally been connected to the rise of magical professionals, who were especially active in large urban centres, such as Carthage, Hadrumetum and Rome. There is less evidence to suggest that these features were employed by individual *defigentes* writing curses on their own behalf.[117] Yet even the higher rate of such elements in these areas does not counter the larger statistical trend: such tablets remain in the minority (or simply are not attested) in some northern provinces. Despite the fact that there are examples of curses that have unusual layouts already in the fourth century BCE, it is not until the High Empire and Late Antiquity that the combination of various languages (transliterations, mixed language texts, etc.) or the use of iconography and *voces magicae* are most widely attested. The fact that these aspects are concentrated in certain areas and times is yet a further reminder that we would be remiss to think of cursing as a monolithic category that was stable across time and space: rather, it was an evolving technology that could be adapted to changing social circumstances.

4.2.1. The text: layout, language and writing

Text is the only element found in the vast majority of the tablets, which generally lack more 'elaborate' features, such as iconography or *charaktêres*. For the most part, text is written and runs in the customary fashion (i.e., from left to right), though depending on a practitioner's ability and knowledge, we occasionally find unusual layouts and/or noteworthy combinations of different languages and ways to organize writing.

4.2.1.1. The layout[118]

Eighty-eight curses (or 14 per cent of the corpus) contain an unusual layout (or *ordinatio*),[119] the majority of which

---

[104] See Faraone and Kropp 2010 and Chiarini 2019: 140–46. See also Poccetti 2002: 38–39.
[105] Piccaluga 2010: 16. Cardona (2009: 141) claims, 'se la forza magica evocatrice della parola detta si spegne quando l'ultimo suono è stato pronunciato, la potenza della formula scritta rimane intatta nel tempo, e non la si può spegnere se non distruggendo il supporto'. For a similar argument, see Ogden 1999: 26.
[106] Cf. **250** B, l. 4. Analogous phrases are found in **486** (A, l. 8: *quandius vita vixerit*) as well as the British curses **350** (ll. 3–4: *usque die ꞌmꞌ quọ moriatur*) and **459** (ll. 6–7: *(ad) diem mortịs*).
[107] Cf. **205**, l. 1.
[108] See *PGM* IV, 304, 2144; V, 360; VII, 459 and 462, etc.
[109] See *PGM* VII, 433 and 459.
[110] For the stylus, see *PGM* VII, 398, 417 and 926; XII, 366 (*defixio* written on a pot for smoked fish); XXXVI, 2, 186 (curse written on unfired clay) and 232. For the nail, see *PGM* LXXVIII, 4.
[111] *PGM* V, 308.
[112] *PGM* III, 18–19.
[113] *PGM* XXXVI, 103 and perhaps also XIXb, 6.
[114] The examples as for the blood of a black donkey (*PGM* VII, 301), a donkey (*PGM* XXXVI, 73), Typhon (*PGM* LXI, 61) or 'in the blood from the womb of a silurus after mixing in the juice of the plant Sarapis' (translated by E.N. O'Neil, *PGM* XXXVI, 362–63).
[115] Examples include the *defixiones* **117–18** (dated to the fourth or fifth century CE), whose texts are written in a mix of Latin and Greek. The

---

tablets also contain iconography, a *charaktêr*, a magical symbol and a sequence of nearly identical *voces magicae*.
[116] Cf. Gordon 2002.
[117] A *defixio* from Eccles (cf. **446**) may be one of the few exceptions, on the reverse of which the Chnoubis symbol is found.
[118] For an extended version of this section, which includes the Latin and Greek *defixiones* from the Roman West, see Sánchez Natalías 2020d: 103–08.
[119] See Poccetti 2002: 47–49. For the layout of the text as a list, see Gordon 1999 as well as Centrone 2010 (though more focused on the Greek world). Also see Urbanová 2018, sections 7.6.1, 8.4, 9.4, 10.4, 11.3 and 12.4 (where the author briefly comments on the layout of several Latin texts as features such as *voces magicae*, iconography and *signa magica*).

Table 4.1. *Defixiones* **grouped by provenance (It. = Italia, Afr. = Africa, Hisp. = Hispania, Gall. = Gallia, Brit. = Britannia, Ger. = Germania, Raet. = Raetia, Nor. = Noricum, Pann. = Pannonia) and their characteristics (*O* = *ordinatio*, L/W = language/writing, I = iconography and *C* = *charaktêres*. *Varia* refers to tablets that contain fewer common elements, such as palindromes, magical symbols, *voces magicae*, etc. The total number of curse tablets in each province is tallied in the right column (that said, even if a *defixio* has several characteristics, it is counted as a single piece in the province's total)**

Prov.	*O*	L/W	I	*C*	*Varia*	Total
It.	20	17	16	13	**22, 117** and **118**: *voces magicae.* **5**: Greek vowels. **6, 20, 22, 24–26, 29–30**: magical symbols. **26–27, 30**: palindrome.	40/119
Afr.	20	28	23	13	*DT* 218, 227, 233, 243, 244, 255: *voces magicae.* *AE* 1907, 165 and 1933, 234-235: *voces magicae.* *DT* 243: magical symbols, "wings", palindromes. *DT* 247, 258 (?) and 260: magical symbols. *DT* 251: *voces magicae* transliterated with the Latin alphabet. *DT* 251 and 253: some Greek letters. *DT* 253: palindromes, *voces magicae.* *DT* 264 and 266: *voces magicae* and magical symbols. *DT* 265 and 268: *voces magicae.* *DT* 272-274: *voces magicae* and identical with respect to *C.* *DT* 286, 288-289, 291-293 and 295: *voces magicae.* *DT* 286 and 292: some Greek letters. *AE* 1907, 68-69: magical symbols. *DT* 270: *voces magicae.*	62/88
Hisp.	10	2	–	1	–	11/30
Gall.	3	12	3	4	**166**: *voces magicae* (?) **156**: alphabetic sequence. **183–184** and **189**: text distributed in three rectangular boxes. **183–184** and **190**: magical symbols. **196–197**: iconography (?). **160**: *voces magicae.*	11/55
Brit.	17	3	–	–	**207**: alphabetic sequence (?). **259**: sign (cross, side A). **446**: magical symbol (SSS). **448**: sign (side A).	21/256
Ger.	14	–	–	–	–	14/59
Raet.	3	–	–	–	–	3/6
Nor.	–	–	–	–	–	0/1
Pann.	1	1	–	–	**530**: magical symbols.	2/9

hail from Africa, Italia, Britannia and Germania. With the exception of the North African *defixiones*, the majority of the rest of these texts were by individual practitioners, who display quite different levels of literacy. For these individuals, writing in a non-standard manner appears to have been a means of making their curses even more effective. Instead of being an attempt to encrypt a message, the distortion of the standard layout, which appears to have always been intentional, has been explained along the lines of persuasive analogy, according to which just as a text is deformed or out of whack, so too shall be that which the text describes.[120] A good example of this can be seen in **19**, a curse from the sanctuary of Anna Perenna in Rome, which is directed against a certain Antonius. On side A, a small anthropomorphic figurine has been etched.

This figure is clearly identified as the victim, whose name is written according to normal conventions. On side B, however, the name appears in a distorted fashion, with the syllables placed in the wrong order. The scrambling of these syllables, or *membra* if you will,[121] should be analysed as a symbolic dismemberment of the victim.

Among the 'atypical' layouts, the most common perversion consists of writing the text in the opposite direction. Of these, the oldest are 12 Oscan tablets, which mostly date between the fourth and third centuries BCE[122] and which hail from southern Italy: the texts are written from left to

---

[120] Cf. Ogden 1999: 30.

[121] For *membrum* as a synonym for *syllaba*, see *TLL s.v. membrum* (8.0.634.30).

[122] The tablets **75–77** are dated to the fourth century BCE, while **78–81** have been dated between the fourth and third centuries BCE. Curses **63–66** have been dated to the Late Republic (first century BCE).

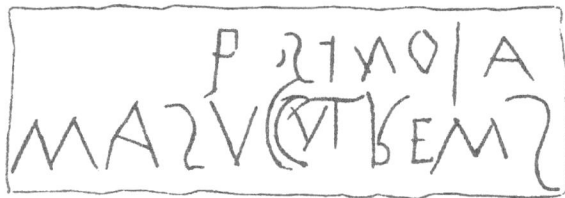

Figure 4.2. Different types of right-to-left layouts: Fectio/ Vechten (cf. **461**; From Bramach 1867: no. 57).

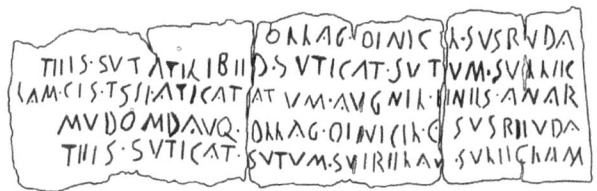

Figure 4.4. Different types of right-to-left layouts: Celti/ Peñaflor (cf. **131**; From Stylow 2012: 151).

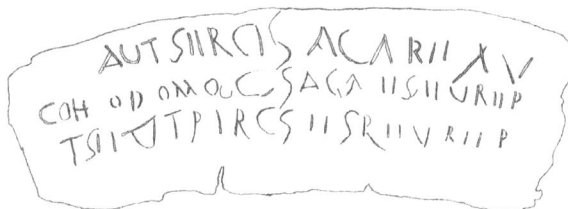

Figure 4.3. Different types of right-to-left layouts: Colonia/ Cologne (cf. **464**; From Blänsdorf *et al.* 2010: 272).

right, instead of right to left, which is standard in Oscan epigraphy. A similar case is documented in Volaterrae/ Volterra (cf. **91**), where, unlike the Etruscan usage, the text runs from left to right.

The remaining cases, all of which are in the Latin language, are written from right to left. These tablets mostly hail from Germania, Britannia and Hispania.[123] From a chronological point of view, there are three early examples from Hispania (first century BCE),[124] but it was not until the High Empire that this sort of layout really took off (with 23 examples); by Late Antiquity, the trend of writing a text backwards seems to have waned with only 5 known examples. Geographically, this type of layout spread along the same lines as cursing practices did generally: the first examples are found in southern Italy (probably under Greek influence)[125] and then spread to the northern provinces. In some examples of texts running from right to left, the orientation of the individual letters was also 'mirrored' (i.e., written from right to left), such as the curse from Vechten (cf. **461**, Figure 4.2);[126] that said, in most of the tablets the orientation of the letters remained standard, as can be seen in the Colonia/Cologne tablet (cf. **464**, Figure 4.3).[127] Another rare but important variation of the normal layout can be found in texts that are double reversed and run from right to left and bottom to top. In other words, to read the text, one must start at the end of

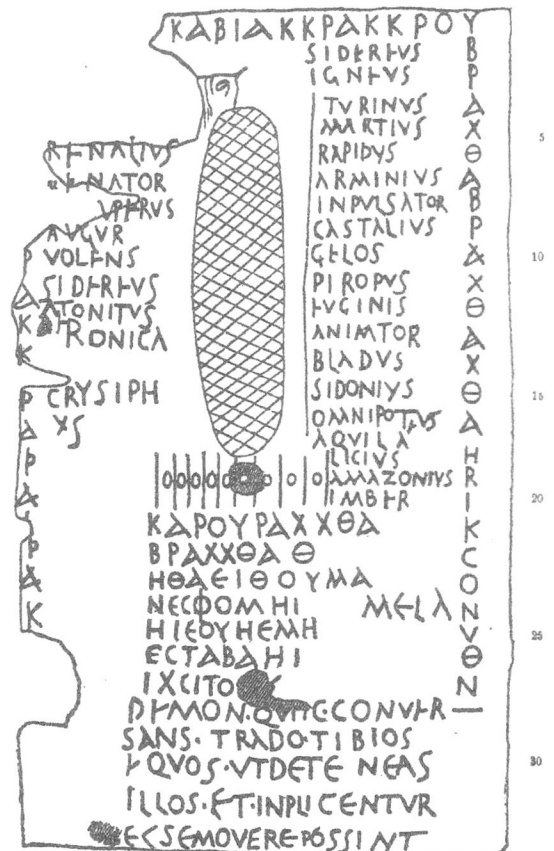

Figure 4.5. *DT* 233: 'Fence'-style layout (From: *CIL* VIII, 12504).

the final line, as can be seen in the Celti/Peñaflor curse (cf. **131**, Figure 4.4).[128]

Another layout that merits mention is the 'frame' or 'fence' type in which a portion of the text follows the edges of the tablet (see Figure 4.5). Such a layout is found in 20 known Latin curses dating from the High Empire and mostly discovered in the North African cities Carthage and Hadrumetum. As Gordon has noted, it is quite possible that this layout was 'derive[d] from the praxis of magical-amulet design, where divine images are regularly enclosed by a text' (2005: 78–79). As I was able to confirm during an autopsy of several North African curses,[129] the inscription of such texts begins with the 'fence' and then continues inward to fill the defined space. Without a doubt, the text chosen to form the 'fence' was

---

[123] These provinces have yielded 12, 8 and 7 items respectively. To this group we must add the three found in Gaul, one from Italy and another from Raetia.

[124] Specifically, **125–26** and **133**, to which **139** (dated to the end of the first century BCE or beginning of the first century CE) could also be added.

[125] Such as the five tablets from Selinunte (mostly dated to the mid-fifth century BCE), in which the lines run from right to left, though the letters maintain their normal orientation. See Bettarini 2005: nos 2, 4, 12, 24 and 25.

[126] The tablets **59**, **133**, **164**, **249**, **442** and **462** could be added.

[127] Other examples are **85**, **125–26**, **139**, **167**, **266**, **341**, **345**, **350**, **450**, **479–80** (these two only in part), **481**, **483**, **485**, **489**, **501** and **503–04**.

[128] To which **134–36**, **149**, **303**, **465** and **524–25** ought to be added.

[129] Specifically, *DT* 276–80 and 282–84.

not left to chance; on the contrary, all evidence shows that the professional practitioners that were producing these curses carefully chose the text to occupy this important and symbolically significant space. Accordingly, in three cases the 'fence' consists of the names of the *daemones* invoked,[130] while in another six curses it is composed of *voces magicae*.[131] In the majority of such texts, however, the 'fence' is reserved for the cursing formula proper.[132] While several of this curses should be categorized as juridical (cf. *DT* 218), erotic (cf. *DT* 227) or commercial (cf. *AE* 1933, 234–35), the bulk of them are agonistic in nature and deal with chariot races.[133] In such cases, it is possible that the 'fence' can be interpreted as a schematic representation of the circus or even of the race itself. Whatever the case may be and irrespective of the content of any particular curse, it seems clear that the intentional layout should be understood in terms of a persuasive analogy, since the 'fence' is an excellent means of symbolically 'confining' the spell's victims, who are accordingly trapped and cannot escape the text's powerful sway.[134]

The *defixio* against Prima Aemilia (from the sanctuary of Isis and Mater Magna in Mogontiacum/Mainz, cf. **484**) is a particular 'fence'-style curse that deserves special mention since the layout seems to be a blunder on the writer's part. Though the author clearly had a good deal of experience with writing practices, he or she did not properly judge the amount of space needed for writing the curse: the author wrote the first four lines following the edges of the tablet (i.e., turning it 90 degrees between each line); then, (s)he continued with the curse beginning just above the centre of the tablet. However, the author miscalculated the space needed to finish and hence had to finish writing on the upper part of the tablet; as a result, there is a space of about 8 mm between ll. 6 and 13. Despite an effort to use the fence-style, it is clear that the result was not quite as planned: the author simply misjudged the needed space for writing the entire text. Something similar can be observed in a *defixio* from Cruciniacum/Bad Kreuznach, (cf. **473**), in which the *defigens* had so many enemies that (s)he had to use the margins of the tablet to squeeze in the final cursing formula. This technique of using the margins to finish a message has been commonly observed in ancient letter writing as well.[135]

Finally, it is necessary to mention other layouts, which, though less common, are quite eye-catching instances. In two curses from Rome (cf. **26**) and Barchín del Hoyo

(cf. **145**), for instance, the circular shape of the curse's media functioned as a guide for its authors, whose texts took on the form of a spiral. In these cases, the layout of the text seems to have been determined by the object on which it was inscribed and hence can be understood as practical rather than a decision dictated by ritual. There are also two tablets from Aquae Sulis/Bath (cf. **308**) and Brigantium/Bregenz (cf. **521**), in which there is a combination of lines running from left to right and right to left (perhaps these are attempts at boustrophedon?). This layout is taken to the next level in a curse from Poetovio/Ptuj (cf. **527**), a tablet in which letters are additionally written mirrored *and* upside down.[136] But it is in two British curses from London (cf. **340** side B) and East Farleigh (cf. **458**), written in capitals with very irregular layouts, that things are taken to an extreme: text runs from right to left, left to right, in ascending and descending fashion; furthermore, letters are sometimes oriented forwards, sometimes 'mirrored' and sometimes upside down (see the commentary in the sylloge for a fuller description).

When a tablet also includes iconography, the inscription is fitted around the images almost as a frame (cf. with **22** and **24**, from Rome). On certain occasions labels are used to identify the represented figures (cf. **6** and **117**, from the 'Sethian' and the Bologna collection, respectively).

4.2.1.2. Language and writing

After the distortion of the layout, the most attested innovation in the curse tablets from the Roman West is the combination of different languages and/or scripts. This is found in almost 10 per cent of the corpus of *defixiones*, which mostly date to the High Empire. Scholars have generally explained the practice of combining different languages and/or writing systems as an attempt on the authors' part to increase the text's magical power. Nevertheless, this is only clear when certain significant words or phrases have been affected.[137] Up to what point these sorts of combinations were thought to ameliorate or facilitate the *defigens*' communication with the powers invoked is a worthwhile question. The topic could be understood in light of the High-Empire trend of using obsolete or at least extremely erudite language in religious writings.[138] But this was not always the case. As we will see in the following paragraphs, some of these cases can also be explained in terms of practicality, like in instances of linguistic borrowings or of an author's insufficient knowledge of the Latin alphabet. Whatever the case may be, it appears that most of the authors who wrote the

---

[130] Documented in *DT* 284 (from Hadrumetum), and *AE* 1933, 234–35 (from Carthage).
[131] Like in the Carthaginian tablets *DT* 218 (juridical in nature), *DT* 227 (possibly erotic), *DT* 233, *DT* 244, *DT* 253 (agonistic) and *DT* 255 (written for unknown reasons).
[132] Among these, we find *DT* 275–84 and *AE* 1907, 68–69 (all agonistic curses from Hadrumetum; for *DT* 275, see Cagnat's commentary *apud* Audollent 1904: 383; Piccaluga 1983: 122–23; Gordon 2002: 92–93).
[133] Cf. *DT* 233, 244, 253, 275–84 and *AE* 1907, 68 and 69 (for the *charaktêres* found in *DT* 276–85 and *AE* 1907, 68 and 69, see Németh 2011).
[134] Cf. Sánchez Natalías 2020d: 105–06.
[135] Sarri 2018: 112; an analogous case is found in **494**.

[136] We can also add **461** (cf. Fig. 4.2) or **479**.
[137] Poccetti 2002: 28; Marco Simón 2012: 128.
[138] Good examples of this are the *Carmen Arvale* (*CIL* VI, 2014, written in archaic Latin during the reign of Augustus), the so-called 'Pillar of the Boatmen' (*RIG* II.1, L-14), which the *nautae Parisiaci* dedicated to Jupiter during the reign of Tiberius. This piece consists of stone blocks which have been engraved with Roman and indigenous deities, which are identified with Latin and Gaulish theonyms. Another example is the small group of Lusitanian inscriptions from Lamas de Moledo and Arroyo de la Luz (cf. Alfayé and Marco Simón 2008). For more examples of linguistic recuperation in religious contexts, see Mancini 1988: 208–09.

tablets discussed in this section of the prolegomena were well-trained professionals who were capable of mixing various languages and writing systems within the confines of a single text. In several cases, this sort of sophistication was combined with other noteworthy features.[139]

Following the typology proposed by J.N. Adams in his study of bilingualism in Antiquity, we can place the relevant *defixiones* into three categories: bilingual, mixed and transliterated (2003: 29–70). While texts can usually be neatly placed in one of these three categories, there are certain cases which could be classified in either the second or third categories.[140] Bilingual curses are those that use two different languages to duplicate the same message. There is only one known instance of such a curse, which comes from Barchín del Hoyo (cf. **145**; dated to the end of the first century BCE or beginning of the first century CE) and written in Greek and Latin by an individual who appears to have been a native Greek speaker.[141]

Adams' mixed type of text is much more common. In this instance, a curse employs various languages to elaborate different content. The causes that give rise to these hybrid texts can be explained by that fact that, as Poccetti explains, 'alla scrittura sovente il potere magico deriva dalla condizione di allografismo e/o di allografia. Si attribuisce, cioè, forza magica alla scrittura o alla parola che appartengono a tradizioni grafiche e/o linguistiche "altre"' (2002: 28). In the Roman West, 48 tablets belong to this group, the majority of which hail from Africa and Italia and were written in a mixture of Latin and Greek.[142] Here, it is important to note that most of these texts were written by professional magical practitioners, who were showing off their Graeco-Egyptian magical know-how in order to impress their audience (human clients and gods invoked). Generally speaking, Greek is used for writing certain 'technical' magical phrases, such as the names of *daemones* or deities,[143] certain *voces magicae*,[144] palindromes[145] and the seven vowels of the alphabet.[146] The inclusion of such Greek language elements undoubtedly constitutes a conscious decision on the part of the author, who sought to imbue his or her text with a powerful boost that would ensure its efficacy.

On certain occasions, the actual invocation of the divinities or even an entire cursing formula were written in Greek, while the rest of the inscription was put in Latin.[147] This is the case with a curse from Lilybaeum/Marsala (cf. **109**), the oldest of this group (dated between the fourth and third centuries BCE), where the author employs a long Greek invocation to summon Persephone, the Titans and the *atélestoi*; the practitioner ask that they take action against a group of victims, whose names are listed in Latin. Another interesting case is found in a pair of Carthaginian tablets discovered in the amphitheatre and dated to the High Empire (cf. *DT* 248–49). In the first, the text is written in Latin except for the final lines, which contain the classic formula ἤδη ἤδη ταχὺ ταχύ (*DT* 248 B, ll. 8–9), while the second curse is completely in Greek except for the brief mention of the victims (*DT* 249 B, ll. 1–3). Given that these two curses target the same individuals, it appears that they were written by the same magical professional and meant to work together in conjunction.

Even though the majority of tablets within the mixed categories combine Latin and Greek, there are other noteworthy mixtures of languages. A good example comes from Cumae (cf. **64**): the curse, which dates to the end of the first century BCE and was inscribed by a Latin-speaking practitioner, uses Latin to name the spell's victims[148] but switches to Oscan for the cursing formula proper.[149] As Mancini has argued, the linguistic diversity of this curse, which is '*intenzionalmente distante* dall'uso quotidiano' (1988: 208), was meant to guarantee the spell's efficacy.

A similar case can be found in the curse tablet from Rauranum/Rom (cf. **159**), which mixes Latin and Gaulish.[150] This tablet, which dates between the third and fourth centuries CE and whose interpretation has proven to be extremely controversial, contains various Latin lexemes (*pura* [A, ll. 7 and 9], *poteat* [B, l. 6] and *decipia* [A, l. 6]) alongside a series of Gaulish verbal forms (e.g., *uoraiimo* [B, ll. 1 and 10], *atepriauimo*

---

[139] E.g., **5**, **117–18** or the North African curses *DT* 251, 253, 286, 289 and 292–94.

[140] Such curses are **5**, **117**, **130** and the curses from Hadrumetum *DT* 295 and 269. All belong to the mixed type (since they are written in Latin and Greek) and to the category of transliteration (since the first four have Greek texts transliterated into the Latin alphabet, while the final one contains a Latin fragment transliterated into the Greek alphabet).

[141] According to the editors (Curbera *et al.* 1999: 283), the text's palaeographical characteristics (such as the use of 'Δ' for 'D' and the final -*n* to mark the accusative in the Latin portion) support this hypothesis.

[142] From Africa are the Carthaginian curses *DT* 218, 227, 233, 243, 244, 248–51, 253, 255, *AE* 1933, 234–35 and Jordan 1988: no. 3; the tablet from Naro/Hammam-Lif (Audollent 1910, no. 1) and those from Hadrumetum *DT* 264, 266, 293–95 and *AE* 1911, 6. Most of these African texts were written by professional practitioners. From Italy are **64**, **109**, **117–18**, and the curses written by professionals discovered in Rome **5**, **24–28**, **33–36**, **38** and **40**. To these, we can also add **150–55**, **166**, **157**, **159** and **530**.

[143] Such as in the Carthaginian curses *DT* 230, 243, 250, 253, *AE* 1933, 234–35; Jordan 1988: no. 3; the curses from Hadrumetum *DT* 264 (?), 293–95 and *AE* 1911, 6; the curses from Rome **5**, **25–27** and **35–36**.

[144] Such as in the Carthaginian curses *DT* 218, 227, 233, 243–44, 253 and 255; that from Naro/Hammam-Lif (Audollent 1910, no. 1); the curse from Hadrumetum *AE* 1905, 171; the curses from the fountain of Anna Perenna in Rome **20**, **24–28**, **33–34**, **38**, **40**.

[145] Such as in **26** and *DT* 253.

[146] Such as in **5** and Jordan 1988: no. 3.

[147] For the Greek invocations, cf. **109**, **117–18**, **166** and the curse from Hadrumetum *DT* 295. Complete formulae in Greek are found in **109**, **530**, *DT* 248, 249, 253 and perhaps 266.

[148] The victim's names, which are in the nominative, use different terminations: the first three employ Oscan morphology (ending in –*is*, ll. 1–2), whereas the last two use the Latin termination (ll. 4–5).

[149] As Mancini (1988: 222–23) points out, 'dove è stato possibile il trascrittore ha operato nel senso di latinizzare la formula originariamente osca. In quest' ambito si spiegano le forme *sint, sit, recta*. L'ovvia sovrapponibilità formale e funzionale ha causato una sorta di riverniciatura latina di queste parole, che in osco dovevano suonare rispettivamente *sins, *sid, *rehtas*'.

[150] Lambert (*apud RIG* II.2) further adds the tablets from Le Mans (cf. **171**) and Les Martres-de-Veyre (cf. **161**). In the first, he interprets *DM* as an abbreviation of the Latin formula *D(is) M(anibus)*, though we must remember that this proposal is extremely speculative due to the complexity of the text, in which only several Celtic personal names can be identified. In **161**, Lambert has taken *DIVOS* (A, l. 2) as Celtic *diuos*, though it could certainly be Latin *divos*.

[B, ll. 7–8] and *bicartaont* [A, l. 5]). Finally, we should perhaps add to this group of mixed curses the six *defixiones* discovered in Amélie-les-Bains (cf. **150–55**, today their whereabouts are unknown) that were written in a language whose precise identification is not agreed upon[151] but are clearly interspersed with a series of Latin words like *rogamos* and *depecamus* ('Vulgar' forms of *rogamus* and *deprecamur*).[152] Generally speaking, there are various factors (our partial understanding of the Gaulish language, the tablets' poor state of conservation and their disappearance) that have impaired the analysis of these texts and kept us from determining to what extent and to what end Latin was mixed with Gaulish, not to mention what role each language played within these curses.

Two other curses should be mentioned in which a text almost entirely in Latin includes several specific words in a different language.[153] The first comes from Montfo (Gallia Narbonensis, cf. **157**), which was found inside of a well and dates to the first century CE. In this text, the *defigens* references the *masitlatida* (B, l. 5), which appears to be a Gallic ritual of unknown characteristics (cf. Lejeune 1981: 52). The second example is a curse tablet from the sanctuary of Sulis Minerva in Aquae Sulis/Bath (cf. **206**), dated to the second century CE, which reads in part: '*qu[i] mihi vilbiam in[v]olavit...*' (l. 1). Russell has interpreted *vilbiam* as a Celtic word that referred to the stolen object mentioned in the curse, perhaps a tool similar to a gouge (2006: 364). In these two cases, the inclusion of an indigenous word is eminently practical and should be considered instances of linguistic borrowing and hence be differentiated from the previous examples.

Now we must turn our attention to a final series of mixed tablets that employ what Adams has called 'alphabet-switching', which is securely attested in seven curses from North Africa. These curses, written in the Latin alphabet, include some Greek letters, such as Chi (χ)[154] or Zeta (ζ),[155] 'for which there was no exact equivalence in Latin' (cf. Marco Simón 2012: 125). As in the previous two examples, these cases do not provide evidence for using a different alphabet as a means of augmenting a tablet's magical potency (these tablets actually employ

onómata[156] or iconography[157] to accomplish that purpose), but rather point to the identity of the magical practitioner from whom the tablet was commissioned. These professionals were probably native Greek speakers who had not achieved mastery of the Latin alphabet and had not found a way to render certain Greek characters in a different alphabet.[158]

The third and final of Adams' categories deals with transliterated texts, that is inscriptions written in one language, but using the writing system of a different language. Among the *defixiones* from the Roman West, those that belong to this category come from the Mediterranean provinces and tend to combine different languages and alphabets. Good examples can be found in five erotic curses that were discovered in Hadrumetum and Carthage: while they are in the Latin language, the magical practitioners who wrote them opted for the Greek alphabet.[159]

Less common are tablets written in the Greek language using the Latin alphabet. In fact, there are only five known curses that fit this category and only partially so. The first example is a Carthaginian curse that contains the *onómata barbariká* as well as some transliterated formulae;[160] the second comes from Hadrumetum and invokes *to autem Domina Canpana*,[161] whereas the third example, from Rome (cf. **5**), ends with *[ed]e ede/ tacy tacy* (ll. 21–22). Perhaps the second fragment from a curse from the Bologna collection, **117**, in which an imaginary(?) language whose meaning is undecipherable but phonetically resembles Greek, should be counted in this group. Furthermore, a fifth curse that hails from Aratispi/Villanueva del Cauche (Baetica, see Figure 4.6 and cf. **130**) should be added. After eight lines of *charaktêres*, it reads *hutos apoleson M(arcum) Domitiu(m) Nigrum Firmanae filium*. In these cases, the use of transliteration has generally been understood as a ritual attempt on the magical practitioners' part to increase the magical power of the spell.

Celtic and Oscan tablets need to be mentioned separately, since they do not belong to the category of transliterated texts: in these instances, the curses were written in the alphabets that their users had taken up for writing their native languages. The use of these writing systems, then, had become traditional and therefore their use in *defixiones* cannot be attributed any sort of magical function.

---

[151] Lambert (*apud RIG* II.2, *L-97) interprets it as a mix of Gaulish and Latin, while Coromines (1975 and 1976) identified it as Sorothapic (the language spoken by the so-called Urnfield culture). For a general discussion, see *RIG* II.2, p. 250.

[152] *Rogamos et depecamus* appear in **150**, I, ll. 2–3, and perhaps in **154**, ll. 2–4, while *rogamus* is found on its own in **151**, A, l. 2 (perhaps this is a case of a mixed language similar to that from La Graufesenque?).

[153] In addition to these curses, a tablet from Orosei (cf. **110**) should be added. Caprara (1978: 152) has interpreted the word *nurgo* (ll. 2 and 5) as a Sardinian word derived 'della radice *nur* –nella sua accezione di "voragine", e quindi probabilmente di luogo infero'.

[154] Cf. *DT* 251 (in which some *onómata* maintain the final c, as in *Psarchyrinχ* (Col. 1, l. 2) and in which the Greek letters π and ω also appear) and *DT* 292–94 (where final χ is maintained in the *vox magica anox*).

[155] See *DT* 253, where the author wrote *Vicentζus* for *Vicentius* (ll. 10, 11, etc.). Poccetti has defined this as 'ricorso a grafemi greci che segnalano processi di affricazione' (2002: 46). Also see *DT* 286 and 289, where the *vox magica basagra* is written as *baζagra*.

[156] Found in *DT* 251, 253, 286, 289 and 292–94.

[157] As is the case in *DT* 286, 289 and 292.

[158] As Adams put it 'If someone writing (e.g.) Latin in Latin script adopts Greek letters from time to time, he was not in total command of Latin script and is likely to have been a Greek with imperfect Latin literacy' (2003: 72).

[159] Specifically, *DT* 267 (ll. 15–25), 269–70 and 304, and the Carthaginian curse *DT* 231. Additionally, we must add **436**, an exceptional curse from the sanctuary of Mercury in Uley (Britannia) that was written in the Latin language and Greek alphabet (for a preliminary note on the curse, see Tomlin 2002: 175).

[160] Cf. *DT* 251, I, ll. 2–10, II and III, l. 2.

[161] See *DT* 295, l. 20–21.

Figure 4.6. Detail from the Aratispi/Villanueva del Cauche *defixio* (cf. 130 From: CIL-Archiv, II_5, 0729 beta).

4.2.2. Other components linked to the text

As Gordon (2002: 17) puts it, 'it was precisely in malign magic, generally considered the most difficult to perform, that special efforts were felt necessary to increase the force of the text'. Among these special efforts, and as mentioned previously, individuals (or better, professional practitioners) could include a range of other components that coexisted in a symbiotic relationship with the curse's text, such as iconography, *charaktêres* and certain *voces magicae*. As can be deduced from Table 4.1, these elements appear (save in rare exceptions) in curses written by professional practitioners coming from North Africa and Italy and mostly date to the High Empire or Late Antiquity, respectively. Iconography, *charaktêres* and *voces magicae* are the most widely attested of such additional components, while palindromes and alphabetic sequences are less common.

4.2.2.1. Imagines magicae[162]

Within the collection of curses from the Roman West, the inclusion of iconography is a relatively rare phenomenon. So far, there are only 42 known examples of *defixiones* that are accompanied by *imagines magicae*.[163] In almost half of the instances, the knowledge that we have of these *imagines* is often limited to an editor's verbal description,

since the publication of curse tablets (which in some cases were edited more than a century ago) sometimes lack visual representations. This omission surely needs to be remedied and further study of these *defixiones'* iconography is sorely missing.

In all of these tablets, iconography is accompanied by the text. That is, there are no *defixiones* with only images, while there are obviously many curses with text without an image. That said, in tablets that have both text and image, where there is always a close connection between the two, it would be inaccurate to claim that the image is somehow secondary. In fact, in these curses it is the text that is fitted around the image, not the other way around. Texts with iconography, then, contain a carefully planned layout which serves to reinforce the power of the image. The text, therefore, can be understood as a secondary element that appears to be dependent on the image. This, of course, is not to say that the text is somehow rendered unimportant. The result of combining these two elements is a clearer, more compelling *defixio* that is better equipped to carry out the practitioners' desires, since his or her message can reach the powers invoked through both image and text.

With the exception of five curses from Mazan and Augusta Treverorum/Trier (Gallia), all of the curses with iconography hail from the places near the Mediterranean, such as Rome, Carthage, Hadrumetum, Cirta/Constantine and Thysdrus/El Jem and were composed by professional practitioners. The earliest examples date to the second and third centuries CE and were discovered in the above-mentioned North African cities. It is only at the beginning of the fourth century CE that *defixiones* with iconography appear in the Roman archaeological record. In the fourth and fifth centuries CE such *defixiones* are well attested in the imperial capital, as can be seen in the Late-Antique collections from the sanctuary of Anna Perenna and the so-called 'Sethian' *defixiones*.

The drawings found on these tablets generally represent either the deity invoked or the curse's victims. There are a few rare instances in which both the deity and victim are represented on the same tablet; while it is even rarer to find other sorts of images.[164] Instances in which 'the images concretize the divinity or power (or a metamorph) whose intervention is required by the spell or rite'[165] are especially common in African curses. In said province, there is an important series of (mostly) agonistic *defixiones* (dated between the second and third centuries CE and composed by professional practitioners) on which the demon invoked is depicted.[166] Such demons tend to be anthropomorphic[167] —though sometimes they

---

[162] An extended version of this section, which includes the Latin and Greek *defixiones* from the Roman West, can be found in Sánchez Natalías 2020d: 108–21. On this same topic, see also Sánchez Natalías 2013c.
[163] See Gordon 2002 and 2018 (for Late-Antique curse tablets with elements of the Graeco-Egyptian tradition, such as those from Anna Perenna or the Sethian collection); Viglione 2010: 119–24 (though she is mostly focused on Greek texts); Németh 2013 (which includes the unpublished sketches that Audollent made while compiling *DT*). For the connection between images, oral speech and writing in the *PGM*, see Crippa 2002 and 2010.

[164] See the classification proposed by Cesano 1961[2]: 1568.
[165] Gordon 2002: 98.
[166] These are the Carthaginian tablets *DT* 229, 244, 247–48 and 260 and those from Cirta/Constantine (*DT* 300), Naro/Hammam-Lif (Audollent 1910: 136–41) and Hadrumetum (*DT* 286–92 and *AE* 1911, 6).
[167] Cf. *DT* 229 and 244 (= Németh 2013: 152, 164–65, where it looks like a bust) as well as those from Cirta/Constantine (*DT* 300; see fig. 16), Naro/Hammam-Lif (Audollent 1910: 137–41) and Hadrumetum (*DT* 286–92= Németh 2013: 200–09 and *AE* 1911, 6).

Figure 4.7. *Imagines magicae: daemon* **Baitmo Arbitto** (From: *DT* 286).

have the heads of a snake,[168] bird[169] or horse[170]— unshod (as a way of marking their divinity) and carry attributes or magical symbols. Sometimes the deity's name is inscribed on his chest. In some tablets, the demons are shown seated,[171] though it is more common to see them standing or on a ship, as can be seen in the famous demon Baitmo Arbitto, who is depicted in an important series from Hadrumetum[172] (see Figure 4.7). We should also mention two curses from Carthage on which the *defigentes* depicted beasts and fantastical creatures, which may be representations of the powers tasked with carrying out the curses' requests.[173]

From Italia (though their precise archaeological context is unknown), there are other noteworthy *defixiones*, such as **117–18**, on which there are possibly representations of Hecate-Selene. In favour of such an identification would be the series of *onómata* composed of φωρ- and the snakes that emerge from her head (which recall a description of the goddess in *PGM* IV 2800–02: '[you] who shake your locks of fearful serpents on your brow').[174] The collection from Anna Perenna also contains some curses with noteworthy iconography. The deity invoked is depicted on various containers from the fountain (cf. **25–27** and **35–36**) and takes the form of a figure with the crested head of a rooster that carries a lamp or a torch in its hand. Furthermore, this figure bears an inscription on its abdomen, which, according to G. Németh (2012b and 2015), is an abbreviation (with slight variations) for the Christian formula Ἰησοῦς Χριστός Ναζωραῖος, Ἰησοῦς Χριστός Ναζωραῖος, καὶ Θεός, Θεός, Θεός. Like the abovementioned case of Baitmo Arbitto or the other North African demons, this formula would have served to invoke and identify the divine power tasked with bringing the spell to fruition. Dating to Late Antiquity and probably made by a single professional practitioner, this series of containers allows us to glimpse the rich environment of religious syncretism in which elements from various traditions came together. Accordingly, and although the rooster-headed figure is reminiscent of Abraxas,[175] the formula inscribed on his abdomen signals a Christian context in which the palindrome Ablanathanabla, which is attested in some Gnostic gemstones that contain all these elements, was also used.[176]

Blänsdorf, the editor of the Anna Perenna curses, has identified another deity invoked in a container (cf. **28**): Seth. The identification, however, is quite suspect, since a new reading of the container determined that the deity is not named in the text, but rather the victim: Seberinus.[177] Thus, the representation would match the curse's text, alluding to the victim of the spell.

This leads us to the other predominant type of iconography found on *defixiones*: representations of the victim.[178] Such representations broadly take the form of portraits or busts, depicted frontally. Even if this model could have been inspired by funerary portraits of the deceased (commonly found in cemeteries), a better way to think of them is as beheaded victims (cf. Martín Hernández 2021). Good examples of this 'bust' style can be seen on a Carthaginian *defixio*, which is probably agonistic

---

[168] Cf. *DT* 247, where Audollent described this representation as 'Homo stans (Typhon-Seth?) serpentis capite insignis, hastam dextra fulmen (?) sinistra'. See Németh 2013: 168.

[169] Cf. *DT* 260, which Audollent described as 'Daemon cuius caput avis (?) capiti simile quasi petaso tegitur duplici crista ornato et brachia extenduntur, nescio quid dextra, tridentem fortasse sinistra tenens'. See Németh 2013: 179.

[170] Cf. *DT* 248, which Audollent described as 'Daemon stans longis auribus et asinino (?) capite insignis, pateras (?) duas, sinistra gerens, fascem (?) dextra'. See Németh 2013: 168.

[171] Cf. *DT* 292, which Audollent described as 'Daemon sedens in structura caementicia obliqueis lineis adumbrata, flagellum tenens sinistra. Ante pedes daemonis humana protome'. Sichet (2000: 190, fig. 24), provides a drawing based on the photograph published in *Cat. Alaoui*, tab. XXVIII. See Németh 2013: 207–09.

[172] Specifically, *DT* 286–91. See Gordon 2005: 69–76 and Németh 2013: 200–05 and 230.

[173] Cf. *DT* 255 and 259 (= Németh 2013: 176 and 178–79, respectively). Audollent described the first as 'imago beluae ingentis delineata est, quam quo nomine adpellem nescio; nam etsi hippopotamo similis est corpore et cornu in naso erecto, elephanta in memoriam revocat hirsuta proboscide (non lingua, ut ait W.), a fronte ad pedes promissa; praeterea alterum cornu et fortasse galli crista in capite eminent, ac tandem cauda draco fuisse videtur; saetae per totum corpus horrent'. The second is *DT* 259, in which the editor identified a cross and 'Ensis aut crux ita

figuratur cum canis aut bestiae cuiusdam imagine in summa hasta'. See the discussion in Németh 2012a: 145 and figs 8–11.

[174] Translated by E.N. O'Neil *apud* Betz 1992². On this iconography, cf. Sánchez Natalías 2013a, with further references.

[175] For the identification as Abraxas, see Blänsdorf 2012e: 619, 622, 624–25 and 2015b: 22f.; Piranomonte 2012a: 167–71 and 2012b: 618 and 625 (with further references).

[176] See Spier 2007: 81–85.

[177] Cf. **28** and Sánchez Natalías 2020b.

[178] For the representations of the victims in the tablets, see Marco Simón and Sánchez Natalías 2022.

Figure 4.8. *Imagines magicae:* Saturnius (From Delatte *et al.* 1906, 323).

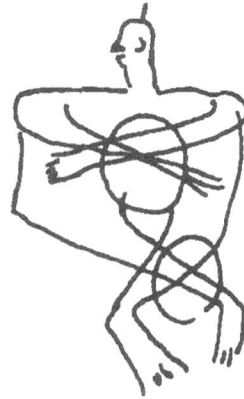

Figure 4.9. *Imagines magicae:* tied charioteer (From Jordan 1988, 130, fig. 2).

Figure 4.10. *Imagines magicae:* victim encircled by snakes (From *DT* 245, *apud* Németh 2013, 166).

in nature[179] (see Figure 4.8), or on a curse from Augusta Treverorum/Trier (cf. **180**) that appears to be directed against a gladiator. Occasionally, there is a full-body representation of the victim, who is shown standing, such as we find on two curses from the sanctuary of Anna Perenna. The first, **19**, targets Antonius, who is shown facing the viewer in standing position with his arms placed against his sides. He looks stunned, like someone that is exposed to and helpless against a magical spell. In a similar fashion, although with less expressiveness, is the abovementioned case of Seberinus, depicted in **28**.

Some practitioners, however, were much more explicit: in certain cases, we find representations of the terrible punishment that victims are meant to suffer. The first examples of this come from Carthage and date to around the third century CE. In an agonistic curse against an *auriga*, the victim is represented with his hands and feet crossed and tied with a rope, in such a way that he surely could not drive his chariot, let alone win a race. The depicted ropes served as a symbolic representation of the desired constraint of the curse's victim[180] (see Figure 4.9). In addition to ropes, we can also find other restrictive elements such as large snakes. In another *defixio* from Carthage of similar date, we see a victim trapped in a sort of wooden coffin from which his head sticks out, entrapped within the coils of a huge snake. Although the head of the reptile has been lost, Audollent's drawing preserves the

bifurcated tip of the snake's tongue, which is just shy of touching the victim's face (see Figure 4.10).

These large winding serpents with their pointy ears, pronged tongues and scaled bodies are clearly found in classical literature and iconography (just think of Aesclepius' snake, the *agathos daimon* or the myth of Laocoön). Nevertheless, during Late Antiquity this reptile enjoyed a new resurgence thanks to Egypt's influence on magical-religious practices throughout the Mediterranean. As proposed elsewhere,[181] it is possible that the image of Osiris wrapped in the coils of a snake could have served as a model for the magical practitioners who drew them on Late Antique curse tablets. Unlike in Egyptian religion where the serpent protected Osiris in the underworld, in these curses the snake becomes a symbol of danger and constriction that is associated with demonic forces.

[179] See Delattre and Monceaux 1906: 222–23 (= *AE* 1907, 165).
[180] Cf. Jordan 1988: 129ff. It is worth stressing that the representation of victims with tied hands and feet is quite common in the collection of 'Sethian' *defixiones*, as can be appreciated in *SV* 20–22, etc.

[181] Sánchez Natalías 2020d: 115.

There are several examples from the fountain of Anna Perenna that match this new conception of the snake. The curse tablet against Sura (cf. **22**), for example, contains a noteworthy representation of its victim with snakes along with other eye-catching features: the judge Sura, whose face is superimposed on a vulva (cf. Gradvohl 2009). This image is connected to the variation of a common matronymic formula, which in this case reads *qui natu(s) est de vulva maledicta* (ll. 14–16). Sura is shown trapped inside of a rhombus, flanked by snakes and hence completely confined by the spell's powers. Another noteworthy case is a curse that appears to target a certain Petronius Cornigus (cf. **33**), if we accept that the curse was targeting the same individual as the magical figurine that was found together with the tablet in the innermost container. In the curse tablet, the victim is shown standing with his arms flat against his sides. In addition to being tied up with dozens of ropes, the victim is flanked by two snake-like monsters that represent the powers meant to destroy him.

Another noteworthy motif that is found several times in Late Antique curses is the mummification of the victim. As Gager has put it, the function of these images was 'to anticipate and enact the desired outcome for the spell itself, to bind or in some other way harm the target' (1992: 11). The mummification of the target, which was surely influenced by the representation of mummified Osiris, served as the ultimate way of depicting the immobility and constriction of a victim, who was left totally helpless and vulnerable to the spell's powers. This is seen in **117**, which finds interesting parallels among the 'Sethian' collection (cf. *SV* 17, fig. 4.7, left) and in a magical figurine from the fountain of Anna Perenna, which are all dated to the same period (fourth–fifth centuries CE).[182] As argued elsewhere,[183] these images are better understood as depicting the victim of the spell. In favour of such a hypothesis, consider the general layout of the curses (with the deities on top and the victims on the bottom of the tablet) as well as the expressions κατὰ κράβατον τιμωρίας ('on (the) bed of punishment') and κακῷ θανάτῳ ('evil death'), documented in these same 'Sethian' curses.

As mentioned above, there are rare occasions in which the victim and a deity are both represented in an attempt to create a narrative structure that served as a sort of script for the divinity tasked with carrying out the *defigens*' wishes. Hence, through his or her creativity, the practitioner shows the deity what it should do and provides it with a *modus operandi*.[184] The curses that securely belong to this category are **117** (against the veterinarian Porcellus) and **5** (which targets the miller Praeseticius), to which we should possibly add **6** (against an unborn child, among other victims). In the first two curses, the divinity is seen in standing position and is placed above its victims, who occupy a lower plane near the deity's feet. In **117**, the victim Porcellus is shown mummified and with his arms crossed or tied, whereas in the tablets from Rome (cf. **5** and **6**) we see three victims schematically represented. In the other instance from the 'Sethian' collection (cf. **6**), we see two figures: the first is bigger, has a large insignia with a *charaktêr* on his chest and is surrounded by magical symbols, seven stars and *charaktêres*. All of this seems to be a means of representing the figure's supernatural status. The second figure is represented upside down and is shown swaddled, which strongly suggests that this is the unborn child mentioned as one of the tablet's victims.

Finally, we must briefly mention the tablets in which neither the victim nor the deity is represented, but rather we find other elements that tend to be related to the spell itself. A good example is found in an erotic *defixio* from Hadrumetum: in the centre there is a representation of intertwined cords that are pierced with nails or swords, which seems to be a visual representation of the union of the *defigens* and his victim.[185] Another noteworthy example can be seen in an agonistic curse from Carthage (Figure 4.5), on which the outline of the circus has been inscribed.[186] Three more *defixiones* (one from Carthage and two from Augusta Treverorum/Trier) where we see a sort of basket or fence (perhaps meant to entrap the victims?) also belong to this category. Finally, a curse from Mazan (cf. **156**) represents what the editors have identified as either a snake or ship, which closely resembles an image found on a curse from Corinth.[187]

4.2.2.2. Magical symbols and charaktêres

The use of magical symbols and *charaktêres* is somewhat more frequent than the inclusion of iconography in the corpus of curses from the Roman West: they are securely found on 53 tablets, which constitutes 8 per cent of the total collection. Audollent grouped magical symbols and *charaktêres* together under the heading *signa magica*.[188] Today in many cases we cannot easily distinguish one from the other, due to the lack of published drawings or photos of many curse tablets. As was mentioned in the previous section, for texts that were published well over a century ago, information about visual components is often scarce or even non-existent. Today, any type of unusual symbol found in a *defixio* or other magical object tends to be included in the group of *charaktêres*.[189]

Charaktêres find their origin in the imitation of various writing systems (such as Egyptian hieroglyphs[190] or letters

---

[182] For the 'Sethian' curses, see *SV* 16–18 and for the magical figurine, cf. **24**.
[183] Cf. Sánchez Natalías 2013c: 10 and 2020d: 113–15.
[184] Cf. Gordon 2002: 101–03.

[185] Cf. *DT* 264 (for an image, see Németh 2013: 182–83).
[186] Cf. *DT* 233 (with an image in *CIL* VIII, 12504).
[187] Cf. Barruol and Barruol 1963: 109. For the Corinthian parallel, see Jordan 1994: 120–21. To these, we must add a recent find from Tongres (see Bélanger Sarrazin *et al.* 2019).
[188] See *DT*: p. LXXII: 'Plures autem multo se praestant litterae singulae, sive mudae sive globulis in extremis hastis ornatae'.
[189] As Gordon has maintained (*per litt.*): 'at any rate, in the meantime it has become usual to use the term "charakteres" for all deliberately estranged signs, whether or not they closely resemble ordinary alphabetic signs'.
[190] Cf. Zago 2010: 848, where the author claims 'sembrano costituire un *alter ego* della scrittura geroglifica egiziana, di cui sopravvalutano però

from the Greek or Latin alphabet)[191] and the use of a series of basic shapes, such as rectangles, rhombi, stars, bars and crosses. Generally, the main feature that distinguishes them from other magical symbols is that they have small circles on the end of lines. As Poccetti has shown, these symbols constitute 'una simbologia grafica allo stato puro, che implica né una lettura né una recitazione, ma solo una visualizzazione'.[192] Their presence in *defixiones,* amulets and 'magical' recipes attests to their range of functions and purposes.[193] One of their defining characteristics is their divine nature, which several *defigentes* invoke. Indeed, they were thought to be sacred elements containing significant power, as is seen in the various invocations documented in several agonistic curses and *phylaktéria*.[194]

Most curses containing *charaktêres* date between the second and fourth centuries CE (cf. Gordon 2002: 90, n. 75), though two tablets from Aratispi/Villanueva del Cauche (Hispania, cf. **130** and Figure 4.6) and Tongres (Gallia Belgica), which have been dated to the first century CE,[195] expands the normal chronological limits associated with the use of *charaktêres*. In a careful analysis of the *charaktêres* found in a considerable number of magical objects (the *PGM*, gems, *defixiones* and *phylaktéria*), Gordon has catalogued around 1,000 different symbols (2011: 27ff.). Within this large collection, Gordon has singled out two important groups, the first of which consists of 12 symbols that are attested more than 15 times (see Figure 4.11); the second consists of 30 symbols that appear around 10 times. The rest of the *charaktêres*, he concludes, 'were simply produced on one occasion. That is why there could be so many of them' (2011: 30).[196]

As is the case with *defixiones* that contain iconography, those that are adorned with *charaktêres* or magical symbols are mostly found in Africa and Italia; indeed, examples from elsewhere are few and far between (see Table 4.1).[197] When used in curse tablets, *charaktêres* are generally given a place of prominence, like the heading (i.e., before the actual cursing formula begins), alongside *imagines magicae*[198] or even alone on one side of the tablet.[199] There

Figure 4.11. *Charaktêres* **attested more than 15 times (Gordon 2011: 28, fig. 3).**

are also instances in which *charaktêres* are used to divide a text into several parts.[200]

As mentioned above, the earliest tablets containing *charaktêres* come from Aratispi/Villanueva del Cauche (Hispania Ulterior, cf. **130** and Figure 4.6) and Tongres (Gallia Belgica), which have been dated to the end of the first century CE. By the second century CE, there are other examples attested in Gallia and Africa.[201] In the latter, the use of *charaktêres* flourished until the third century CE. The proliferation of this trend is in fact so strong that it is possible to identify specific series that point to the existence of prolific magical professionals in Hadrumetum during the High Empire.[202] By the end of the third century CE and the beginning of the fourth century CE, the first curses containing *charaktêres* begin to appear in Italy, though it was not until the fourth and fifth centuries CE with the appearance of the 'Sethian' and Anna Perenna collections that this visual element truly reached the height of its popularity.[203] Furthermore, during the same period there are other curses with *charaktêres* or magical symbols from Gaul (cf. **183–84** and **190**) and even further afield in Britain (cf. **446**) and Pannonia (cf. **530**).

4.2.2.3. *Other voces magicae*

On rare occasions, *defixiones* from the Roman West contain other *voces magicae* alongside the use of iconography or *charaktêres*. This less common category includes items such as the *onómata barbariká*, palindromes or letter sequences containing the vowels of the Greek alphabet. Although they may have been incomprehensible, these elements could be pronounced and hence (in contrast to the *charaktêres*) played an important role in the oral portion of the *actio magica*.

As is the case with *charaktêres*, the *onómata barbariká* are not only found in *defixiones*, but are also used in other magical objects, such *phylaktéria*, gems, papyri and *ostraka*. The *onómata barbariká* are first attested in the Mediterranean in the first century BCE and then reached the height of their popularity during the High Empire.[204] According to the Neo-Platonic philosopher Iamblichus (*Myst.* VII, 4–5), the *onómata barbariká*, which were

---

il carattere ideografico rispetto a quello fonetico'. Likewise, Frankfurter 1994: 207 states that 'the heavenly "letters" in fact denote Egyptian hieroglyphs'. For a contrary view, see Mastrocinque 2004: 98 and Gordon 2011: 27, 30–31 (who notes some exceptions).
[191] Cf. Gordon 2011: 28 and 30.
[192] Cf. Poccetti 2002: 42; Gordon 2011: 26–27.
[193] Cf. Zago 2010: 847, n. 60.
[194] Good examples include the tablets mentioned by Gager (1992: 11) from Apamea, Beth Shean and Hebron (= Gager 1992, no. 6, 77 and 106, respectively). We can also add the curses from Hadrumetum *DT* 273 (ll. 11–13) and 274 (ll. 11–13; cf. Németh 2011: 101), among others. For the *phylaktéria*, see the examples discussed by Mastrocinque 2012: 537–38.
[195] To the editor's surprise, who writes, 'Litterarum formae saec. I vix posteriores videntur, quamquam charakteres saec. II demum frequentiores apparuerunt' (*CIL* II²/5, 729). For the tablet from Tongres, see Bélanger Sarrazin *et al.* 2019.
[196] Cf. also Gordon 2002: 90.
[197] There is one *defixio* from Hispania (**130**), five from Gaul (**166**, **183–84**, **190** and **203**) and one from Pannonia (**530**).
[198] As in the cases of **6**, **25–26**, **117–18** (where they appear on the chest and pubic region of the deity invoked), etc.
[199] E.g., **20**, **166**, **184**, **259** (?), **446**, and **448**.

[200] E.g., **30**, **183** and the curses from Hadrumetum *DT* 275–83.
[201] Cf. **166** and *AE* 1907, 68 and 69 (from Hadrumetum).
[202] The following Carthaginian curses share the same date: *DT* 243–44, 247, 258, 260, Jordan 1988: no. 3 and *AE* 1996, 1717 and 1718 as well as the following from Hadrumetum *DT* 264–65 and 272–83. For the sequence of *charaktêres* as evidence for the existence of *officinae magicae*, see Németh 2011.
[203] See **6**, **18**, **20**, **22**, **24**, **29–30** and **117–18**.
[204] For a discussion of dating and diffusion throughout the Mediterranean, see Zago 2011: 115f., esp. n. 20. For the *onómata barbariká* in general, see Graf 1995: 211–15.

immutable and eternal, had a divine origin, since they were consubstantial with the gods. As M. Zago has argued, these *onómata* are the product of 'una babele linguistica, che ricorre a diversi sistemi di lingua (ebraico, egiziano, greco, aramaico, babilonese, copto) e li fonde in neologismi' (2010: 835). It is precisely in this otherness that the power of the *onómata* resides. As Poccetti argues, these *onómata* were intentionally distinct from common languages (or even human language) to assimilate themselves to superhuman beings (2002: 35). Accordingly, the inclusion of the *onómata* in *defixiones* (something which was always intentional) was meant not only to increase the potency of a given spell, but also to improve communication between a *defigens* and the deities invoked. Thus, the use of this extraordinary special language was thought to guarantee a spell's efficacy.

In the Roman West, the *onómata barbariká* are securely found in 30 tablets that mostly hail from Carthage[205] and Hadrumetum.[206] Additionally, there are several tablets of interest from Italy (cf. **22, 117–18**) and Gaul (cf. perhaps **160**). Besides the three Italian examples (dating to the fourth and fifth centuries), the rest of the relevant cases belong to the High Empire. Generally speaking, the *onómata* are written using the Latin alphabet, just like the curses that they accompany.[207] That said, there is a small, but noteworthy, group of nine tablets in which the *onómata barbariká* were written in the Greek alphabet, while the remainder of these texts was written in Latin with the Latin alphabet: by switching the alphabet, these professional practitioners had found a further way to difference between the *onómata* and the language found elsewhere in the same curses.[208] While the majority of these *onómata* come from unknown languages or have been so distorted from their 'original' form that they are now utterly unintelligible, specialists have determined that some of the words that are found (mostly) on *defixiones* from Carthage have an Egyptian origin.[209]

As is well known, the *ephesia grammata* belong to the larger group of *onómata barbariká*. Although they are often associated with Ephesus due to their name, scholars such as D. Ogden have argued that these *grammata* should actually be linked to the Babylonian word *epesu* ('enchant').[210] According to Androcides (*apud* Clem. Al., *Strom.* VIII, 45.2), there are six of these powerful *nomina*: ἄσκιον, κατάκιον, λίξ, τετράξ, δαμναμενεύς and αἴσια.[211] It must be noted that the *ephesia grammata*, which

remained largely unchanged over a long period of time, are hardly found in the corpus of curses from the Roman West. In fact, δαμναμενευς only appears in three tablets from Hadrumetum and (so far) one from Gaul.[212]

Another category of *voces magicae* that ought to be mentioned separately consists of palindromes, which, of course, are the same whether read from left to right or right to left. Gordon has suggested that the mysterious origin of these words should be located in the Greek world (2002: 86). So far, in the corpus of curses from the Roman West there are only a few examples of such palindromes: αραρακαραρα and (its variant?) αραραχαραρα are attested in two curses from Carthage that date to the High Empire.[213] The classic αβλαναθαναβλα, for its part, appears on a series of containers from Anna Perenna (dated between the fourth and fifth centuries CE; cf. **25–27, 35–36**).[214]

Even less common is the use of alphabetical sequences in the *defixiones* from the Roman West. In this group we must highlight the vowels of the Greek alphabet. Due to their association with the seven planets, it was believed that the ritual recitation of these seven sounds summoned all the sounds of the cosmos.[215] Such sequences are found on two agonistic tablets (that also have iconography): the first comes from Carthage and dates to the third century CE:[216] the tablet contains the partial sequence ααα/εεε/ooo. The second curse, from Rome (cf. **5**), belongs to the so-called 'Sethian' collection (fourth or fifth century CE). Along with the visual representation of the deity invoked, we find the Greek vowels arranged in sequences of seven and more or less forming a *plinthion*.[217] Finally, another alphabetical series that deserves mention is the Latin alphabet itself. According to Ogden, the complete or partial recitation of the alphabet was thought to be powerful. There are two such examples found on curses from the Roman West. The first, an erotic curse from Maar (cf. **173**, Gallia Belgica), contains the entire alphabet written on a small clay jar

---

[205] Specifically, these are *DT* 218, 227, 233, 243–244, 251, 253 and 255; *AE* 1933, 234–35 and Jordan 1988: no. 3.

[206] Cf. *DT* 264–67, 270, 272–74, 286, 288, 289 and 292–95.

[207] Like in the following from Carthage *DT* 244, 251, *AE* 1933, 234–35 and Jordan 1988: no. 3, the following from Hadrumetum *DT* 264–67, 270, 272–74, 286, 288–89, 292–95, **22** and **160**.

[208] Like in the following curses from Carthage: *DT* 218, 227, 233, 243, 244, 253 and 255 as well as in **117–18**.

[209] Zago 2010: 831, n. 2 identifies those from *DT* 243, 251 and 253, to which we should add those found in **22**.

[210] Cf. Ogden 1999: 47. For its origin and relation to Orphism, see Bernabé 2003.

[211] See Gager 1992: 5–6 with further bibliographical references, and Zago 2011: 116–17, esp. n. 22.

[212] Cf. *DT* 267 (l. 7), 268 (l. 8), *AE* 1968, 620 (l. 4) and the curse from Autun (**166**, col. III, l. 2).

[213] They are, respectively, *DT* 243 (ll. 11–26) and 253 (ll. 2 and 67). For the first, we must mention that this palindrome as well as other *onómata barbariká* are arranged in decreasing triangles. As R. Martín Hernández (2010: 495) has maintained in a discussion of certain *PGM* recipes, 'most spells in which a word… have been written in a decreasing triangle… are spells in which the intention is to make something disappear.' This idea jibes well with the aims of *DT* 243, which is directed against a group of *agitatores*. For the performative value of triangles, see Mastrocinque 2010: 5ff. For the *carmina figurata*, which involve the construction of triangles (*klima*), rectangles (*plinthion/pterugion*) and wings (*pterygion*), see Frankfurter 1994: 199–200; Gordon 2002: 85; Poccetti 2002: 53–56, who has underscored the interesting combination of the acoustic effect with the visual impact generated by the layout of the writing.

[214] Cf. **26** (container c, correctly written in Greek: Aβλαναθαναλβα), **27** (container b, in the Latin alphabet: *abla<na>tanabla* (!)), **35** (container b, in the Latin alphabet: *abla<na>tan<a>bla* (!)) and **36** (container b, in the Latin alphabet: *abla<na>tanabla* (!)). If the editor's reconstruction is correct, we should add **30**, which reads *abl[anatabla]* (l. 7; cf. Blänsdorf 2010c: 46–49). For this theonym of Hebraic origin and disputed interpretation, see Mastrocinque 2004: 99–100.

[215] See *DT*: p. LXXIIIf.; Frankfurter 1994: 200–01; Zago 2010: 846, n. 57.

[216] Cf. Jordan 1988: no. 3.

[217] For the *plinthion*, cf. n. 213 above and Mastrocinque 2010: 7, who maintains that the magical power of this shape rests in the multiplication of the letters.

and upside down when compared to the text of the curse proper.[218] The alphabetical sequence found in Aquae Sulis/Bath (cf. **207**), however, is partial and reads *abcdefx*.

4.3. *Formulae defigendi*

In a chapter dedicated to the writing of curses, it is necessary to save space for a discussion of the formulae found in *defixiones*. Since this is one of the questions that has attracted the greatest amount of scholarly attention, it is not my intention to propose a new system for classifying these formulae, as others have done. Thus, the following pages outline the main taxonomies established by C. Faraone, A. Kropp and D. Urbanová, which have been the most recent and/or influential approaches to the issue.[219]

The oldest and also most simple cursing formulae consisted simply of inscribing the victim's name on a lead sheet, which could be further specified with the addition of several other identifying details, such as the patronymic, matronymic or specification of the victim's profession).[220] This technique is likely based on the principle that names were considered to be fundamental parts of the people to whom they refer, with all the magical implications that such a tight connection implies. The first attestations of names (or lists thereof) are found in Greek curse tablets dating to the fourth or fifth centuries BCE and continued to be used until the fourth century CE, though at a lower rate.[221] That said, at the same time that these minimalistic ways of cursing enter the archaeological record we also have evidence for the use of more complex formulae, which Faraone has divided into three categories. It is worth laying out this classificatory system in some detail.[222]

1. 'Direct Binding Formula' refers to cases in which a *defigens* uses a first-person singular verb (e.g., καταδῶ, παραδίδωμι or καταγράφω) to curse a victim (occasionally also making pointed reference to vital organs or possessions). In such instances, the *defigens* also carried out a ritual act of manipulation in which he

or she would pierce or fold the tablet. If any divinity is mentioned in the text, it was in the role of a witness who was meant to supervise the *actio magica* (cf. Faraone 1991a: 5).

2. 'Prayer Formula' refers to instances in which the *defigens* uses second-person imperatives (e.g., κάτεχε) to spur the deities invoked to take action and carry out the *defigens'* request. The deities found in this type of curse tend to be chthonic and referred to with their respective epithets. By the High Empire, other components could be included, such as iconography or *voces magicae* (see section I.4.2.2). As Faraone has argued, this type of formula is securely attested from the fourth century BCE onwards. As was the case with direct binding formulae, prayer formulae could include the ritual manipulation of the physical curse.

3. 'Wish Formulae' (or *similia similibus* formulae), attested in the Attic curses starting in the fourth century BCE, are traditionally linked to the principle of sympathetic magic; more precisely, he connects it to the principle of persuasive analogy (cf. Tambiah 1973: 212). This type of formula establishes a comparison between a characteristic or phase of the *actio magica* and the victim due to 'a strong belief in the persuasive power of certain kinds of formulaic language' (Faraone 1991a: 8). Often, *similia similibus* formulae are followed by an explicitly stated wish, in which the victim is the grammatical subject.

Kropp, for her part, has built upon the research of Kagarow and Faraone and has deeply analysed the *formulae defigendi* from the perspective of speech-act theory.[223] As a result she has proposed four main categories:

1. Manipulation Formulae (Manipulationsforme):[224] this category, which is analogous to Faraone's first category ('Direct Binding Formula'), includes formulae in which there is explicit reference to the ritual manipulation of the tablet, which would have physically taken place during the *actio magica*. For Latin texts, common verbs in this type include *defigo, implico, describo, immergo* and *ligo* as well as its compounds *alligo, colligo, deligo* and *obligo*.

2. Committal Formula (Übergabeformel):[225] this typology, also derived from Faraone's first category, includes both formulae for consigning victims to the deities invoked as well as formulae that refer to the deposition of the *defixio* (with verbs like *commendo, devoveo, do, dono, mando, trado*, etc.). The 'consignation' could be carried out through either explicit or implicit performative expressions, which would immediately take effect after being pronounced.[226] The first kind depends on

---

[218] In full, though with an error in the sequence *p r r*, for *p q r*.

[219] See Faraone 1991a; Kropp 2008: 137–79 and 2010. Additionally, we must add the contributions of Audollent 1904: pp. LVIff. ('verba devotoria') and LXXIVff. ('formulae defigendi'); Kagarow 1929: 28–49 (for Greek curse tablets); Cesano 1961²: 1570–76; Tomlin 1988a: 63–74 (for the formulae founded at the sanctuary of Aquae Sulis/Bath; this classification can be applied to the whole corpus of curses against thieves from Britannia); Graf 1995: 117–25; Ogden 1999: 26–28; Curbera and Jordan 2007; Murano 2010 and 2012 (for Oscan formulae); Urbanová 2018: 60–77 (for the structure, auxiliary formulae and a summary classification of the formulae founded in Latin curse tablets) and 102–26 (where the author explains her own typology, which results from the mix of Faraone's and Kropp's work).

[220] This should be understood to a certain extent as a magical version of the proverbial idea *pars pro toto*, according to which the name that is used for referring to a certain person is essentially linked to him/her. Therefore, and given that the name is a vital part of the individual, it is possible to harm someone through their names (cf. Rossenblat 1977: 27). Ogden has also noted that 'initially, the very act of writing a name, of "freezing" it permanently in lead, could in itself have been considered a way of tying it down by comparison with the transience of uttering it' (1999: 10). Also see Gager 1992: 5; Piccaluga 2010: 13–20.

[221] E.g., **19**, **178**, **180**, **360**, **362** and **368**.

[222] See Faraone 1991a: 4–10, who based his taxonomy on that of Kagarow (1929: 28–49) for Greek *defixiones*.

[223] Kropp 2008: 137–79 and 2010.

[224] Cf. Kropp 2008: 145–46, table 4.1 and 2010: 361.

[225] Cf. Kropp 2008: 146–49, table 4.2 and 2010: 362–64.

[226] Cf. section I.4.1, esp. n. 98. The recitation of this sort of expression in a determined context could lead to concrete effects in the real world. A classic contemporary example is the phrase 'I now pronounce you man and wife' which has an immediate legal effect. Cf. the classic volume by Austin 1962.

first-person singular verbs in the present indicative that are followed by an accusative. A good example is found in the tablet from Baelo Claudia/Bolonia: *Isis Muronem tiḅi çọnmendọ furtu(m) meu(m)* (cf. **128**, ll. 1–3). Implicitly performative expressions are those that betray a more reserved and humble attitude on the *defigens'* part, who seeks to 'shield' him- or herself from the dangerous consequences of directly communicating with a deity.[227] These formulae are often in the passive voice, as can be seen in a curse tablet from Ratcliffe-on-Soar (cf. **349** A, ll. 1–2), which reads: *donatur deo Iovi Optimo Maximo.*

3. Request Formula (Aufforderungsformel):[228] this category is similar to Faraone's second type, though it differs in so far as the stress is placed on the act of asking for something (which does not entail any relationship between the person who asks for help and the one who is asked). This replaces the idea of 'prayer', which implies a hierarchical relationship.[229] This category includes all formulae that are used to solicit the intervention of the evoked deities and that offer up instructions.

Generally, orders are given directly or through performative expressions (again either explicit or implicit). The first option entails the use of a second person imperative (e.g., **118**, ll. 8–13: *Fistu<m> occidiȋe inicaȋe*). In performative expressions, we normally find *verba rogandi* (like *rogo, oro,* etc.), as can be seen in a curse from Emerita Augusta/Merida **120**, ll. 1–6: *Dea Ataecina Tuȓibrig(ensis) Proserpina per tuam maiestatem te rogo oro obsecro uti vindices quot mihi furti factum est.*

In instances when the text does not directly name the deity to whom it is addressed (who, in all likelihood would have been named orally during the ritual deposition of the curse), practitioners could solicit a deity's intervention either directly or by means of an analogy; these two strategies are equivalent to Faraone's third category ('Wish Formula-*Similia Similibus*'). A direct petition is expressed as a desire with a subjunctive verb and the indication of the desired results (e.g., **210**, ll. 3–6: *qui illas involavi(t) ut mentes sua(s) perd[at]*). Analogies are spelled out with *similia similibus* formulae, which are usually introduced by *quomodo* and meant to set in motion a process that would lead to a favourable outcome (e.g., **157**, ll. 1–3: *quomodo hoc plumbu(m) non paret et decadet sic decadat aetas membra vita*).

4. Curse Formula (Fluchformel):[230] this category, which does not have a clear analogue in Faraone's typology,

consists of formulae that use a performative expression to directly reference to the act of cursing itself. So far, there is only one known example from Aquae Sulis/Bath: cf. **304**, 1. 1: *ẹxẹcro qui involaverit....*

Recently, Urbanová has based her classification on Faraone's and Kropp's typologies, bringing together the pragmatic, semantic and syntactic aspects of the various formulae attested in Latin curse tablets and 'prayers for justice'.[231] Following the work of R. Risselada (1993), she has distinguished three main categories within which there are up to nine different types of formulae. Furthermore, these individual formulae can be found on their own or in conjunction with another type, forming 'simple' or 'combined' curses.

1. 'Simple nominal list of cursed people' (or formula 0): this merely consists of a list of the name of the victim(s), which can be accompanied by further details (e.g., matronymics, professions, etc). A good example would be **99**: *Secundula aut qui sustulet.*
2. 'Direct cursing formula': this is equivalent to what Faraone called 'Direct binding formula' and Kropp referred to as 'Manipulation formulae' and also includes what Kropp called 'Committal formulae'. This kind of formula contains a first-person verb in the present indicative followed by:
   a. A 'predicate of cursing' or 'formula 1', in which we find verbs like *defigo, ligo, deligo, obligo, describo,* together with the name, body parts or properties of the victim(s); such as in **339**, ll. 1–2: *Tretia(m) Martia(m) defico et illeus vita(m) et me(n)tem...*
   b. A 'predicate of committal' or 'formula 1a', in which we find verbs for handing over the victims of the curse (such as *do, dono, voveo, mando, trado, commendo, desacrifico, defero*), together with the name and/or body parts of the victim(s). On occasion, we also find the mention of divinities. A good example is **56**, ll. 4–5: *Dii i(n)feri vobis com(m)e(n)do illius mem<b>ra colore(m)...*
3. 'Invoking formulae': this category partially corresponds to Kropp's request and committal formulae (which were based on Faraone's first two categories). 'Invoking formulae' include any formula in which invocations take on a more substantial role. For Urbanová, there are various subtypes, depending on the types of verbs, their moods and grammatical constructions (e.g., verbs of requesting and giving, with purpose clauses, imperatives, wishes or *similia similibus* formulae).[232]

As I mentioned before, it is not my intention to propose yet another system for taxonomizing every single type of formula according to linguistic categories, an endeavour that at times can over complicate things. What is clear is that the work Faraone did back in 1991 remains extremely influential for later authors, such as Kropp and Urbanová, whose discussions fruitfully take further considerations

[227] Cf. Kropp 2008: 148–49 and 2010: 366, where the author notes that 'the *defigens* articulates his awareness of the status difference between him and the god invoked, insofar as he gives his request a non-peremptory character and, at the same time, qualifies his own position as dependent and inferior'.
[228] Cf. Kropp 2008: 149–55, 174–76, table 4.3 and 2010: 365–69.
[229] Kropp 2010: 365, notes, 'the term "prayer" implies a hierarchical relationship between orant and addressee, with the latter occupying the dominant position. I adopt the more general term "request"... [because it] has the advantage of not excluding any kind of communicative setting'.
[230] Cf. Kropp 2008: 155 and 2010: 369.
[231] See specifically, Urbanová 2018: 127–36.
[232] On the *similia* formulae, see Franek and Urbanová 2019a and 2019b.

into account without radically changing the picture. While Urbanová's classificatory system is by far the most detailed, it is also the least user friendly. Furthermore, the scholarly desire to classify and organize can also make us forget that, as Gordon has recently pointed out in relation to the curses from Italy, most of the texts do not follow a general model (2019b: 421). This same idea can be further extended to the entire Roman West, where most of the texts were written by individual practitioners. Consequently, instead of thinking strictly in terms of formulae, Gordon has proposed that 'it seems ... more useful to distinguish between different degrees of religious competence, drawing upon different kinds of cultural resources in an attempt to gain illocutionary authority vis-à-vis the (implied or expressed) addressee(s)' (2019b: 421–22).[233]

Given the general priorities of this volume to elucidate the cultural and archaeological contexts of curse tablets, in the following catalogue I resist the urge to fit each text into a neat box based on linguistic and formulaic features. That said, I do use useful phrases such as '*similia similibus* or persuasive analogy', 'all-inclusive' formulae, as a useful shorthand to refer to common features across the corpus.

---

[233] On this, see also Gordon 2019a on religious competence and the pragmatics of cursing.

5

The Manipulation of *Defixiones*

5.1. Introduction: technical considerations

On certain occasions, after inscribing the tablet, the practitioner would physically manipulate the curse, either as part of ritual or for more practical reasons. There are three main types of manipulation that are found in the archaeological record: folding, rolling and piercing. Additionally, tablets could be folded and pierced or rolled and pierced.[234] Although these are by far the main ways of manipulating *defixiones*, Table 5.1 shows that there were other *modi operandi* of great interest.

As the data collected in the table shows, over half of the known *defixiones* from the Roman West were manipulated after being inscribed. Unfortunately, these results do not give us the complete picture, since many *editiones principes* do not comment on the absence or presence of any signs of ritual manipulation. As a result, we simply do not know whether the tablets were deposited 'open' (i.e., without having been deliberately manipulated)[235] or whether they had been manipulated, but archaeologists did not record such details, which has resulted in the loss of important information.[236]

5.2. Folded tablets

With a total of 172 examples, folding is the most frequently attested type of manipulation (see Figure 5.1). Folded tabulae come predominantly from Italia, Gallia and Britannia.[237] This technique is already attested in the fourth century BCE (with the Cirò Marina curse, cf. **75**)[238] and endured until the fifth century CE (with the Giuncalzu tablet, cf. **114**). As Tomlin has pointed out, 'its purpose may have been… to conceal what had been written' (1988a: 84). That said, the fact that other inscribed tablets were simply left 'open' without undergoing any type of manipulation suggests that folding was not meant to hide the texts (which, after all, were quite often deposited in

places that were inaccessible to 'mortal' eyes). Another possibility is that practitioners folded the tablets as part of an attempt to protect the text from being physically damaged (either scratched or otherwise harmed). However, the archaeological record also yields examples that complicate this hypothesis: uninscribed curse tablets which were nevertheless folded before being deposited.[239] In these instances, the practitioners had no text to protect or conceal; perhaps they were just performing what was perceived to be 'the usual' ritual procedure: orally performing the curse and a series of physical gestures, with the folding of the tablet being the only one visible in the evidence. Finally, we are left to wonder if folding could simply have been a pragmatic means of easily transporting a *defixio* from where it was manufactured to where it was finally deposited.

Generally speaking, tablets were folded in half longitudinally, as can be seen in the *defixiones* from Nomentum/Mentana (cf. **49**, where the tablet was folded only once) or Cremona (cf. **105**, folded twice) to give just two examples. Sometimes after being folded longitudinally, a tablet was then folded transversally, thus being reduced to an even more compact unit. A curse from London (cf. **342**, folded twice) and one from Savaria/Szombathely (cf. **531**, folded seven times) provide good examples of tablets being folded multiple times.

While these are the most common types of folding, the archaeological record contains other, less conventional ways of folding a tablet. A curse tablet from Aquae Sulis/Bath (cf. **244**) for example, was folded four times towards the centre, while another from Old Harlow (cf. **353**) was folded in the 'accordion' style; another from Dalheim (cf. **203**) was folded thrice, first in half before each side was folded in towards the centre. The number of folds attested ranges from one to nine, and we cannot give any general rule concerning how many times a text would have to be folded. Presumably, the size of a particular lead sheet played a role in influencing each practitioners' choice in this regard.

As mentioned above, a tablet could both be folded and pierced. Thus, some curses (cf. e.g., **49–51, 56** and **73**) were clearly pierced before being folded and then deposited. Conversely, we have examples of tablets that were folded

---

[234] In general, see Gager 1992: 18; Ogden 1999: 13–14; Bailliot 2010: 77–81; Martin 2010: 20. More specifically, see the analysis of binding gestures found in McKie 2018: 118–20.

[235] Ten per cent of tablets are 'open'. Some of these *defixiones* were left 'open' due to the characteristics of the medium. The marble plaques or altars (cf. **4, 57, 120**) the slate plaques (cf. **72, 146–47**), lamps (cf. **3**), busts (cf. **15**), cinerary urns (cf. **16**), lead containers (cf. **24–27** and **35–36**), *ostraka* (cf. **113**), jars (cf. **173**) and *tegulae* (such as the one from Thysdrus/El Jem, see Foucher 2000) could obviously not be folded.

[236] This is the case for over a quarter of the tablets, some of which were found during nineteenth-century excavations.

[237] Of these, 134 were just folded, 25 were folded and pierced and 12 were folded and further manipulated (see Table 5.1). These 171 tablets comprise 27 per cent of the total corpus.

[238] We could also add the tablets from Laos/Marcellina (cf. **78–80**), which likewise belong to the group of fourth- or third-century Graeco-Oscan curses.

[239] Cf. for instance, **159**, which was accompanied by other uninscribed but folded curse tablets. Also, at the sanctuary of Mercury in Uley, 140 tablets were found, mostly 'rolled and then flattened' (Woodward 1993: 113). Of these, only 86 were uninscribed. That said, it seems clear enough that the practitioners still felt that it was necessary to roll them in order to comply with all the steps of the cursing ritual.

Table 5.1. *Defixiones* classified according to provenance (It. = Italia, Afr. = Africa, Hisp. = Hispania, Gall. = Gallia, Brit. = Britannia, Ger. = Germania, Raet .= Raetia, Nor. = Noricum, Pann. = Pannonia) and type of manipulation (F= folded, R= rolled and N= nailed). The total number of manipulated curse tablets in each province is tallied in the right column.

Prov.	F	R	N	F & N	R & N	*Alia*	Total
It.	14	13	14	14	1	**1**: F and tied. **48**: attempt of F and N. **52**: F and tied. **53**: R around a nail. **61**: F and tied. **88**: F and tied. **92**: attempt of N. **97–98**: R and crushed. **103**: F, cut, R and N. **109**: R around a nail.	67/119
Afr.	8	33			2	*AE* 1907, 69: F or R.	44/88
Hisp.	4	5	3	1	1	**132**: F and closed with an iron pin. **139**: cut. **148**: F and cut.	17/30
Gall.	18	7	4	–	–	**175**: thrown in a fire. **188**: hammered.	31/55
Brit.	72	6	12	7	–	**206**: cut. **269** and **309**: F and cut. **338**: N and thrown in a fire. **432**: punctured with a pointy object. **433**: hammered. **441**: R, with label.	104/256
Ger.	14	11	4	2	–	**483**: R and stuck to a nail. **488–489, 498**: R and thrown in a fire. **493**: R, F and thrown in a fire. **504**: F and cut. **508**: F or R. **512**: beat with a blunt object.	39/59
Raet.	–	1	–	–	–	–	1/6
Nor.	–	–	–	–	–	–	0/1
Pann.	4	–	–	1	–	**528**: thrown in a fire.	7/9
						530: R around a nail.	

Figure 5.1. Folded *defixio* (cf. **485**, before opening. Landesarchäologie Mainz).

and then pierced. The best examples of this practice are the five first-century BCE tablets from Rome that are now housed at Johns Hopkins University (cf. **10–14**). These curses were all folded up together and then transfixed with a single iron nail.

5.3. Rolled tablets

After inscribing a *defixio*, the *PGM* recommend to 'roll up the lamella in the usual fashion',[240] a habit that scholars have generally analysed as a reflection of epistolary practices.[241] In this regard, we must mention papyrus rolls more generally, which were normally rolled up. In a different vein, authors such as Ogden have interpreted this type of manipulation as a symbolic act that was meant 'to achieve a sympathetic binding and perhaps a sympathetic confusion of the tablet's contents' (1999: 13). While his proposal is doubtlessly suggestive, the lack of concrete evidence means that it remains little more than a tantalizing theory.

---

[240] *PGM* XXXVI, 234 (translated by R.F. Hock [*apud* Betz 1992²]), which recommend τὴν λάμναν ἑλίξας κατὰ τρόπον and also *PGM* VII, 463–64, which advise to 'roll (the curse) up and throw it into the sea' (ἕλιξον καὶ βάλε εἰς θάλασσαν; translation by E.N. O'Neil [*apud* Betz 1992²]). On these passages, see also section I.6.3.
[241] Thus, Gager 1992: 18 and Ogden 1999: 13.

Figure 5.2. Rolled *defixio* (cf. 486, before opening. Landesarchäologie Mainz).

Figure 5.3. *Defixio* rolled around a bird bone (Courtesy of GDKE, Landesarchäologie, Mainz).

Based on the available data, there are 92 confirmed instances of tablets being rolled up in the Roman West,[242] dating from the second half of the fourth century BCE (the Graeco-Oscan curse from Castiglione di Paludi [cf. **77**]) to the fourth century CE (a curse from Hamble [cf. **451**], for example). This type of manipulation was especially important in the North African cities of Hadrumetum and Carthage. Most curses from these two sites were inserted into cinerary urns via the libation-tube. To do so, the practitioner had to roll the tablet up 'comme un cigare'.[243] It seems that in the case of these North African tablets, the rolling up of a *defixio* should not be understood in terms of sympathetic magic but rather be seen as practical solution to assist with the goal of depositing the tablet in a certain context.

Generally speaking, tablets were individually rolled without anything placed inside before being deposited in a chosen place (see Figure 5.2). When two curses dealt with a similar theme, however, they could be rolled up together, as happened with two *defixiones* from Corduba/Cordoba (cf. **125–26**), which were found deposited inside a cinerary urn. On rare occasions, *defigentes* rolled their tablets around things like iron nails or bones, objects which could have been used during the cursing ritual (see Figure 5.3).[244]

Since it was physically difficult to pierce a *defixio* that had already been rolled up, piercing would precede rolling.

The curse from Roccagloriosa (cf. **76**), for example, was first pierced and then rolled up.[245] Though it itself was not pierced, the curse from Caistor St Edmund was rolled up and then deposited with an uninscribed lead label that had been pierced with an iron nail (cf. **441**).

5.4. Pierced tablets

Nails have undoubtedly become an emblematic part of *defixiones*: no element of these tablets better embodies the ideas of binding, joining or constricting. The piercing of a tablet was a symbolic gesture through which the spell itself materialized, as the etymology of the verb *defigo* ('to fix, fasten down, render immovable') makes clear. In fact, as Cesano has maintained, 'il chiodo trapassante la *tabella* significava che doveva di necessità avvenire ciò che vi era scritto; come dal fautore della *defixio* il chiodo era confitto nel piombo così il defisso venina indissolubilmente legato' (1961²: 1562).[246] Only one recipe from the *PGM* gives specific information about what kind of nail should be employed, recommending the use of a 'copper nail from a shipwrecked vessel'.[247] In this case, the nail's provenance (i.e., from a context related to the *biaiothánatoi* [see section I.6.2.1]), it would undoubtedly have been endowed with considerable magical power. In the archaeological record, however, we most commonly find iron nails with unknown origins and of various lengths. At times, they are still found transfixing the *defixio*,[248] while at others they are simply found nearby.

Despite the nail's iconicity, in the Roman West there are only 72 known instances of *defixiones* closely associated with nails, which amount to a relatively small percentage of the overall corpus.[249] These examples date from the fourth century BCE (the Graeco-Oscan curse from Roccagloriosa [cf. **76**]) to the fourth or fifth century CE (the *defixiones* from Augusta Treverorum/Trier). Most of the pierced tablets date to either the Republic or High Empire. While there are examples of pierced curses from each province in the Roman West, the greatest concentration is found in Italia and Britannia.

We can distinguish between three different categories of curses associated with nails: those that were deposited alongside nails,[250] those that were still transfixed with the nail *in situ* at the time of discovery[251] and, finally, cases in

---

[242] Specifically, there are 76 rolled tablets, 4 rolled and pierced, as well as 12 in which rolling is combined with another type of manipulation (see the preceding table). This amounts to 14 per cent of the total corpus.

[243] Delattre 1898: 218.

[244] The tablets rolled around a nail come from Lilybaeum/Marsala (**109**, third century BCE), Ostia (cf. **53**, second century CE) and Carnuntum/Petronell (**530**, fourth century CE), while one of the curses found in the sanctuary of Isis and Magna Mater (Mogontiacum/Mainz) was rolled around a bird bone (see Fig. 5.3). Here we should also include Choppard and Hannezo's observation that some curses from Hadrumetum: 'On trouve quelquefois [lamminam]... roulée sur un ossement' (*apud DT*, p. CXV, n. 3).

[245] For other examples, see the North African curses *DT* 253 and 264 and perhaps the *defixio* from Carmo/Carmona (cf. **129**).

[246] Cf. Piccaluga 1983; Gager 1992: 18; Ogden 1999: 14; Gordon 2015: 158–61.

[247] *PGM* VII, 466: ἥλῳ κυπρίνῳ ἀπὸ πλ[ο]ίου νεναυαγηκότος (translated by E.N. O'Neil, *apud* Betz 1992²)

[248] Such as those found with the tablets **10–14**, **119**, **124**, **345**, etc.

[249] Of these, 37 were pierced, 25 folded and pierced, 4 rolled and pierced, and 6 belong to the group of otherwise manipulated *defixiones*. In total this is 11 per cent of the entire corpus.

[250] Such as a curse from Groß Gerau (cf. **483**), which was rolled up and deposited together with a nail, though it does not appear to have been pierced.

[251] Such as **119** (which still has both nails) and **345** (pierced five times with four nails still preserved *in situ*). In addition to these, see Gager 1992: 19 for a discussion of tablets nailed up in the Carthaginian circus (also see section I.6.5.3 n. 336), and also the Carthaginian tablets 'fixées

Figure 5.4. Pierced *defixio* (cf. 119; Getty Museum).

Figure 5.5. Pierced *defixio* from Pompeii (cf. 72, detail; Ministero dei Beni e delle Attività Culturali e del Turismo-Soprintendenza Pompei).

which a tablet was pierced before or after being inscribed but now the resulting hole provides the only evidence for this ritual manipulation (i.e., we do not have the nail). This final category is the largest.[252]

Within this larger practice of piercing tablets, there are two motivating reasons that can explain the practice: magical considerations linked to ritual or more practical reasons. In the first group, the holes coincide with significant words or formulae found in the text as a way to stress the symbolical and unavoidable bond formed by the victim(s) and the spell. A good example of this phenomenon is the curse from Mediolanum Santonum/Villepouge-Chagnon (cf. **160**), in which we find a *similia similibus* formula referring to the victims that reads: *sic tra(n)specti sin<t> quomodi ille* (Tab. II, ll. 4–5). This phrase, referring to the moment when the puppy was harmed (or perhaps even killed) is followed by the hole left by the nail. Similarly, a *defixio* of unknown provenance and dated to the first century CE (cf. **119**, Figure 5.4) refers to the victims with the expression *quorum nom[ina] hic sunt perea[nt]* (col. II, ll. 3–5). In this phrase, the hole coincides with the word *nomina*. Given that victims' names were considered a vital part of an individual, like an additional body part, piercing the word for name enacts the insoluble link between the victims and the spell.

We must also add two British curses, one from Aquae Sulis/Bath (cf. **213**) and the other from London (cf. **339**), to this group. As Tomlin has noted,[253] the former is an opisthographic tablet that contains lists of names on both sides, though they are ordered differently. This allowed the practitioner to pierce the name *Anniola* (A, l. 6 and B, l. 1)

on both sides of the tablet. The curse from London was pierced nine times: the largest of the holes comes between the victim's name and the word *vita(m)* (l. 2), which is certainly no accident.

Currently there is only one known case of a curse tablet that was pierced for magical and practical reasons: the Pompeiian curse against Faustus (cf. **72**, Figure 5.5) which was written on a slate plaque that was pierced in its four corners in order to attach it to the front of tomb 23OS in the Porta Nocera necropolis. The tablet, however, also has a fifth nail, which is larger and placed between the words *meae innocentiae* (l. 6). In this case, and as Elefante noted (1985: 433), the fifth nail serves as a means to stress and reinforce the importance of this phrase.

As mentioned above, certain tablets were only pierced for more practical reasons. There are instances of tablets being pierced at their corners, perhaps so that they could be mounted and 'displayed'. This practice can be clearly seen in a curse from Caere/Cerveteri (cf. **95**), dated to the second or first century BCE. The *defixio*, which contains a list of personal names, was found in the *dromos* of a tomb in the Banditaccia necropolis. The tablet was pierced in its four corners, as a means of mounting it on the wall (there is no indication of a magical reason for these holes). In a similar vein, two other first-century BCE curses from Hispania (cf. **129** and **133**, both without an exact archaeological context) were pierced in their corners. Finally, it is also worth noting a different curse tablet from Pompeii (cf. **71**) that was written on two tablets that resemble *tabulae ceratae*. This curse was pierced twice in order to make it into a type of diptych. In all these instances, rather than piercing the tablets with magical purposes in mind, it seems that the practitioners were imitating the usual practices of displaying inscriptions employed in the realm of public epigraphy (e.g., in the cases of Caere/Cerveteri and Hispania) or of common writing practices (e.g., in Pompeii).

---

aux parois du cippe à l'aide d'un clou de cuivre qui en transperçait tous les plis' (Delattre, *apud DT*, p. CXV) as well as the two from Hadrumetum that were 'trouées par un gros clou, encore adhérent à la plaque, comme si on avait voulu les maintenir appliquées contre une des faces du tombeau' (Cagnat, *apud DT*, p. 361).

[252] If the nails used in rituals were as valuable as is implied at *PGM* VII, 466 (cf. n. 247), it is possible that professional practitioners chose to use such nails on later occasions instead of just depositing them.

[253] Cf. Tomlin 1988a: *Tab. Sul.* 8.

5.5. Other *modi operandi*

As Graf has aptly put it, the inscribed text of a *defixio* is itself the representation of the victim (1995: 128), a sort of effigy that could be harmed and injured in various ways. Admittedly, examples of this are rare, but those that we do have are undeniably fascinating. In all likelihood, the cruelty shown to the physical tablets took place while the author of the text recited verbal curses. This type of ritual performance should be interpreted in terms of sympathetic magic: based on the principle of persuasive analogy, the victims would suffer the same damage that the *defigens* inflicted upon the physical curse tablet.

Two curses from Classis/Classe (cf. **97–98**), which only contain the names of their victims were discovered rolled up and crushed inside cinerary urns. Other curses (such as **103**, from Ateste/Este, see Figure 5.6, **139**, **148** and **504**) were cut with a sharp object after being inscribed, which led to different types of damage. The lead tablet from Emporion (cf. **139**), however, was so mutilated that only a small fragment of the tablet has been preserved. This extreme act of chopping up the tablet could be seen as a symbolic method of dismembering a victim.

In the same vein, other texts were beaten after being inscribed. A curse from Uley (cf. **433**), for example, was stabbed with a pointed object until it was totally disfigured, while a text from Mogontiacum/Mainz (cf. **512**) was pounded eight times with a blunt object. A *defixio* from Augusta Treverorum/Trier (cf. **188**) was beaten with a hammer with the result that today its text is barely legible. Throwing texts into a fire is also a well-documented type of manipulation. Good examples of this practice are seen in a curse from London (cf. **338**) and another from Emona/Ljubljana (cf. **528**), whose edges show tell-tale signs of smelting). Additionally, we ought to add three *defixiones* from Mogontiacum/Mainz (cf. **488**, **493** [see Figure 5.7] and **498**), all of which were thrown into the fire on the altar

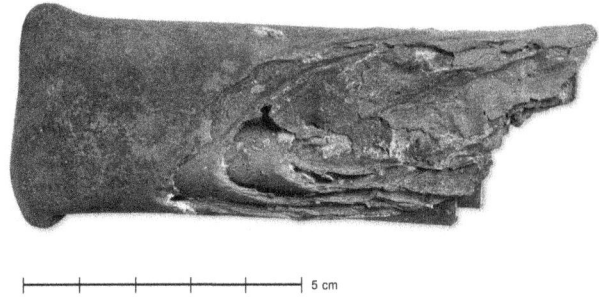

Figure 5.7. Melted *defixio* (cf. 493, before opening; Landesarchäologie Mainz).

of the sanctuary of Magna Mater so that the victims would melt just as the lead melts (**488**, B, ll. 2–5: *sic illorum membra liquescan(t) quatmodum hoc plumbum liquescet*). This *modus operandi* (throwing the tablets into the altar) was the usual in this sanctuary.

Finally, we must turn to a small group of tablets that were tied up before being deposited. All such examples hail from Italian necropoleis and have been dated between the second century BCE and the first century CE. A curse tablet from Volaterrae/Volterra (**88**) was discovered with two other *defixiones* (**89** and **90**), which, according to Lanzi, were inserted in the first one, which is folded as a dyptich and tied up with a lead strip.[254] A similar case can be observed in a tablet from Rome (cf. **1**), which was folded and 'filoque ferreo clausa' after being inscribed.[255] An already mentioned curse from Pompeii (cf. **71**) was written on two lead sheets in a way that is reminiscent of *tabellae ceratae*; after being inscribed, these two were closed like a diptych, connected with two small nails and then tied together with a strip of inscribed lead (which today is lost).[256] In a similar fashion, two curses, one from Cumae (**61**) and the other from Ostia (**52**), were folded in half, pierced (once and five times, respectively) and then tied with a metallic(?) thread.[257] In these instances, the authors of the texts were probably thinking of the curses as letters to the underworld; accordingly, they employed the same system for sealing their texts.[258]

Figure 5.6. Cut *defixio* from Ateste/Este (cf. 103, detail; Soprintendenza per i Beni Archeologici del Veneto. Museo Atestino di Este).

[254] *Apud CIE* 52 a.
[255] According to *CIL* I², 1013.
[256] For a possible formal parallel, cf.*CIL* IV, 9252.
[257] These threads have not survived. However, based on documented parallels, it seems likely that they were made of lead or iron.
[258] Letters written on wood (such as *tabulae ceratae*) were usually notched and enclosed with a string. See Sarri 2018: 83.

6

Deposition Contexts: Where the Curses have been Discovered

6.1. Introduction: putting 'context' into context

Once the curse tablet had been manufactured, 'the final stage of a tablet's activation was its deposition', as Ogden (1999: 15) has put it. As was the case with other parts of the ritual, *defigentes* did not choose a place to deposit a curse at random, but rather took a series of considerations (e.g., the desired outcome or evoked divinity) into account for increasing the tablet's efficacy. Relying on literary and archaeological sources, traditional scholarship has differentiated four main contexts where *defixiones* could be deposited: necropoleis (often taken as the archaeological context par excellence for curse tablets), sanctuaries (both dedicated to chthonic and uranic deities), aquatic spaces or areas somehow linked to the curse's victim.[259] As is the case with my typology, this classificatory scheme is problematic and upon further scrutiny can be woefully simplistic. By neatly separating every single deposition into one of these four categories, scholars can overlook two key questions: the possible overlapping of these categories and the cultural significance that these contexts could have in different times and places throughout the history of the Roman West.

Let's start with the first question. The proposed contexts do not necessarily fit into neat categories, and therefore, they cannot be completely differentiated from one another. At times, deposits are superimposed, creating new, mixed and polysemic contexts that were conducive to aggressive magic for various reasons. This is certainly the case with amphitheatres or circuses, since both of these were closely connected to the victims (who are often explicitly named as gladiators, charioteers or even horses), but also were spaces inhabited by the 'restless dead' and stained with *miasma*, a characteristic that is also shared by funerary contexts.[260] The professional practitioners who wrote a series of curses directed against the *venatores* from the amphitheatre in Carthage were in all likelihood aware of this double valence: they deposited their *defixiones* in a *cella* within the amphitheatre complex where, according to Audollent, 'caesorum gladiatorum trahebantur corpora' (1904: CX, cf. *DT* 246–54). Accordingly, this space is doubly conducive for depositing a curse since it was extremely close to its victims and was also linked to the spirits of the *aoroi* and *biaiothánatoi*.

The second question to be considered is the cultural significance attached to the various contexts. Any analysis must be carried out by taking culturally and historically relevant frameworks into account, since the principals who wrote (or commissioned) the curse were people of their time, who were likely—as we shall see—able to perceive and interpret these contexts from different viewpoints. In this vein we can examine the tablets found in two British amphitheatres (from Isca Silurum/Caerleon and London, cf. **337** and **343**, respectively), which can serve as a good counterpoint to the agonistic tablets from the Carthaginian amphitheatre. In these tablets, which are both *defixiones in fures*, Diana and Nemesis are urged to punish the guilty party. Given the content expressed in these curses, the choice of depositional context does not seem to be linked too much with the proximity to the victims (in both cases the identity of the thief was unknown) or with the morbid undertones of the amphitheatre; instead the choice seems to have been taken along different lines: the amphitheatre was a sacred space dedicated to the very divinities whom the *defigentes* evoked. In short, we can see how these categories can quickly breakdown and, in the process, lose much of their interpretative value.

Accordingly, the present study of contexts seeks to analyse the different places where *defixiones* were deposited, while taking these interpretative problems into account. I do this while continuing to work within the traditionally sanctioned categories (i.e., funerary, aquatic, sacred and spaces linked to the victim). The goal is to examine each of these spaces through the information gleaned from the sylloge along with the different temporal and geographical data about the curses. As hinted at above, however, there are several cases (which are clearly marked) in which is difficult or even somewhat arbitrary to assign a *defixio* to a specific type of context, either because it can comfortably be placed within two categories ('mixed' deposits) or because a more culturally sensitive analysis of the context can change its meaning and distinguish it from superficially similar cases.

6.2. Funerary contexts

Funerary contexts are understood as those spaces that were permeated with death and inhabited by the so-called restless dead (cf. Johnston 1999), all of which meant that these spaces were suffused with *miasma*. While within this context, tombs and necropoleis undoubtedly play the leading role, we cannot overlook other spaces like certain *cellae* in amphitheatres (see section I.6.5.3) or specific aquatic spaces (see section I.6.3).[261]

---

[259] For a general discussion of magical contexts, see Wilburn 2013: 40–53; for curse tablets in particular, see Audollent 1904: CX–CXVII; Cesano 1961²: 1587–89; Preisendanz 1972: col. 5, Vb and col. 20, IV; Gager 1992: 18–21; Graf 1995: 123; Ogden 1999: 15–25; Kropp 2008: 90–94; Bailliot 2010: 81–83; Martin 2010: 25–28; Urbanová 2018: 58–60.

[260] See Tremel 2004: 31–33; Le Glay 1990: 222; Gómez Pantoja 2007: 69.

[261] On curse tablets in funerary spaces, see a preliminary Spanish version of this section in Sánchez Natalías 2012b. For another discussion of

Table 6.1. *Defixiones* **discovered in funerary contexts, categorised by date and provenance (It.= Italia, Afr.= Africa, Hisp.= Hispania, Gall.= Gallia, Brit.= Britannia, Ger.= Germania, Raet.= Raetia, Nor.= Noricum, Pan.= Pannonia). The final line shows the total number of tablets from funerary contexts against the total number of tablets from that province**

Provenance \\ Date	It.	Afr.	Hisp.	Gall.	Brit.	Ger.	Raet.	Nor.	Pan.
Republic	21	2	5						
High Empire	23	64	5	10		13	3	1	4
Late Antiquity	6			1		1			
Unknown	3	6		1	1	1			
Total	53/119	72/88	10/30	12/55	1/256	15/59	3/6	1/1	4/9

The practice of using necropoleis to deposit *defixiones* has traditionally been explained through recourse to two different theories, which in my opinion are not mutually exclusive. The first theory views funerary spaces as sites impregnated with *miasma*. Given that one's name was considered a fundamental part of any individual in Antiquity, by engraving someone's name on the tablet and depositing it in a space tinged with *miasma*, the victim would automatically become infected with that very *miasma* from the necropolis.[262] The second theory stresses that funerary environments were privileged sites of communication with the chthonic powers and the spirits of the deceased who could thus be recruited to act as a practitioners' assistant.[263] The validity of this second theory has been questioned by J. Curbera, who has argued that, although the oldest curses from Sicily originate in necropoleis,[264] invocations to the gods or epistolary formulae only appear at a later date. Therefore, for Curbera this suggests that any attempt to communicate with supernatural forces was not a top priority for practitioners at that time (1999a: 160).

It should be pointed out, however, that from its earliest stages, the *actio magica* was performed both through writing and oral recitation (see section I.4.1). In these rituals, the recitation of certain formulae is recommended both for the invocation of the *numina* and for the enumeration of the practitioners' desired outcomes.[265]

Therefore, it stands to reason that despite the fact that the earliest curse tablets in the Roman West do not preserve such invocations,[266] these may have been uttered by the practitioners during the ritual act in an attempt to communicate with the deities and spirits of the 'restless dead' who presided over the site. Something similar is at play in the sanctuaries where some, but certainly not all, curse tablets explicitly mention the deities to which these spaces were consecrated (see Table 8.1 on page 64). Nevertheless, we still can assume that the *defigens* was addressing the same deities that presided over the site. All that is to say that Curbera's observation may not invalidate this second theory about communicating with the deities or the restless dead.

6.2.1. Geographical and temporal data about funerary deposits

In the Roman West, necropoleis and tombs are among the most well-attested depositional contexts. As Table 6.1 shows, nearly a third of the curse tablets studied in this volume come from such contexts.

The geographical distribution of these *defixiones* is even more noteworthy, seeing that most of them originate in major cities in Italy and North Africa, such as Rome, Carthage and Hadrumetum. Over one third of all the curse tablets found in necropoleis come from these two North African cities.[267] The popularity of this context is later reflected in the *PGM*, whose recipes recommend the use of the graves of *biaiothánatoi* as a place for

---

funerary contexts that takes into account Greek curses from the Roman West, see Alfayé and Sánchez Natalías 2020: 45–48.

[262] See Ogden 1999: 16 and Curbera 1999a: 160. In Antiquity the name was considered a fundamental part of the individual. By virtue of the performative power of script (see section I.7.2), etching a name on a curse tablet automatically led to that individual becoming infected by the *miasma*.

[263] Faraone 1991a: 9 claims that 'The rationale behind the placement of the tablets in graves and chthonic sanctuaries has been similarly misinterpreted. It is true that contact with the coldness and inertia of corpses provides the motivation of some *similia similibus* formulae, but ... these formulae seem to rationalize ... the practice of communicating with the gods or the dead.'

[264] In particular, see Curbera 1999a, nos 15 (dating from between the sixth and fifth century BCE or to the fifth century BCE), 1, 4–7, 12 (whose chronology goes back to the fifth century BCE), 2–3 (dated to the fifth–fourth century BCE), 8 (from the late fourth century BCE), 47 (dating from the third century BCE), etc. For an updated corpus of Sicilian curse tablets, see Sommerschield 2019.

[265] Here I provide several good examples: *PGM* III, 30 ff., which provides the recitation of formulae during the deposit of the tablets; *PGM* IV, 332 ff., where it is recommended to recite the formula written on the *defixio* and to utter another one during its deposit; *PGM* IV, 1747 ff., which

urges the practitioner to engrave the formula and to recite it afterwards; *PGM* IV, 2235 ff., where the recitation of the text takes places after being written; *PGM* V, 319 ff., where a series of formulae are uttered while piercing the tablet and another series are spoken during its deposit.

[266] For just a few examples, see **49–51, 55, 71, 78, 94, 95, 125–26**.

[267] Thirty-five per cent of the total number of *defixiones* found in a funerary context originate in this province. When it comes to Hadrumetum, according to Audollent (1904: 360), 'inter sepulcra coemeterii romani iuxta viam quae ducit Kairouan effosi diversis temporibus erutae sunt omnes hadrumetinae tabellae (263–98)'. In Carthage, 35 of the 43 *defixiones* were found in a funerary context: 27 were found in graves and 8 (*DT* 247–54) were found in the *cella* of an amphitheatre where the corpses of gladiators would have been stored. This, then would constitute a 'mixed' archaeological context, undoubtedly linked to the funerary world (see section I.6.5.3 and n. 341 below). Beyond these cities, three other curses deserve mention: one from Cirta/Constantine (see *DT* 300), one from Thysdrus/El Jem (see Foucher 2000) and one from Naro/Hammam-Lif (see Audollent 1910).

deposition.[268] The preference for using funerary contexts as sites for depositing curse tablets is also reflected in Italy and Hispania, where a third of these curse tablets were found. Nevertheless, it should be pointed out that further north this type of deposition is not as common as sacred spaces. Thus, just one tenth of the curse tablets found in funerary contexts originate in provinces like Gallia or Germania, the figure drops to almost zero in the case of Britannia, where (so far) we only know of a single curse tablet that was deposited in a grave (cf. **345**). This is all to say that practices and preferences were not uniform throughout the Roman West. In fact, this diversity deserves explanation.

As shown in Table 6.1, chronologically, funerary contexts were used for depositing curse tablets from a very early period: in the Republican period, Italia, Africa and Hispania are already represented. Even if it is true that in Africa and Hispania there are not many early cases, we should stress that in Italy there are more tablets from funerary contexts dating to the Republic than to the High Empire. During the High Empire, funerary contexts were used as a site for deposition throughout the Roman West, except for in Britannia where sanctuaries were by and far the favoured context. Unless archaeology should prove the opposite, during Late Antiquity the use of necropoleis fell out of favour and sacred and/or aquatic deposits became much more prevalent.

6.2.2. *The various* modi operandi

The fact that tombs and necropoleis were spaces presided over by the deities of the underworld, populated by all kind of spirits and filled with *miasma* made these spaces into an ideal environment for depositing curse tablets. Thus, necropoleis are used for not only depositing the oldest *defixiones* from the Roman West (cf. **68**, **74–75** and **78**), but there are also a good deal of tablets dated to the High Empire, irrespective of the presence (or lack thereof) of invocations to chthonic deities or references to Hades. Although depositing a curse in a funerary environment was thought sufficient for achieving the desired outcome without the need of more 'invasive' practices, the archaeological record gives examples of *defigentes* going above and beyond.[269] In the following paragraphs, we will examine these different practices and comparing them to the recommendations found in the *PGM*, which are later in date, but the only source with which we can compare the

archaeological evidence. The evidence is organized in a crescendo, beginning with the deposits furthest away from the dead to those closest to the corpses.

Within the *PGM*, at least four different formulas refer to the time and method of depositing the tablet in a funerary context. The Great Magical Papyrus of Paris contains three of these. The first urges the practitioner to deposit the tablet next to the grave of a person who had died prematurely or violently.[270] This necessarily involved a certain proximity with the burial site (and probably depositing the curse in the dead of night so as to avoid detection), though without direct contact with the deceased. And indeed, this is documented in numerous cases where the tablets were placed near funerary monuments, mausolea or graves; in such cases, however, the *defigens* always maintained some distance between the deceased and him-/herself. For some examples of this, we can cite some *defixiones*, such as a curse from Rome (against Caecilia Prima, found next to a mausoleum in Via Ostiense, cf. **48**), one from Copia Thurii/Sybaris (discovered in the outside wall of a mausoleum, cf. **82**), a tablet from Aventicum/Avenches (found, still folded, behind a funerary monument, cf. **481**) and another from Celti/Peñaflor (found about five metres away from two graves in a cavity wall, cf. **131**).

Yet, when approaching a burial area, practitioners could employ more imaginative strategies. For example, in Mazan (Gallia Narbonensis, cf. **156**), next to grave no. 1 in the necropolis of Saint-Andéol and near the head of the deceased (but outside the tomb), an urn was found containing the remains of a small bird under which a Latin curse tablet had been placed. According to the editors of this *defixio* and taking the characteristics of the deposit into account, this ensemble may have been buried at the same time as the deceased. While the tablet in question, of unknown date, contains a fragmented text that is still unpublished, the presence of this small bird appears to be an offering to the chthonic deities addressed to by the practitioner. Another interesting case comes from Roßdorf (Germania, cf. **480**), where a curse tablet was found together with organic remains and a small iron nail inside of a cinerary urn. Perhaps, as Nuber has suggested (1996: 241 and 243, n. 3), the remains found inside of this urn might have been *ousiae* (i.e., something that had belonged to the curse's victims). Be that as it may, the most interesting aspect is that the urn was deposited upside down (hence 'spilling out') at the very limits of the necropolis, a liminal area that was conducive to magical practices, since these border zones were often reserved for burying more marginalized members of society (e.g., prostitutes or gladiators; cf. Hope 2000: 116–18).

Even though depositing curses near graves was both effective and feasible for the activation of the tablets, some

---

[268] See, for example, *PGM* IV, 333 and 2215–16 or *PGM* V, 330–40. Also note other relevant rites: *PGM* VII, 466, where the practitioner is told to write a *defixio* using a nail from a shipwreck; *PGM* XV, 8–10 and 16–19, where it is suggested that the curse be placed in an aquatic context since those who died prematurely inhabited this space; *PGM* XXXVI, 370, where the mouth of a dead dog is used as the place for depositing the tablet. There are other such examples.

[269] Despite the information that we do have, we must also stress that there is lamentably little information about the archaeological context of many curses that were discovered during nineteenth-century excavations. For many of these, even if we know that they were found in necropoleis, we have no further details about many important questions, such as the type of tomb, the exact position of the curse or whether it was touching human remains.

[270] *PGM* IV, 333, where it is recommended τίθεσαι ἡλίου δύνοντος παρὰ ἀώρου ἢ βιαίου θήκην (to place it 'as the sun is setting, beside the grave of one who has died untimely or violently' [Translated by E.N. O'Neil, *apud* Betz 1992²]).

rites in the *PGM* actually recommend burying them inside the grave of a person who had died prematurely.[271] As if that were not enough, there are some occasions in which practitioners were given even more precise instructions: sometimes we learn the exact moment when the act of deposition ought to take place ('when the moon stands in opposition to the sun')[272] or even the ideal depth for the deposit ('four fingers deep').[273] While these prescriptions are hard to document archaeologically,[274] it should be pointed out that over half of the *defixiones* originating in necropoleis were found inside a grave (both burial and incineration graves). Access to such graves not only depended on the characteristics of the site but also on the skill (and at times, the audacity) of practitioners. As a result, there are a wide range of practices that deserve a more minute analysis.

The safest of all the options is broadly documented in North African necropoleis, where libation tubes connecting cinerary urns with the outside world were used to 'send' the curses inside a grave. Thus, according to Chopard and Hannezo, *defixiones* from Hadrumetum were rolled up and then slid down through these conduits. Sometimes this did not work so well: in fact, there are cases in which cinerary urns had been stuffed with so many tablets that *defixiones* got stuck in the tube itself.[275] This *modus operandi* is also attested at the necropoleis of Bir-ez-Zitoun and Bir-el-Djebbana (Carthage), where *defixiones* were rolled up 'like cigarettes' (Delattre 1898: 218). It must have been so common to deposit *defixiones* in this manner that even a *cippus* was found whose tube had deliberately been sealed with a perforated lead sheet through which only fluids could be introduced. This device demonstrates an effort on the part of the deceased's relatives to prevent this deeply rooted praxis from affecting the grave of their loved one.[276]

If there was a lack of libation tubes, practitioners at times opted for bolder procedures, breaking into the funerary monument and depositing curses at a grave's entrance. This riskier method was used in the case of three curses from Volaterrae/Volterra (cf. **88–90**) that were found in 1755 in the entrance to the lower chamber of a hypogeum and among broken urns and ashes. Similar instances are documented in other tombs, such as no. 336 from the necropolis of Banditaccia (Caere/Cerveteri, cf. **95**), where a *defixio* was fixed to the wall in the *dromos*. Another interesting case comes from tomb no. 10 from the Pompeiian necropolis located outside the Porta Stabia, where a *defixio* which looked like a diptych (cf. **71**) was found on the ground at the entrance to a grave.

There are, however, other examples in which there was even distance between the practitioner and the deceased: curses were at times deposited next to the grave goods, as in Maar (Gallia Belgica), where a *defixio* was found in 1893 written on a clay pot next to the incineration urn, remains of oil lamps and three coins (cf. **173**). There may be another instance of this from Faviana/Mautern (cf. **526**) if we accept Scherrer's reinterpretation of the context (1998: 77–79). According to this scholar, the area where the tablet was deposited was not a sanctuary (as Thaller 1948 had proposed) but a grave, as is suggested by the presence of copious ashes, 2 pieces of pottery, 13 iron nails and some 40 coins. The *defixio* in question was used as the cover of a small jug containing the remains of organic materials, sand and some human hair-like fibres, which have been explained by Faraone and Kropp (2010: 388, n. 27) as the remains of a burnt magical figurine. Although this hypothesis cannot be proven, it is doubtlessly suggestive.[277]

Nonetheless, in an attempt to create a close link between the remains of the deceased and the tablets, the latter were at times deposited inside the cinerary urns themselves. This *modus operandi* was unquestionably riskier than others, given that it not only involved entering the columbarium or opening a grave, but also the direct handling of an urn (at least when it lacked a libation tube for 'sending' the lead tablet inside). Of the total number of curses found in funerary contexts, about 20 were discovered inside cinerary urns. These *defixiones* mostly come from Italia, although we also know of examples from Africa, Hispania, Germania and Gallia. These tablets are generally found mixed together with the cremated ashes and bones. There are, however, some noteworthy exceptions, such as the *defixio* from L'Hospitalet-du-Larzac (cf. **158**, Gallia Narbonensis): in 1983, during the excavations of grave no. 71 at the necropolis at La Vayssière, which included an impressive collection of 40 vases, a Gaulish *defixio* was discovered. The curse, inscribed on two tablets, had been carefully placed on top of a cinerary urn serving as a sort of a lid that 'protected' the charred human bones within. The fact that the tomb was not ransacked during Antiquity strongly suggests that the tablets were deposited at the same time as the burial, as was the case from Mazan mentioned before (cf. **156**).

---

[271] *PGM* IV, 2215–16: κατορύξεις δὲ ἐπὶ ἀώρου θήκην τὴν λεπίδα ἐπὶ ἡμέρας γ´.

[272] *PGM* IV, 2220–25 (translated by H. Martin, Jr. *apud* Betz 1992²): καὶ καταχώσεις εἰς ἀώρου μνῆμα σελήνης οὔσης διαμέτρου ἡλίου.

[273] *PGM* V, 333 (translated by M. Smith, *apud* Betz 1992²) ὄρυξον ἐπὶ δ´ δακτύλους καὶ ἔνθες.

[274] It is obviously impossible to determine the exact moment when a *defixio* was deposited. Likewise, it is only in rare instances that we can know whether someone was deemed to have died prematurely. See, for just some examples, **96** (deposited next to the burial of a child), **125–26** (where two tablets were found inside a cinerary urn containing the charred remains of a child), or a curse tablet from Naro/Hammam-Lif (found next to a child's grave; cf. Audollent 1910, 136–41).

[275] Chopard and Hannezo 1894: 194: 'étaient au préalable roulées et que l'on glissait pour les faire pénétrer jusqu'aux ossements contenus dans le récipient; souvent même, en raison de l'encombrement du récipient et du tube, la lamelle de plomb était arrêtée dans le tube et mélangée aux os calcinés'. In the case of the *defixiones* found in Hadrumetum, *DT* 275–84 are believed with a high degree of certainty to have been found in this context.

[276] Delattre 1898: 218: '…était fermé par une lamelle de plomb percée de petits trous formant passoire et ne permettant que l'introduction des liquides'.

[277] In this regard, it is worth noting an interesting parallel from the sanctuary of Anna Perenna (Rome), where a small ceramic jug was found with the remains of bones and parchment and had been sealed with an apparently uninscribed lead sheet (Polakova and Rapinesi 2002: 39 and 49).

At times, when curse tablets were deposited in burial graves, the practitioner deliberately sought to put the curse in direct contact with the remains of the deceased. This intentional and morbid contact has been documented on rare, though noteworthy, occasions when the skull or the chest of the deceased was chosen as the place to deposit a curse tablet. Indeed, some *defixiones* were found placed directly under the deceased's skull, such as in Minturnae/Minturno where the tablet was actually nailed to the back of the cranium (cf. **56**). According to Delattre (1888: 158), in Carthage, some curses were found on top of the skulls of two decapitated individuals. The chest of the deceased could also be a good place to deposit a curse tablet. There is an interesting case from Durocortorum/Reims (cf. **174**), where a Gallo-Roman burial was found in 1894 that contained the remains of a person whose skull was malformed (hence, probably, the use of this grave for magic purposes) and on whose chest (next to the left shoulder), a coffer was found which contained 14 coins and a rolled *defixio* (Jadart 1901: 66). Another case from Paris (cf. **165**) could be added, where according to Vacquer (1879: 111) 'une lame de plomb mince, pliée en deux et reposant sur la poitrine du mort' was found.

As can be seen, the archaeology attests to a great heterogeneity of practices. This diversity can be explained in terms of the *defigens*' attempt to do his/her best to deposit a curse in a necropolis. That said, during the High Empire, in places like Carthage and Hadrumetum, the existence of professional practitioners provides us with a different pattern, that is, the repeated use of the very same tombs over and over as places for depositing *defixiones* (something similar also took place in the Late Antiquity in cities such as Rome with the 'Sethian' corpus). In general, even if the recommendations recorded in the much later *PGM* are attested in the archaeological record, the imagination of actual practitioners went well beyond suggestions found in the literary record.

6.3. Aquatic contexts

The phrase aquatic context is generally used to refer to any space that is composed of water, such as rivers, seas, fountains, wells, etc. Even if scholars have traditionally used this category as if it were straightforward and easily separated from the other contexts in which *defixiones* were deposited, it is actually one of the more problematic contexts, not only because it intersects with other categories but also because the coherence of the category itself is challenged by the diverse cultural meanings that water could have in Antiquity.[278]

Scholars have explained the use of aquatic contexts in three different ways. The first one links this space with the principles of sympathetic magic. In other words, the

coldness of the water would symbolically 'freeze' the victim of the curse (Ogden 1999: 23).[279] This theory is quite compelling for the *defixiones* found in the wells from the Athenian agora, among which we frequently find formula like ὡς ταῦτα τὰ ὀνόματα ψύχεται, οὕτω καὶ Ἀλκιδάμου ψυχείσθω τὸ ὄνομα... ('as these names grow cold, so too let Alkidamos' name grow cold').[280] Here, as the water cools the tablet, the practitioner asks that the name and hence victim himself be frozen and paralysed. Even though this explanation is clearly correct for describing curses from this specific context (the Athenian wells), it would be a mistake to try to give the same explanation to the curses from the Roman West, where (so far) no similar formulae have been attested.

In a different vein, other authors have linked aquatic contexts to Hades. As M. Martin (2010: 27) states, water can come from the depths of the earth, where, thanks to its perpetual movement, it was thought to be linked with the chthonic deities who lived below the earth's surface.[281]

There is another theory put forth by authors like Wünsch, who suggested that *defixiones* were deposited in aquatic settings since shipwrecked sailors resided there (1898: IV, col. 2).[282] This interpretation is also recorded in the *PGM*, where some recipes recommend depositing tablets in water, thanks to the widespread belief that the souls of drowned men wandered the bottoms of the sea since they were unable to reach Hades.[283] In the *PGM*, it is recommended that curses be thrown into rivers or the sea 'late in the evening or in the middle of the night'[284] or 'before sunrise'.[285] Another possibility was to 'glue it to the dry vaulted vapor room of a bath',[286] to 'throw it into the heating chamber of a bath',[287] or deposit it 'where there is a stream or the drain of a bath, having tied a cord [to the plate] throw it into the stream or into the sea'.[288] At least in these recipes from *PGM* VII, it is clear that different

---

[278] A different version of this section, which included Greek curse tablets and magical figurines from the Roman West, has already been published (see Sánchez Natalías 2019b).

[279] In a similar vein and for a discussion of the verb καταψύχω, see Guarducci 1978: 255 and Jordan 1985b: 241, n. f, where he argues that in curses from the Athenian wells this verb 'may refer to the chilling effects of the waters in the wells'. That said, in *SV* 16 (from a necropolis) the verb alludes to 'the chill of the lead itself'. For the idea of depositing a *defixio* in a well so as to 'freeze' the victim's name, see the brief mention in Jordan 1990: 437.

[280] Translated by Jordan 1985b: no. 6, ll. 27–29. The same analogy is found in Jordan 1985b: nos 1 (ll. 16–18), 2 (ll. 13–15), 3 (ll. 13–15), 4 (ll. 21–25), 5 (ll. 10–12), etc.

[281] See also Guarducci 1978: 242 and Graf 1995: 123.

[282] On this, also see Fox 1912b and Cesano 1961²: 1589.

[283] See Stramaglia 1999: 194–95, where there is a discussion of the explicit passage of Achilles Tatius V, 16, 2: λέγουσι δὲ τὰς ἐν ὕδατι ψυχὰς ἀνηρπαμένας μηδὲ εἰς Ἄιδου καταβαίνειν ὅλως, ἀλλ' αὐτοῦ περὶ τὸ ὕδωρ ἔχειν τὴν πλάνην, that is: 'They say that the souls of those who have met their end in the deep never go down to Hades, but wander in the same spot about the face of the waters' (Translated by S. Gaseke, Loeb 1984).

[284] *PGM* VII, 435. Translated by M. Smith, *apud* Betz 1992².

[285] *PGM* VII, 420. Translated by M. Smith, *apud* Betz 1992².

[286] Translated by E.N. O'Neil, *apud* Betz 1992², *PGM* XXXVI, 75: κόλλα εἰς τὸν ξηρὸν θόλον τοῦ βαλανείου.

[287] *PGM* VII, 469: βάλε εἰς ὑποκαυστήριον βαλανείου. Translated by E.N. O'Neil, *apud* Betz 1992².

[288] Translated by M. Smith, *apud* Betz 1992², *PGM* VII, 436: ὅπου ῥοῦς ἐστιν ἢ παραρέον βαλανείου (...) βάλε φέρεσθαι εἰς τὸν ῥοῦν (ἢ εἰς θάλασσαν).

41

aquatic contexts (i.e., the stream, the bath, the sea) were seen as equivalent places for depositing tablets.[289]

The reason that the *PGM* recommend practitioners to use this depositional context can be deduced from erotic spells (*agōgai*) collected in *PGM* VII, which can be dated to either the third or fourth century CE. One curse tells the reader to the curse ought to be written 'with a copper nail from a shipwrecked vessel'[290] and subsequently thrown into the sea. In this case, the nail used to write the curse is an element that links aquatic and funerary contexts. The second relevant spell urges the reader to use a lamp whose wick is made 'of [the hawser from] a wrecked ship'.[291] As was the case with the previous recipe, the material used in the ritual is an element that is linked to both funerary and aquatic contexts, each of which brings its own magical valence, as Wünsch and his contemporaries had already noted.[292]

Provocative though these three hypotheses may be, they are all difficult to verify archaeologically. Theories concerning the value of aquatic settings in terms of sympathetic magic or their ability to summon the infernal gods or restless dead can only be judged by examining the textual remains of the *defixiones*, which generally omit any reference to this issue. A few exceptions, however, do exist. Thus, **206**, deposited in the sacred spring of Sulis Minerva in Aquae Sulis/Bath, does attest to the magical valence of the aquatic contexts in terms of sympathetic magic. Written in response to a theft, this tablet asks the goddess to make the thief 'as liquid as water' (l. 2), thus directly alluding to the dissolution of the victim. This same idea of dissolution is found in the persuasive analogies found in three curses from the sanctuary of Isis and Mater Magna (Mogontiacum/Mainz), where the victims and their property ought to dissolve 'like salt in water' (cf. **490**, **492–93**). We must note that in these three instances the analogy is not connected to the context in which the curse tablets were actually deposited (they were tossed into the fire on the altar at the back of the temple).

Although to date there is no further textual evidence that connects aquatic contexts to the principles of sympathetic magic, the findspot of two British curses could possibly point in this direction. More specifically, there are two *defixiones* from Bravonium/Leintwardine (cf. **347–48**) that were discovered inside a small drain in the *frigidarium* of the local bath complex. Since the texts of these curses consist only of lists of names in the nominative case, we cannot determine whether the practitioner sought to 'freeze' symbolically the victims. Furthermore, the fact

that we cannot determine a date for these texts means that we do not know whether the practitioner deposited the curses in a space that was still in use (perhaps linked to the victims?) or had been abandoned (perhaps inhabited by ghosts who could help with the curses' activation?).[293]

As far as the aspects that could potentially favour communication with infernal deities, we ought to highlight (though not without some reservation given that difficulty involved in deciphering the text) a Gaulish curse from Arverni/Chamalières (Gallia Aquitania, cf. **163**) which was deposited in the 'Source des Roches', a Gallo-Roman sanctuary where there was an aquatic cult. The text invokes *andedíon uediíumi diíiuion risun-/ artiumapon aruerιίatin*' (ll. 1–2), which Lambert translates as 'Au nom de la bonne force des divinités chtoniennes, j'invoque Maponos d'Avernion'.[294] That said, the fact that the tablet was deposited in a space that could have been a sanctuary dedicated to Maponos could also explain this invocation.

6.3.1. Geographical and temporal data about aquatic deposits

With the aim of clarifying the use of aquatic spaces for the deposition of curse tablets, it is fruitful to turn to a more archaeological (and less theoretical) perspective and to study the various contexts in which tablets have been discovered (see Table 6.2).

6.3.2. Aquatic contexts as sacred spaces

To start, I would like to suggest that we ought to divide aquatic contexts into two separate categories: sacred and non-sacred spaces. In the first category, we find sites such as the British sanctuaries of Sulis Minerva in Aquae Sulis/ Bath and Mercury in Uley, where water played a key role, since the spring itself was the centrepiece of cultic activity.

---

[289] Although it is possible that many North African tablets ended up being deposited in the sea or other aquatic contexts, so far we only know of four *defixiones* from the 'Fontaine aux Milles Amphores', in Carthage (on this, see Audollent 1933b). Of these, the two Latin curses were written for economic reasons.

[290] Translated by E.N. O'Neil, *apud* Betz 1992², *PGM* VII, 466: γράφε ἐν ἥλῳ κυπρίνῳ ἀπό πλ[ο]ίου νεναυαγηκότος.

[291] Translated by E.N. O'Neil, *apud* Betz 1992², *PGM* VII, 594–95: ποίησον ἐλλύχνιον [ἀπ]ὸ πλοίου νεναυαγηκότος.

[292] See n. 282 above.

[293] The idea that bath complexes were infested with demons is well attested in the Imperial period, which could explain why the tablet was deposited in this context (see Bonner 1932a and Stramaglia 1999: 191 ff.). On these tablets, see Alfayé 2016, who does not address their date. The same author suggests that all the curses from Bath/Aquae Sulis could be seen as coming from the same context (2016: 28). This, however, does not take into account that these tablets were thrown along with votive offerings into the sacred spring). Alfayé also identifies four other British tablets as coming from baths (**336**, **456–57** and **446**); since the archaeological context of these four items is uncertain, I have excluded them from the present analysis. Among the *defixiones* that evoke the aquatic context in the terms of sympathetic magic, a curse from Salerno has traditionally and incorrectly been included (cf. **69**): discovered in a grave, it reads: *Locus · capillo-/ribus · expect-/at · cap-/ut · su-/um.* Several authors (Mommsen, *apud CIL* X, 511; Fox 1912b: 305; Ogden 1999: 24; Marco Simón and Velázquez 2000: 271, n. 44) have ignored the interpuncts and singled out the letters *ribus*, which they have incorrectly analysed as a Vulgar form of *rivus*, hence falsely understanding the tablet in terms of sympathetic magic: just as hair is submerged, so too should the victim be submerged. As Mancini already noted (1884–86: 81), the reading *capilloribus* (por *capillis*) invalidates this hypothesis. Accordingly, the place that awaits the victim of the curse is the tomb where the hair and tablet were found, not the supposed brook mentioned by the above-mentioned authors.

[294] According to Lambert (*apud RIG* II.2, L-100), -*mapon(on)* (l. 2 formed from **ma(k)kʷo-* 'young man' and the suffix -*ono*-) is Maponos, while the following word, *aruerιίatin* (l. 2), ought to be identified as an epithet referring to the place of god's cult worship, in this case Maponos 'of the underworld'.

Table 6.2. *Defixiones* discovered in aquatic contexts, organised by provenance. The number of pieces from this sort of context is compared to the total number of pieces from each province

Provenance	*SD*/site	Archaeological context	Total
Italia	19–47	Fountain of Anna Perenna.	33/119
	57	Grotto of Tiberius (abandoned pool).	
	83	*Lacum Fucinum* (?).	
	92	Fountain.	
	104	Channel.	
Africa	Carthage (Audollent 1933)	Fountain 'aux milles amphores'.	2/88
Hispania	121	Sanctuary (pool).	2/30
	137	Beach (?).	
Gallia	150–155	Fountain 'Le Gros Escaldador'.	10/55
	157	Fountain 'Source des Roches'.	
	159	Well.	
	163	Well.	
	164	Fountain 'Chaude'.	
Britannia	206–335	Sanctuary of Sulis Minerva (spring).	224/256
	340	Riverbank (Thames River).	
	347–348	Thermal complex (*frigidarium*).	
	354–440	Sanctuary of Mercury (pool).	
	441	Riverbank (Tas River).	
	449	Little Ouse River (metal detector).	
	451	Hamble's estuary (metal detector).	
Germania	479	Fountain (?).	1/59 (?)
Raetia	–	–	0/6
Noricum	–	–	0/1
Pannonia	529	Kupa River.	1/9

In these sanctuaries, curses were deposited together with other votive offerings, such as coins, lamps and *paterae*. While in Aquae Sulis/Bath these were deposited in the sacred spring, at Uley, they were originally deposited inside a pool located in the *cella*.[295]

Another series of sites that fall into this category includes fountains such as the one of Anna Perenna in Rome but also at places like Arretium/Arezzo, Amélie-les-Bains and Arverni/Chamalières. These sites were cult centres for the Nymphs (cf. **19–47** and **92**), the Niskas (cf. **150–51** and **155**) and Maponos (cf. **163**), respectively. In these fountains, the presence of deposited coins as well as other cultic objects (e.g., altars, votives, ceramics and organic remains) suggest that all these places were indeed sacred. Probably, the 'Fontaine aux 1000 amphores' (Carthage[296]) should also be added to the list of such sacred aquatic spaces, even though the curses found there do not invoke aquatic deities. Ritual wells formed yet another subset of sacred aquatic spaces. Among these, we can point out two examples from Gallia (Montfo and Rauranum/Rom; cf. **157** and **159**), where different cultic offerings were also found.

Besides these manmade sites, we must mention the 'natural' ones, which were typical of 'Celtic' religion. Within this category of natural sacred spaces, we ought to mention flood plains, rivers and beaches. All these contexts have a common denominator: they were thought to be sacred places that were consecrated to aquatic divinities such as Neptune,[297] Niskus[298] and Savus.[299]

When it comes to spaces that were apparently not consecrated but were nevertheless used to deposit curses, we can mention a canal (in Altinum/Altino, cf. **104**)[300] and baths (at Bravonium/Leintwardine, cf. **347–48**).[301] The absence of any written invocation of gods connected to aquatic contexts makes it difficult to determine why these places were chosen to deposit a curse, although the invocations could also have been uttered while performing the ritual. A *defixio* found in

---

[295] See Woodward 1993: 113 and below, section I.6.4.
[296] On this, see Audollent 1933b. For the discovery of the site, see Carton 1920: 258–68.

[297] Neptunus is invoked in the following texts: **441**, **449** and **451**.
[298] Niskus is invoked together with Neptunus in **451**, a curse discovered in the estuary in Hamble.
[299] As is found in the *defixio* from Sisak (cf. **529**), which was deposited in the River Kupa and whose text evokes the river god Savus in order to send the victims to the riverbed.
[300] Specifically, the *defixio* was discovered, according to Scarfi (1972: 55) 'a 2 metri di profondità, all'esterno delle palificazioni di sostegno di una grande costruzione in blocchi parallelepipedi di trachite, ubicata ai limiti meridionali dell'area urbana antica'.
[301] On these, see above and note 293.

an abandoned pool in the so-called 'Grotto of Tiberius' (from Fundi/Fondi, cf. **57**) dates to the fourth century CE and was written on a reused piece of *opus sectile*. This curse, which contains various references to biblical passages, seems to have been intentionally deposited in an abandoned space for several reasons. First, the belief that such areas were inhabited by all sorts of spirits and ghosts made it an ideal place to deposit a curse, since these supernatural beings could assist the practitioner. Second, the persuasive analogies established in the text between the archaeological context (an area in ruins) and the physical and economic ruin of the tablet's victims could also explain the choice of deposition.[302] Finally, in the examples from Marsi Marruvium/San Benedetto and Emporion (cf. **83** and **137**), the lack of information in the texts (just lists of personal names), as well as the scarce and contradictory accounts about exactly where they were found prevents us from knowing the reasons why the curses were deposited in apparently aquatic contexts.

With only these few rare exceptions, the so-called aquatic sites from the Roman West are, at heart, better understood as different types of sacred spaces. For this reason, it seems more fruitful to study them as such.

6.4. Sacred contexts

Within this category, we ought to include all spaces firmly associated with a divinity, whether or not marked with a monument. Accordingly, even if temples and sanctuaries are the most common contexts within this category, we must also remember that there is a much larger range of sacred places for depositing a curse. Among these contexts, there are fountains, ritual wells and pits, amphitheatres and other 'natural sites' that were not built upon. As alluded to above, 'natural sites' are central to 'Celtic' religions in which cultic rites were celebrated in places like rivers and lakes. Again, this only goes to show the difficulty and danger in drawing a stark line between 'different' contexts.

The general popularity of sacred contexts for deposition can be attributed to the desire to communicate with the deities invoked, whom traditional scholarship has generally categorized as chthonic.[303] As Ogden stated, 'the progression from grave to chthonic sanctuary as a deposition site is easy and explicable: the chthonic gods, like the dead, dwelt under the earth, but could be expected to be much more reliable and powerful' (1999: 23). Surprisingly, the *PGM* do not discuss this context save for a single possible exception in the Great Magical Papyrus from Paris: in a recipe for an *agōge* in which Hekate is evoked it *defigens* is told to deposit the tablet at a crossroad (*PGM* IV, 2955), a space that was suitable for this goddess.

6.4.1. *Geographical and temporal data about deposits in sacred spaces*

In the Roman West, sacred spaces were beyond a measure of doubt the most common archaeological context: indeed, over a half of the tablets studied in this volume were deposited in sacred spaces.

As Table 6.3 suggests, a large portion of these tablets have been found in the northernmost regions of the Roman West. The most represented *provincia* is Britannia, where over three quarters of the *defixiones* belonging to this category were discovered, mostly at Aquae Sulis/Bath and Uley. In Germania, most of the lead tablets have been found at Mogontiacum/Mainz. In Italy, the fountain of Anna Perenna in Rome deserves special attention. Besides this fountain, hardly any texts deposited in sacred contexts have been found in the Italian peninsula, Gaul or the Iberian peninsula.[304] To date, there is not a single example from North Africa.

Regarding chronology, the first tablets from the Roman West discovered in a temple are the Greek *defixiones* deposited in the Sicilian sanctuaries at Selinunte and Morgantina.[305] Interestingly enough, there is a Oscan curse (cf. **76**) dated to the fourth century BCE that came from the sanctuary of Roccagloriosa, which was found with the remains of another 13 lead tablets (today lost). If these tablets were, as it seems, curse tablets, this findspot would be the oldest from the Italian peninsula, dating to just after the sanctuary of Demeter Malophoros in Selinunte. As Poccetti has suggested, this should be understood as a reflection of Greek practices.[306] That said, from the fourth century BCE to the first century CE, there are no known examples of *defixiones* deposited in sanctuaries, since (so far) in the Republican era the use of curse tablets seems to

---

[302] Alfayé 2019: 268–70 and also section I.3.3.2.
[303] See section I.7.2 below.

[304] In Italy this amounts to roughly a quarter of the total. Something similar can be observed in Gallia, where the tablets from sacred spaces amount to nearly a quarter of the total number of curses from the province. To these we would add the two tablets from Arlon and Dalheim (Gallia Belgica, cf. **203–04**): the first was found during the survey of the area near a Gallo-Roman *fanum*, while the second was discovered by a metal detectorist near the sanctuary and the residential zone of the *vicus*, which means that it should be attributed to one of these two contexts. In Hispania, the curses found in sanctuaries only amount of 6 per cent of the total number from the province; we could perhaps add a further five tablets from Saguntum that treasure hunters found among the ruins of a building that some scholars have identified as a sanctuary (cf. Corell 2002: 67). Nevertheless, the lack of secure information about the archaeological context means that we ought to exclude these tablets in the interest of being cautious. From Abusina/Eining (Raetia), there is one *defixio* to which we ought to add four more curses that were recently published by Blänsdorf and have not been included in the sylloge (cf. Blänsdorf 2019).
[305] For these tablets (dated to the fifth and first centuries BCE, respectively), see Curbera 1999a: nos 22–33 and 56–64. Faraone 1991a: 22, n. 7 provides a list of Greek *defixiones* deposited in chthonic sanctuaries.
[306] According to Poccetti, the transmission of cursing technology from the Greek to Roman world went through the Oscan populations (cf. Poccetti 1993d: 80, 1999: 555, 2015: 383–86; on this, see section I.9.2). As different scholars have pointed out, Oscan curses contain elements taken from the Greeks (from Sicily and abroad; cf. McDonald 2015: 133–66) and also share certain elements with the early Latin texts (cf. Poccetti 2015). On the patterns of influence and the spread of curses throughout the Italian peninsula, see Vitellozzi 2019.

Table 6.3. *Defixiones* discovered in sacred spaces, organised by provenance (It.= Italia, Afr.= Africa, Hisp.= Hispania, Gall.= Gallia, Brit.= Britannia, Ger.= Germania, Raet.= Raetia, Nor.= Noricum, Pan.= Pannonia) and the site of discovery; there is also reference to the archaeological context, date and the total number of tablets from each province

Prov.	*SD*/site	Context	Date	Total
It.	19–47	Fountain of Anna Perenna.	4th–5th CE.	31/119
	76	Sanctuary.	2nd CE.	
	92	Fountain.	4th BCE.	
Afr.	Carthage (Audollent 1933)	Fountain 'aux milles amphores'.	–	2/88
Hisp.	121	Sanctuary.	1st CE.	2/30
	128	Sanctuary of Isis.	2nd CE.	
Gall.	150–155	Fountain 'Le Gros Escaldador'.	–	15/55
	157	Well.	3rd–4th CE.	
	159	Well.	50–60 CE.	
	162	Sanctuary.	–	
	163	Fountain 'Source des Roches'.	1st CE.	
	164	Fountain 'Chaude'.	4th–5th CE.	
	171	Pit.	–	
	182–183 and 189	Amphitheatre.	4th–5th CE.	
Brit.	205	Sanctuary of Nodens.	4th–5th CE.	226/256
	206–335	Sanctuary of Sulis-Minerva.	175–400 CE.	
	340	Riverbank (Thames River).	–	
	341	Pit.	4th CE.	
	353	Pit or well (?).	3rd–4th CE.	
	354–440	Sanctuary of Mercury.	75–400 CE.	
	441	Riverbank (Tas River).	–	
	447	Sanctuary (metal detector).	4th CE.	
	449	Little Ouse river (metal detector).	4th CE.	
	451	Hamble's estuary (metal detector).	4th CE.	
	455	Sanctuary.	3rd CE.	
	458	Sanctuary (?).	–	
Germ.	487–517	Sanctuary of Isis and Mater Magna.	1st–2nd CE.	36/59
	518–519	Sanctuary of Mater Magna.	2nd–3rd CE	
Raet.	525	Sanctuary.	–	1/6
Nor.	–	–	–	0/1
Pann.	529	Kupa River.	1st–2nd CE.	2/9
	531	Sanctuary of Isis.	1st–2nd CE.	

be restricted to the Mediterranean basin, where funerary contexts were favoured (see section I.6.2.1 and Table 6.1).

From the first century CE onwards, however, this absence is brought to a close with examples from Gallia (cf. **157** and **163**), Britannia (cf. **337**), Pannonia (cf. **529** and **531**), Germania (cf. **487–517**) and Hispania (cf. **121**). During the second and third centuries, important sanctuaries emerged, such as that for Sulis Minerva at Aquae Sulis/ Bath (cf. **206**, **233**, etc.) and to Mercury at Uley (cf. **355**, **359**, etc.). In addition to these sanctuaries (which were heavily frequented until the beginning of the fifth century), we also find scattered finds across the island (cf. **343–44**, **205**, etc.) and Gallia (cf. **159** and **204**). And of course we must add the fountain of Anna Perenna in Rome (cf. **19–47**), which was most actively used for magico-religious activities during the fourth and fifth centuries CE.

6.4.2. Spaces for communicating with the divine

As pointed out earlier, the archaeological record attests to an impressive heterogeneity of sacred spaces used for depositing *defixiones*. Still, we must note that the knowledge that we possess about these sacred spaces has often been limited due to the far from ideal techniques used during some excavations. Many nineteenth-century excavations, not to mention secret or illegal ones, offer little or no information about an object's exact context with the result that it is more difficult to put together an accurate large-scale analysis. Despite these difficulties and relying on the known characteristics of these sites, it is possible to distinguish two main categories: developed sites and natural ones.

In this first category, sanctuaries and temples predominate, given that they were privileged spaces for communicating with divinities. Accordingly, these two contexts count for the vast majority of tablets found in sacred spaces. As alluded to, in the Roman West, the sanctuaries of Sulis Minerva and Mercury have yielded the largest number of tablets, with over 200 *defixiones* from these two places alone (i.e., almost two-thirds of the total). Among the other sites where *defixiones* have been discovered, we should highlight the importance of the sanctuary dedicated to Isis and Magna Mater in Mogontiacum/Mainz which has given us 34 tablets dating to the first and second centuries CE. Within this same chronological span, there are another two texts coming from the *isea* of Baelo Claudia/Bolonia and Savaria/Szombathely (cf. **128** and **531**). The texts from Centum Prata/Kempraten (cf. **518f.**) have been dated between the second and the third centuries and were found in a sanctuary dedicated to Magna Mater; this is also the case for the ones from Abusina/Eining (cf. **525** and Blänsdorf 2019). Of later date is the curse tablet discovered at Lydney (cf. **205**), a site that was dedicated to the Roman-Celtic deity Nodens. The remaining sanctuaries from the Roman West, which were dedicated to deities whose identity we can no longer determine are found in Hispania (cf. **121**), Gallia (cf. **162**) and Britannia (cf. **447**, **455** and **458**) and have only yielded few isolated items.

In these contexts, we can observe different trends and patterns in the ways that curses were deposited (although it is not always clear the reasons why these particular locations were selected). The resulting diversity of practice is seen in the particular places chosen, which include the area around the temple (cf. **162**, **447**, etc.), within the tenemos (cf. **128** and **455**), in the portico (cf. **76**) as well as near or even behind the podium (cf. **531**). In the case of Mogontiacum/Mainz, 24 curse tablets were found in the rear part of the temple and placed inside of a rectangular well above which two altars were later built (Witteyer 2005: 116 and 2013; *DTM*, pp. 1–6, 39f.). On these altars offerings, among which we must count several curses, were thrown directly into the sacred fire.

In other instances, tablets have been uncovered within sanctuaries, as is the case at Aquae Sulis/Bath and Uley. Both of these complexes fit the mould of a Roman-Celtic sanctuary, where the sacred space is marked by a cella and is surrounded by an ambulatory upon which worshipers would walk. At Aquae Sulis/Bath, curses were thrown directly into the sacred spring, which was located in the centre of the complex (cf. **206–335**). At Uley, on the other hand, there was a small pool placed in the centre of the *cella*, which likely served as the place to deposit curses (cf. **354–440**). Although this *cella* seems to have served as the original deposit for these curses, where they were actually found spread throughout all the archaeological strata of the sacred complex (mostly among the secondary votive deposits).[307] Finally, we should add to the list the

sanctuary at Salacia/Alcácer do Sal (cf. **121**), where one *defixio* was found inside a small tank in the smaller of the temple's two *cellae*, was dedicated to a deity whose identity is today unknown.

Pits, which were structures similar to the Roman *favisae*, are also generally associated with sanctuaries. In this contest, votive offerings were deposited.[308] So far, in the Roman West, we know of at least two *defixiones* thrown into these pits, which have been found in Gallia (cf. **171**) and Britannia (cf. **341**). The Gallic pit was discovered in the Cité Judiciaire of Le Mans during an emergency excavation about which we have hardly any information (cf. *RIG* II.2, p. 296). The pit, dated to the first century CE, contained a reused lead tablet (cf. **171**), which, because of the material and context, seems to have been a *defixio*. Turning to Britannia, we know of at least one pit that held a *defixio*: excavated in 1988 in Southwark (London), it held a single curse that only bore its victim's name (cf. **341**). The tablet was found alongside other artefacts that have been dated to the fourth century CE: a coin from the reign of Constantine II (cf. Hassall 1992: 310) and some household rubbish, as well as 'the remains of a partially articulated dog' (cf. Seeley and Wardle 2009: 153), an animal that can possibly be connected to the underworld (cf. Green 1992: 111–13).[309]

Within this same category of built-up sacred spaces there are also fountains, from which we have some 20 texts. Whether clearly marked as sacred or not, *fontes* possessed a strong religious character from the Greek Archaic period onwards, because of the power associated with the flowing water and the belief that underground water provided a way to communicate with the underworld.[310] In the Roman West, five such fountains were used as a place for depositing curses: Arverni/Chamalières, Amélie-les-Bains and Aquae Tarbelliacae/Dax (all in Gallia) as well as at Arretium/Arezzo and Rome (in Italia).

Among these different archaeological sites, we ought to highlight the hot water spring at Arverni/Chamalières, known as 'Source de Roches', where 3,000 votive offerings[311] were found inside of the principal basin

---

[307] Of the 140 curses, 62 were found within secondary votive deposits dated to phase 5; we do not have precise details about the strata of 47 tablets; the remaining 31 were found among strata 4, 6, 6b, 7a and 7b. For a discussion, see Woodward 1993: 113 and Woodward and Leach 1993: 330–31, fig. 225.

[308] On this, see Green 1997: 170–71, *s.v.* 'pit'.

[309] To this British pit, we should perhaps add that from Old Harlow, although it is not clear whether it ought to be classified as a pit or a well. The excavation (carried out in 1970) determined that the structure was 3 m deep and had a curse (cf. **353**) as well as ceramic sherds dated to the third and fourth centuries CE (see Conlon 1973: 34 and 40). Furthermore, we should note that the structure where the tablet was found was located near two others that contained animal bones, shells, pieces of glass and pottery (dated to the second and third centuries CE), as well as fibulae and bronze votive offerings. Furthermore, near the top of one of these structures, archaeologists found 90 coins dating between the third and fourth centuries CE. All of this suggests that this was a sacred context.

[310] See Romizzi 2005: 242, s.v. '*Fons* (mondo romano)', in *ThesCRA IV*, 242–44.

[311] Romeuf 2007: 88, where it is specified that 1,500 complete votives along with some 8,500 additional fragments were found (best estimates suggest that there was a total of some 3,000 items). The majority of these were anthropo- and zoomorphic sculptures and wooden plaques (which were inscribed or painted), as well as mallets, coins, fibulae, pottery and other offerings. For a further discussion, see Romeuf 2000 and 2007: 88–93.

(Romeuf 2007: 87). Among these votives and deposited in what appears to be a haphazard manner, a Gaulish *defixio* was discovered that invokes Maponos, the god to whom the sanctuary may have been dedicated (cf. **163**).[312] Less is known about the six *defixiones* from Amélie-les-Bains (cf. **150–55**), which were discovered in 1845 in the main fountain ('Le Gros Escaldador') of a bath complex: they were uncovered along with coins dated to the first century CE, which attest to the site's religious function.[313] The final example from Gallia is the so-called 'Fontaine de la Nèhe' or 'Fontaine Chaude' in Aquae Tarbelliacae/Dax, which was of Gallo-Roman origins and was built up during the reign of the Severans (Watier and Gauthier 1977: 323). An excavation in 1976 brought to light a curse tablet written after a theft (cf. **164**) together with ceramic sherds and a group of coins that had been deposited between the end of the fourth century and beginning of the fifth century CE.[314]

In Italy two fountains have also been discovered. Little is known about the first, which is in Arretium/Arezzo and surveyed in 1869. In this fountain, archaeologists found a *defixio* together with a group of coins dating to the reign of Antoninus Pius; it has been speculated that the fountain was dedicated to the nymphs who are invoked in the curse (cf. **92**). The fountain of Anna Perenna, which was dedicated to the goddess and her nymphs and which was discovered in 1999, deserves special attention.[315] The fountain was supplied by a *krene* (i.e., a spring) in which there were three altars dedicated to this deity (cf. Friggeri 2002: 26–33). Its cistern contained a rich votive deposit made up of more than 500 coins, some 70 lamps, a *caccabus*, organic remains and, most important for our purposes, 32 *defixiones* (cf. **19–47**).

Ritual wells are also a type of sacred space that was used for depositing *defixiones*. Two such cases have been recorded in Gaul (cf. **157** and **159**). Generally, it is thought that these wells, which are found in Celtic areas, probably served as Roman *mundi* (gates to the underworld) or as openings to the inner parts of the earth. These had a chthonic quality and were in use before the Roman conquest of the regions in question.[316] The first Gallic well was discovered in 1975 in the *oppidum* Montfo, which was inhabited from the sixth century BCE until the first century CE. This well, which is some 13.5 m deep, contained wooden objects (tablets, combs, pegs), ceramics (including nearly complete jugs) and animal remains, which, according to Bacou and Bacou, 'sont tombés ou ont été envoyés dans

le puits' (1975: 22; there were five dogs, one cat or lynx, a deer and an ox).[317] Among these remains, archaeologists uncovered a *defixio* (cf. **157**) dating to the mid-first century CE, which was deposited in the well when it was still in use. We should note that this text includes an intriguingly persuasive analogy that compares the falling of the lead tablet to the bottom of the well to the downfall of its victims (cf. **157**, A, ll. 1–4). The well at Rauranum/Rom was discovered and excavated in 1887 in a Roman villa. Measuring 1.8 m in diameter and 20 m in depth, this well contained surplus building materials, animal bones and bronze coins. At a depth of 10 to 12 m, 40 lead tablets were unearthed. Some of these were rolled up, others were pierced with a nail. None of these seems to have been inscribed, though it is believed that they were nevertheless curses, like other uninscribed lead tablets deposited in sanctuaries (e.g., at Uley; cf. Jullian 1897a: 132, n. 1). Below this, archaeologists found a collection of tablets, a sickle, a pick and a curse tablet (cf. **159**; note that this is the only published curse from this site), which has been dated to either the third or fourth century CE and has proven quite difficult to decipher. Though we are short on reliable details concerning this well and its contents, the discovery of this important collection of tablets nevertheless provides evidence that the well served as a site for communication with divine powers.

Finally, we can turn to natural sacred spaces, in which five tablets have been uncovered. Four of the five were found in Britain (cf. **340**, **441**, **449** and **451**), while the fifth hails from Pannonia Superior (cf. **529**). Among the British examples we must note that the curses from Brandon and Hamble, which date to the fourth century CE, were found by metal detectorists (cf. **449** and **451**). We do not know the date nor the exact circumstances in which a curse from London was found along the banks of the River Thames (cf. **340**), where the curse from Venta Icenorum/Caistor St Edmund (cf. **441**; of unknown date) was discovered on the riverbank of the River Tas. Only the curse from Siscia/Sisak (cf. **529**), which is dated to either the first or second century CE, was found during an actual archaeological excavation, in this case those carried out on the shores of the River Kupa in 1913.

Though our knowledge about the discovery and context of these tablets is rather hazy, it seems likely that they were originally placed in a flowing river and then were later deposited in a river bank, mud or beach. Such a narrative would certainly fit with the deities invoked in these texts, who are all associated with water, such as Neptune,[318]

---

[312] According to Lambert *apud RIG* II.2, p. 274, 'Maponos est ici invoqué en tant que divinité de la source de Chamalières'. But see the objections proffered by Romeuf 2007: 94–95.

[313] On the archaeological context, see the brief notice from Puiggari *apud* Henry 1847: 410.

[314] See Nony and Tobie 1977: 324–25, who maintain that, even if the hoard of coins dates between 364 and 375 CE, 'ces émissions sont pratiquement au seules à circuleur au Vᵉ siècle', a date which would match that of the curse tablet (*contra* Alfayé 2019: 264).

[315] We are still awaiting the full publication of the fountain. For the present time, see Piranomonte 2002, 2005, 2009, 2010a, 2012a, 2013 and 2015.

[316] See Green 1997: 224, *s.v.* 'well.'

[317] For the well's contents, see Bacou and Bacou 1975: 17–22. Given the presence of dogs deposited in wells, Green has argued that these animals were connected to the underworld (1992: 111–13, esp. 112).

[318] Neptune is evoked in all the British curses, though in **340** the theonym appears in the Vulgar form Metunus and in the *defixiones* from Brandon and Hamble (**449** and **451**) he is alluded to as *dominus*. In the case from Brandon, the phrase *cor´u´lo pare(n)tator* (l. 7) is used to offer the victim to Neptune and could be linked to the punishment mentioned by Tacitus (*Germ.* XII, 1) for *ignauos et inbellis et corpore infamis caeno ac palude, iniecta insuper crate, mergunt*. On this, see Marco Simón 2020.

Niskus[319] and Savus.[320] As is well known, in 'Celtic' religion, water was thought to be one of the privileged sites of communication with the divine.[321] Indeed, water was viewed as a sacred liminal space that not only was the fount of life but also provided an entrance to the world beyond. Accordingly, such aquatic spaces often served as the site for ritual practice. Among these cultic activities, the deposition of metal is one of the best known, thanks to both ancient textual testimony and also to the archaeological record[322] that attests to a flexible practice which evolved to include the deposition of *defixiones* during and subsequent to the period of 'Romanization.'

6.5. Spaces associated with the victim

As the name implies, this depositional context was chosen due to its proximity to the target. This purpose could be accomplished by hiding tablets in the victim's house or place of work (as happened in cases when the victim was a gladiator or a charioteer and the tablets were placed in the amphitheatre or the circus). It is hard to discern the main motive behind this type of deposit, since not only do we have a lack of literary references, but also (and more generally) because of the lack of good information about the tablets' archaeological contexts.

Classical literature, however, does provide us with some relevant information about aggressive magical practices that relied on proximity to the victim. One of the best-known sources comes from Tacitus' description of the death of Germanicus. As the historian puts it:

> Germanicus' conviction that he had been poisoned/put under a spell [*veneni*] by Piso aggravated the disease. They dug up the floor and the walls and found remains of human bodies in them, spells and binding curses [*devotiones*], and the name of Germanicus inscribed on lead tablets, ashes half-burned and smeared with gore and the other evil devices by which it is believed that souls are devoted to the infernal powers.[323]

In this instance, the walls of Germanicus' house served as the place where the curses were deposited, together with other human remains. We are left to wonder if this final detail could be an embellishment of Tacitus' part, who was 'imagining' the magical praxis rather than recounting what actually happened (though note that Dio Cassius tells the same story).[324] We learn of a similar event from Libanius, who recounts suffering from a protracted illness that no physician could cure, until 'a chameleon, of uncertain origin, was discovered in the classroom. It had been there a long time and had been dead for many months. We saw that its head had been placed between its hind feet. Of its forefeet, one was nowhere to be seen, and the other was closing its mouth to keep it silent'.[325] Once the animal was discovered, Libanius managed to recover from the mysterious illness.

Likewise, thresholds, which are the liminal spaces par excellence, were also an ideal place to deposit a curse, as Saint Jerome describes. In his *Life of Saint Hilarius the Hermit*, the author tells the story of a deranged young virgin against whom a man had written 'some verbal monstrosities and monstrous forms on plates of copper and buried them under the threshold of the girl's house'.[326] Furthermore, we can also add the testimony of of Sophronius who mentions in his story about the doctor Theodorus of Cyprus who was ill and had a revelatory dream that uncovered the cause of this sickness and the cure to his suffering:

> 'send one of your servants to Lapithos and tell him to dig in front of your bedroom next to the doorway. There he will find the wicked instrument of the sorcerer. Once it is uncovered, its maker will disappear immediately.' Theodoros sent (him) to the place, as commanded, and he found the cause of the disability.[327]

Apparently, this was some sort of magical artefact (the author does not give further details) whose powers were lost upon being discovered.

[319] Niskus is invoked together with *domino Neptuno* in the curse from Hamble (cf. **451**). Determining the identity of this Niskus has been somewhat difficult given the absence of other parallels. Scholars have associated him as the masculine counterpart of *Niskas* from **150–51** and **154**, or as a 'Celticized' version of Neptunus (see Tomlin 1999a: 562, n. 52).

[320] The deity of the river in which the curse from Sisak was deposited and upon whom the *defigens* calls to drown the curse's victims (cf. **529** B, ll. 1–6).

[321] For the symbolic value of water in Celtic religion, see Cunliffe 1988: 359–62; Webster 1995: 449–50; Green 1997: 223–24 (*s. v.* 'water').

[322] When it comes to classical sources, one of the most well-known passages is from Strabo (IV, 13), where the geographer mentions the lacustrine deposit of precious objects made by the *Volcae Tectosages* in the vicinity of modern-day Toulouse. Archaeologically, we should mention the discoveries at La Tène and Llyn Cerrig Bach (see Webster 1995: 450, with further bibliography).

[323] Tacitus, *Ann.* II, 69 (translated by Ogden 2002: 217): '...*et reperiebantur solo ac parietibus erutae humanorum corporum reliquiae, carmina et devotiones et nomen Germanici plumbeis tabulis insculptum, semusti cineres ac tabo obliti aliaque malefica quis creditur animas numinibus infernis sacrari*'. On this episode, see D'Erce 1969; Tupet 1980; Dickie 2010.

[324] Dio Cassius, LVII, 18, 9 (translated by E. Cary, 1968): 'His death occurred at Antioch as the result of a plot formed by Piso and Plancina. For bones of men that had been buried in the house where he dwelt and sheets of lead containing curses together with his name were found while he was yet alive' (ἀπέθανε δὲ ἐν ᾿Αντιοχείᾳ, ὑπό τε τοῦ Πίσωνος καὶ ὑπὸ τῆς Πλαγκίνης ἐπιβουλευθείς· ὀστᾶ τε γὰρ ἀνθρώπων ἐν τῇ οἰκίᾳ ἐν ᾗ ᾤκει κατορωρυγμένα καὶ ἐλασμοὶ μολίβδινοι ἀράς τινας μετὰ τοῦ ὀνόματος αὐτοῦ ἔχοντες ζῶντος ἔθ' εὑρέθη).

[325] Libanius, *Orat.* I, 249 (translated by Ogden 2002: 260). On this, see Bonner 1932b; Cracco Ruggini 1996 (esp. p. 162 ff., for an analysis of the metaphorical value of the chameleon which represents the orator's own political ambiguity); Maltomini 2004 (for a different analysis that focuses on three magical recipes in which chameleons are used to silence an enemy).

[326] Jerome, *vit. Hilar.* XI (translated by Ogden 2002: 230 and slightly modified): *...et subter limen domus puellae portenta quaedam verborum et portentosas figuras sculptas in aeris Cyprii lamina defodit.* On the media for writing the curse, see section I.3.2, n. 58.

[327] Sophronius, *Narratio*, LV (Migne, P.G., LXXXVII, 3, col. 3625, *apud* Audollent 1904: CXXII. English translation by Gager 1992: no. 166): τινα τῶν σοι διακονουμένων εἰς Λάπιθον, καὶ πρὸ τοῦ κοιτῶνος τοῦ σοῦ παρὰ τὸ πρόθυρον σκάψαι διάταξον · ἐκεῖσε γὰρ εὑρήσει τὸ τοῦ δεδρακότος κακούργημα, ὑπὸ τὸ πρόθυρον ἀφανῶς καλυπτόμενον · ὃ καὶ φανερούμενον, εὐθὺς ἀναιρεῖ τὸν ποιήσαντα. Πέμψας δὲ Θεόδωρος ὡς κεκέλευστο κατὰ τὸν λεχθέντα τόπον, τὸ τῆς ἀρρωστίας εὕρισκεν αἴτιον...

Table 6.4. *Defixiones* discovered in contexts closely associated with the victim, organized by provenance (It.= Italia, Afr.= Africa, Hisp.= Hispania, Gall.= Gallia, Brit.= Britannia, Ger.= Germania, Raet.= Raetia, Nor.= Noricum, Pan.= Pannonia). Reference is also made to the archaeological context, date and the total number of curses found in each province.

Prov.	*SD*/Site	Context	Date	Total
It.	17	Domestic ('house of Livia')	1st CE	2/119
	113 (?)	Domestic (monumental area)	3rd CE	
Afr.	*DT* 247–251	Amphitheatre	1st CE	8/88
	DT 253–254	Amphitheatre	1st CE	
	Jordan 1988: no. 3	Circus	3rd CE	
Hisp.	127	Domestic (on a floor)	2nd CE	4/30
	139	Domestic	1st BCE–1st CE	
	145	Domestic (entrance of the settlement)	1st BCE–1st CE	
	148	Domestic (wall, chryptoporticus)	–	
Gall.	172	Domestic (ditch)	1st CE	29/55
	175–202	Amphitheatre	4th–5th CE	
Brit.	336	Domestic (Roman fort)	–	8/256
	337	Amphitheatre	1st–2nd CE	
	343	Amphitheatre	2nd–3rd CE	
	344	Amphitheatre	–	
	346	Domestic (oven)	3rd–4th CE	
	456–457	Domestic (patio of a *mansio*)	2nd–3rd CE	
	446	Domestic (on a floor)	4th CE	
Ger.	463	Domestic (Roman fort)	1st–2nd CE	2/59
	482	Domestic (ditch)	1st–2nd CE	
Raet.	522	Domestic (wall)	1st CE	2/6
	524	Domestic (foundations)	2nd–3rd CE	
Nor.	–	–	–	0/1
Pann.	528	Domestic (entrance of a dwelling)	1st–2nd CE	2/9
	530	Amphitheatre	2nd–3rd CE	

Finally, we should turn to the *PGM*. It is noteworthy that only a single recipe calls for the deposition of a curse tablet in a space closely associated with its victim.[328] More specifically, we find this instance in a spell desiring the separation of lovers (*PGM* XII, 365–75), where the practitioner is asked to deposit the spell 'where they [i.e., your victims] are, where they usually return'.[329] So far, this is the only known case about curse tablets from the papyri. Nevertheless, such a strategy is widely recommended in a distinct context: the *PGM* tells its readers to place amulets within the walls of houses or businesses that they want to see thrive.[330]

6.5.1. *Geographical and temporal data about deposits closely associated with the victim*

Despite these dramatic stories, we are hard pressed to find good archaeological cases of this same practice, as Table 6.4 makes clear.[331]

As the above data demonstrates, the use of curses in this context is almost anecdotal in the Roman West, accounting for less than 10 per cent of the total. As explained in previous pages, the vast majority of *defixiones* were deposited in funerary contexts (especially in Africa, Italia and Hispania; see section I.6.2 and Table 6.1) or sacred contexts (especially Britannia and Germania; see section I.6.4.1 and Table 6.3). Chronologically speaking, this kind of context first appears around the end of the first century BCE, around a fifth of the attested cases date from the

---

[328] Wilburn 2013: 45, n. 130 also mentions several recipes from *PDM* xii. Nevertheless, their contents are too fragmentary to be discussed here.
[329] Translation by R.F. Hock (*apud* Betz 1992²).
[330] For *phylakteria* deposited in the house or workplace of the interested party, see the following two examples: *PGM* IV, 2360–440 (meant to make a house or business thrive); *PGM* VIII, 53–63 (a request to Hermes to bring success). For amulets, see *PGM* VII, 390–94 (meant to bring victory in a horse race and hence written on a horse's hoof) and *PGM* VII 919–24 (to secure victory, it should be carried in one's sandals), among others.

[331] To this evidence, we should add an extraordinary curse recently published by A. Varone (2019), which was inscribed on the walls of room 28 of Villa Arianna (Stabiae/Castellammare di Stabia, Regio I). The room was part of the villa's *termae*.

High Empire and the majority date from Late Antiquity, the period to which more than half of the known cases date. Within this context, we can distinguish two main subcategories: domestic and agonistic spaces (e.g., the circus or amphitheatre).

6.5.2. Domestic spaces

In this first group, we can include the tablets found in military and civilian settlements. Among the former, we can count the *defixio* from Chesterton-on-Fosse (Britannia, cf. **336**), which was discovered during the excavations of a Roman fort (though the exact context is unknown). Another similar case is that from Bodegraven (Germania Inferior, cf. **463**), which was probably discovered within a Roman fort, 'between the barracks of the *praetentura sinistra*' (L. Swinkels, *per litt.*). As far as civilian settlements are concerned, we can point towards the *defixio* from Neapolis/Terralba (cf. **113**), which was written on an *ostrakon* and can be dated to the third century CE: this curse was found in the monumental area in the southern portion of the city. In this kind of settlement, the archaeological record attests to a diversity in the actual means of depositing curses in this context: sometimes tablets were simply placed in the vicinity of a house, as it happens with **17** (Rome), which was found near the 'house of Livia', in an exact context that is hard to define, seeing that, as Panciera (2006: 146) explains, 'il terreno appariva profondamente sconvolto ed il materiale trovato con la *tabella* è risultato estremamente eterogeneo'. Tablets could also be placed in a nearby ditch, as is the case with **482** (Groß Gerau, Germania Superior), where the tablet was found inside the ditch of a dwelling together with stucco fragments, a *tegula* and a coin dating to the reign of Vespasian.

On certain occasions, curse tablets were deposited inside of the house itself. Thus, some curses were hidden in the courtyards of large homes. This is the case with **456–57**, which were found in the patio of a *mansio* from the north-eastern part of Ratae Corieltauvorum/Leicester. The curse from Canonium/Kelvedon (Britannia, cf. **346**) was found in an oven where it had been 'folded up in a third- and fourth-century stratum' (Wright 1958: 150). This context, which is unparalleled, does not seem to be linked to the kind of curse (it seems to be a *defixio in fures*) nor to the deities invoked (Mercury and Virtus). I am left to wonder if this context could somehow be explained in terms of sympathetic magic. In parallel to the stories found in Saint Jerome and Sophronius, curses have been discovered in the entrances of the houses, such as the tablet from Emona/Ljubljana (Pannonia, cf. **528**), that was found in the entrance of a dwelling (between rooms 52 and 53 to be precise), a liminal space through which the curse's victims surely passed. Finally, we know of three curse tablets that were deposited in the walls of houses. One is from Cabrera de Mar (Hispania Citerior, cf. **148**) and was found among the material used to fill the walls of a *cryptoporticus* (see Bonamusa *et al.*, 2000: 169). Upon its discovery, the curse from Cambodunum/Kempten (Raetia, cf. **522**) contained traces of grout, which led the editor to suppose that it had

originally been placed inside a wall (Egger 1957: 72). The tablet from Peiting (Raetia, cf. **524**), was found among the foundations of a Roman villa.

Generally, scholars have interpreted these spaces as those in which victims either lived or worked. Though this seems likely in certain cases (when the target is a charioteer or a gladiator and the curse was deposited in the circus or the amphitheatre), at times it is impossible to confirm whether the victims lived or worked where a curse were deposited, simply because the texts do not provide any specifics. Just to give one example, the curse tablet from Barchín del Hoyo (Hispania, cf. **145**), dated between the first century BCE and the first centuries CE, was deposited in the Iberian settlement Fuente de la Mota, which was abandoned around 210 BCE. Although there is some controversy about the exact findspot, it seems that the tablet was deliberately deposited in the south-eastern entrance of the settlement, among ruins, since 'these were considered a place in contact with the nether world' (Curbera *et al.* 1999: 280).[332] For the editors, it could also be explained by the fact that the victims of the text were workers on one of the active mines located near the Iberian settlement. Such a hypothesis is simply impossible to prove. In addition to the Hispanic text, a Gaulish text from Autricum/Chartres (Gallia Lugdunensis, cf. **172**) also deserves special mention: dated to the first century CE, it contains three lists of personal names. Given that the curse tablet was discovered in a ditch running along a path, near a ceramic workshop, the excavators have supposed that the curse had intentionally been deposited in a space close to their victims, who could have worked at the workshop. Again, such a hypothesis is purely speculatory.

When the victim was indeed living in a domestic space, it is unknown whether—as Tacitus and Dio Cassius claim was the case for Germanicus—these curses were accompanied by the remains of human corpses or other items, which were thought to increase a spell's potency (Ogden 1999: 19). If such practices did indeed take place, we would again find ourselves in the situation where apparently separate contexts—in this case the domestic and the funerary—overlapped and were blurred. Such a mixed or polysemic context would certainly be thought to have wielded extraordinary power.

6.5.3. The agonistic sphere

The second subcontext that comprises places closely associated with the victim is the agonistic sphere, which is well represented by a considerable group of *defixiones* unearthed in circuses and, above all, amphitheatres.[333]

A good example from the circus comes from Carthage, which was excavated between 1982–90 by a team from

---

[332] In addition, we could also suggest the deliberate placement of the tablet in this landscape if the practitioner sought to establish a persuasive analogy between the victims and the depositional context: thus, ruins would bring ruin upon the targets of the curse (see Alfayé 2019).

[333] See Sánchez Natalías (2020c: 67–68 and 70–73).

the University of Georgia who found 13 curse tablets.[334] We must stress that the fact that these curses were found within the circus itself makes this cache into a unique find among the *defixiones* from the Roman West. To date, all other circus tablets have been found in tombs.[335] Accordingly, we are left to ask for what reason these 13 *defixiones* were deposited in this space. The tablets were discovered opposite the *carceres* and near the *spina*,[336] spaces of a liminal nature where two of the crucial moments of the race occurred (Heintz 1998: 340f.). Thus, the *carceres* were the place where the *daemones* invoked were expected to attack first, frightening the horses and —at least— hindering the charioteers' start.[337] In addition, the risky turn around the *metae* of the *spina* constituted the perfect spot for teams to fall and get injured, just as the texts request. Some ask for an accident 'so that tomorrow morning they are not able to run in the hippodrome (…) or circle around the turning post; but may they fall with their drivers...'.[338] That said, of the 13 curses found in the Carthaginian circus, only 3 have been published (cf. Jordan 1988). While two of them seem to deal directly with chariot races, the other makes no sense.[339]

In any case, the decision to deposit these curses in the circus should not be seen as random: we must remember that it was a building contaminated with *miasma*, given that numerous accidents (at times fatal) took place there.[340] Consequently, these areas were inhabited by *aoroi* and *biaiothanatoi*, whose ability to activate *defixiones* was generally assumed. Accordingly, we can glimpse the attractiveness of this location for depositing curse tablets, above all when the curses were targeting chariot races. In addition to the contamination of *miasma*, this building was related to the infernal world from its very origin. Thus, Homer already described a race where the cut timber used for the turning posts was thought to be the marker of an

ancient grave (Homer, *Il.* XXIII, 331), while in the Roman world the cone shape of the *metae* also evoked a funerary monument, since this shape was a recurrent motif on tombs (Humphrey 1988: 256). Nevertheless, and as mentioned above, so far the use of the circus as a deposition context for curse tablets should be seen as an exception to the rule: most practitioners from the Roman West preferred the use of necropoleis and graves for depositing curses related to games and spectacles.

Within this agonistic sphere, we must also examine amphitheatres which provide a hefty number of curses, some of which were directed towards gladiators. It must be noted that the reasons for using the amphitheatre as a place for the deposition of curse tablets are not univocal, given that this enclosure could be conceived of as both a religious space and as one connected to the restless dead and underworld. In fact, it all came down to how the practitioner understood this space, which could serve his/ her various needs in different ways.

As shown in the previous table, we know of curses from the amphitheatres of Carthage, Isca Silurum/Caerleon, London, Augusta Treverorum/Trier and Carnuntum/ Petronell. From the first of these, we have 55 curses[341] that were discovered by Delattre in 1895 'dans l'arène un souterrain aboutissant à une sorte de cul-de-sac carré, ouvert à la partie supérieure, au niveau même de l'arène' (1897: 318). According to Audollent's analysis, the presence of so many curses in this space means that it was used for funerary purposes (1901: 303), which has led to it being identified as the *spoliarium*. This area, where the corpses of gladiators and *venatores* were stored, had obvious links to the *aoroi* and *biaiothanatoi* (Audollent 1904: CX). Of the 55 curses found in this space, the 9 published *defixiones* target gladiators and *venatores* who participated in the games celebrated in the same amphitheatre. Accordingly, this context can be seen as having a double valence, mixing the funerary with closeness to the victims.

Concerning the amphitheatres from Britannia, so far we know of three curse tablets from Isca Silurum/Caerleon (cf. **337**)[342] and London (cf. **343–44**).[343] The first was found in the arena, while those from London were discovered among the material used to fill a drain in the arena. Although one of the texts (cf. **344**) just contains a list of names, the other two can be confidently identified as curses against thieves. These curses, whose victims' identity was unknown, evoked Diana and Nemesis. This led us to think that, at least in the case of these two texts, it seems as if the practitioners sought out a context connected

---

[334] On the excavations, see Pintozzi and Norman 1992; for the lead of the tablets and their stratigraphy, see Pintozzi 1991.

[335] For example, the 'Sethian' *defixiones*, which were discovered in the columbarium on the Via Appia (cf. Wünsch 1898), or the curse found in the columbarium of the Villa Doria Pamphili (Rome; see Bevilacqua 1998) as well as another from Astigi/Écija (cf. **132**). From Hadrumetum there is an important series of circus curses that were found inside of tombs (see *DT* 265 and 272–95; Grenier 1905: nos 1–2; Audollent 1906: nos 1–2; perhaps Audollent 1910: no. 2, though the exact provenance is unknown).

[336] According to Pintozzi (1991: 51–61), of these 13 curses, 1 was found next to the *podium* 'but it may have been disturbed from an original location at the arena's edge' (1991: 54; US 82-3-948= Jordan 1988, no. 3), 2 in the arena (tablets US 83.1B and US 81-13-2= Jordan 1988, nos 1 and 2) and 4 near the *spina* (curses US 90.3-206, US 90.3-588, US 90.3-260 and US 90.3-279). The exact provenance of the other six *defixiones* is unknown.

[337] Cf. *DT* 187 (l. 59) and *DT* 234 (ll. 21–22)= Heintz 1998: 340, no. 22 and 23, on the ancient belief that horses were able to perceive demonic presences. See also Gordon 2012: 48, no. 111 and Faraone 2019: 183.

[338] As put in *DT* 237, l. 35–42 (English translation by Gager 1992, no. 9). There are other examples, such as *DT* 237 (l. 48–73) and *DT* 239 (l. 42–48).

[339] Although, as the editor has pointed out, one of the tablets 'does not yield any continuous sense, but its purpose is no doubt related to its findspot' (Jordan 1988: 119).

[340] Regarding the death of charioteer Scorpus, see Martial *Epigrammata*, X.50 and 53.

[341] Of the 55, 7 are in Latin and only 9 have been published (*DT* 246–54). For the amphitheatre in Carthage, see Golvin 1988: no. 95 and Rossiter 2016.

[342] Found in the amphitheatre's arena, the curse contains the following invocation: *Dom(i)na Nemesis do tibi palleum et galliculas...*

[343] It reads: *[d]eae Dea[na]e dono çapitûlarem...* This curse was found in the drainpipe of the arena in London along with two other tablets that were quite poorly preserved. The first (**344**) simply contains a list of names, while the second, which is illegible, was still folded up (see Tomlin 2003: 362–64).

to the deities rather than to their victims (even though they could possibly be aficionados of the games). Following this hypothesis, the practitioners who wrote these tablets understood the amphitheatre as a religious space rather than a space connected with the restless dead and the underworld. In this regard, we ought to remember that within amphitheatres there were cultic spaces dedicated to divinities associated with the games, such as Diana and Nemesis, who were invoked in the British texts. [344]

Something similar is at play with at least 3 of the 28 Latin curse tablets discovered in the basement of the amphitheatre at Augusta Treverorum/Trier.[345] Unfortunately, little is known about the original deposit of this ensemble from Trier (cf. **175–202**), which was found in 1908 in the so-called 'östlichen Kammer'.[346] While some of the *defixiones* were found 1 m below the surface, others were found on the ground level, while still other tablets were discovered 1.5 m deep. Wünsch (1910: 2f.), who was surprised by the different strata of these finds and the way that the tablets were spread out, offered forward two hypotheses. The first one suggested that the *defixiones* could have originally been buried in the arena and later fallen down to the basement when it collapsed sometime around the fifth century CE. His second hypothesis proposed that the curses could have been nailed to the wooden posts of the basement where they were eventually buried by the debris after the entire structure collapsed. Yet, only three curses from this collection seem to have holes from nails. Therefore, the first hypothesis—which defended the burial of the *defixiones* in the arena—seems more plausible. In any case, the lack of data regarding the context of the tablets prevents us from tracing the exact location of the original deposit, rendering any hypothesis far from certain, as Wünsch himself admitted (1910: 2). In addition, the contents of the curses do not further our understanding of why they were deposited in the amphitheatre: 10 of the 30 curses remain unedited (being illegible or not inscribed), while 13 were written for unknown reasons.[347] Only three of the tablets could possibly belong—with reservations, given the fragmented condition of the texts—to the group of judicial *defixiones*.[348] Therefore, we are left to wonder why these practitioners chose to deposit their curse tablets in this context.

Evidently, given that none of the *defixiones* are aimed against gladiators or *venatores*, proximity with the victim was almost certainly not the key issue, as was the case, for instance, with the tablet from the amphitheatre of Carthage. Although the funerary connotations of the amphitheatre could be one key for understanding the deposition of the tablets from Augusta Treverorum/Trier (Wünsch 1910: 3), we must remember that this location was also a religious site. This, in my opinion, is the more compelling explanation (see Grenier 1958: 709, n. 2), particularly if we bear in mind that two of the *defixiones* invoke Mars and Diana (the latter being a deity who was worshipped in that precise location, as shown by an inscription discovered in the amphitheatre, cf. *CIL* XIII, 11311, and **182–83**),[349] while a third summons a female divinity with the formula *bona san(c)ta nomen pîa* (cf. **189**, l. 1).[350] These texts from Augusta Treverorum/Trier further underline the difficulty and problematic nature of trying to neatly fit texts into one context over another. Nevertheless, our lack of information about the findspot as well as the fragmentary nature of these curses (which today are largely lost and therefore cannot be examined)[351] ultimately prevent us from offering a satisfactory solution to the question of the tablets from the amphitheatre in Augusta Treverorum/Trier.

We find a similar case with the curse from Carnuntum/Petronell (Pannonia, cf. **530**), where during the archaeological excavations carried out between 1923 and 1925 at the amphitheatre in the civilian settlement a *defixio* was discovered. Little is known about the curse's archaeological context, which was found on the ground next to the enclosure's southern door and where a tank was built in Late Antiquity (cf. Egger 1926: col. 137). The curse targets a certain Eudemus and should be classified as a *defixio in fures*. The tablet evokes infernal deities, such as Dis Pater, Veracura and Cerberus.[352] As was the case with the tablets from Augusta Treverorum/Trier, it is difficult to determine why this curse was deposited in this particular context: the practitioner may have been attracted to the chthonic associations of the place or perhaps (s)he chose the area near the gate through which the victim of the curse may very well have passed, thus coming into close contact with the *defixio*.

---

[344] According to Marcattilli (2005: 185), 'i sacelli erano allestiti in uno dei *carceres* dell'anfiteatro, ad una delle estremità dell'asse minore dell'edificio, per lo più al di sotto del *pulpitum editoris*, comunque in stretto rapporto con il percorso delle *pompai*' (*ThesCRA* IV, 2005, *s. v.* 'Arena': 184–86). For these cultic spaces with amphitheatres, see Golvin 1988: 337–40. In addition, the possible existence of a *nemeseum* in the amphitheatre in Isca Silurum/Caerleon would reinforce the religious aspect of the depositional context (cf. Golvin 1988: 129, n. 344).

[345] Where, according to Golvin (1988: 338), 'une chapelle devait aussi exister à l'une des extrémités du petit axe de l'arène', from where the base of a statue dedicated to Diana (found in 1909) may have come (cf. *CIL* XIII, 11311).

[346] Wünsch 1910: 2. For the amphitheatre of Trier, see Golvin 1988: no. 41 and Kuhnen 2017.

[347] **194**, **197** and **201** are not edited; **193** and **202** are illegible, while **198–200** are anepigraphic. **175**, **177**, **179–81**, **184–85** and **187–92** were written for unknown reasons.

[348] **176** and **182** could be judicial *defixiones*, since they contain terms such as *adv̯o[ca]tu̯ṣ* (**176**, ll. 2–3) and *inimicum* (no **182**, l. 1).

[349] Specifically, **182** l. 7 reads: *Marti et Diane*, while **183**, ll. 5–7 reads: *[Di]anam et Martem vinculares ut me vindicetis de Ququma...* The presence of Mars in this context can be explained by the connection with the fighters in the amphitheatre, as attested by Martial, *Spect.* XXII, 3 and Statius, *Silv.*, I, 6, 62 (cf. Golvin 1988: 337: n. 169).

[350] In **189**, where this same deity is evoked (maybe Diana?) as *santne dia* (l. 4) and *domina* (l. 7).

[351] L. Schwinden (Rheinischen Landesmuseum Trier) has said (*per litt.*) 'Die *defixiones* von R. Wünsch, *Bonner Jahrbücher* 119, 1910, sind zum Teil bei uns ausgestellt, nicht mehr alle Bleitäfelchen aus dem Amphitheater 1908/1909 sind erhalten'.

[352] Together with the *ministeria infernorum d̯eu[m]* and the *larvae* (ll. 18–20).

7

Categorization of the *Defixiones*

7.1. Introduction

Based on an analysis of the curses' contents, it continues to be possible to categorize *defixiones* following the typology that Audollent first proposed back in 1904. He distinguished between the following: 'tabellae iudiciariae et in inimicos conscriptae'; 'in fures calumniatores et maledicos conversae'; 'amatoriae' and 'in agitatores et venatores immissae'.[353] While it is true that this taxonomy has generally stood the test of time and has been employed in various subsequent studies,[354] it is equally true that scholars have proposed various modifications and/or additions. In 1991, for instance, H. Versnel suggested that the *defixiones in fures* ought to be reconceived of as 'prayers for justice' (and hence questioned their status as curses per se).[355] Faraone, for his part, has proposed adding a new genre of *defixiones*: 'commercial curses', which are mostly attested in the Greek world.[356] This same author has maintained that the earliest Greek *defixiones* all arose in agonistic contexts (to which the Latin curses also belong). In such contexts, the *defigens* and his/her victim compete with one another and use curses as a tool to increase their odds of winning that competition.[357]

7.2. A tacit agreement

Audollent had already recognized that 'obscurae nimis sunt tabellarum magna pars quam ut diiudicare valeamus quem ad finem exaratae sint'.[358] And indeed this could undoubtedly be applied to many curses from the Roman West. As Table 7.1 shows, in more than half of the known *defixiones*, only the *defigens* and (probably) the deities with which (s)he invokes knew the reason that led to the writing of the curse.[359] That is, the practitioner did not think it was necessary to spell out in writing the circumstance that led him/her to compose the curse. While the poor state of conservation of a *defixio* often impairs

our understanding,[360] we cannot forget that even more often we are left in the dark simply due to the abbreviated nature of the texts. Obviously, it is difficult to identify the exact reason why these texts can be so terse. However, it does seem plausible that in many cases the practitioners orally gave more details and pertinent information. Another option would be that they took the omniscience of the deities invoked for granted: these powerful forces would surely be able to understand the message and take appropriate action.

On occasions, this 'tacit agreement' between the *defigens* and deity results in the practitioner simply listing the victims' names. Providing this apparently minimal information was extremely important, because in magical thinking the very nature of an individual was intimately linked to his or her name.[361] Simply inscribing personal names (whether in the nominative or accusative,[362] whether alone or as part of a list) proved to be a long-lasting technique, which is attested from the fourth century BCE to the fourth century CE. Examples of listing names come from all corners of the Roman West, though this practice was most common in Italia, Britannia and Germania. Sometimes this frugal form was enhanced through the addition of other details, such as the naming of a victim's profession or parents, that could be used to help identify the correct victim.[363] As Gordon has noted, the proliferation of such lists should be explained by the influence that the everyday use of writing and public epigraphy had on magical practices.[364]

Within the larger group of curse tablets written for reasons that are today lost to us, there is an interesting sub-group of 40 texts written by somewhat loquacious *defigentes*. In certain texts, the author uses verbs, such as *mando*,[365] *commendo*[366] and *devoveo*,[367] to refer to the handing over of

---

[353] *DT*, p. XC (for his taxonomy, see pp. LXXXVIII–XCI).
[354] Cf. Cesano 1961²: 1564f. and Graf 1995: 117. On the different types of curse tablets, in general, see Edmonds 2019: 65–74; Eidinow 2019: 351–52 and 356; Watson 2019: 62–64.
[355] Cf. Versnel 1991 and 2010 (with previous references). His approach has been taken to the extreme by Urbanová 2018: 18–33, who neatly distinguishes between both categories in her book.
[356] Cf. Faraone 1991a: 10–11. The category of 'commercial curses', which are mostly attested in a Greek context, are not considered in the present chapter, since there are only two known examples from North Africa (see Audollent 1933b).
[357] See Faraone 1991a: 11ff. and Graf 1995: 153–54.
[358] *DT*, p. LXXXVIII.
[359] The tablets written for unknown reason constitute 390 of 623 or over 60 per cent. In Greek contexts we find something similar: according to Faraone, 'more than three quarters of the published Greek κατάδεσμοι are inscribed with names only or are so laconic that they give us no hint whatsoever of their specific purpose' (1991a: 10).

[360] These are generally quite fragmentary, as is the case with **8**, **32**, **139**, **167–70**, **224–27**, **513**, and the North African tablets *DT* 214, 255, among many others.
[361] On this, see section I.4.1 and note 220.
[362] There is no scholarly consensus about why both nominatives and accusatives are used in the same list of names. For some, this alternation is just a mistake, while for others it would denote practitioners (in nom.) *versus* victims (in ac.). For the Oscan texts, it has been argued that both nominative and accusative could be a way to distinguish different types of victims, which seems unlikely for the Latin curse tablets.
[363] A matronymic qualifies the victims in **20**, **235**, **461** as well as the North African curses *AE* 1996, 1717–18 and *DT* 263, just to mention several examples. For the use of the matronymic, see López Jimeno 1991–92; Curbera 1999b (who stresses the Egyptian origin of this practice); Poccetti 2002: 36. The victims' professions are named in **52**, **101–02**, **117**, **495** and **502**, among others.
[364] Cf. Gordon 1999 and Centrone 2010.
[365] Cf. **67** (ll. 6–7), **3** (ll. 1–2: *Helenus suom nomen eimfereis mandat...*).
[366] Cf. *DT* 228 (A, ll. 2–4 and B, ll. 2–3: *...commendo tibi Iulia Faustilla...*).
[367] Cf. **92** (A, ll. 9–10 and B, ll. 1–4: *...aput vostrum numen demando devoveo desacrifico...*) and **145** (B).

Table 7.1. *Defixiones* **from the Roman West, according to provenance (It.= Italia, Afr.= Africa, Hisp.= Hispania, Gall.= Gallia, Brit.= Britannia, Ger.= Germania, Raet.= Raetia, Nor.= Noricum, Pan.= Pannonia) and typology (E= erotic; A= agonistic; J= juridical; *IF= in fures;* U= unknown)**

Provenance / Purpose	E	A	J	*IF*	Uncertain/other categories	U
It. (119)	3	1	9	2	E?: **48**, **73**. J?: **65**, **105**, **113**. *IF*?: **112**. Personal revenge: **4**	97
Afr. (88)	14	37	12	1	A?: *AE* 1907, 165 A?: *DT* 290-291 Commercial: *AE* 1933, 234 and 235.	19
Hisp. (30)	1	1	7	5	E?: **129** J?: **148** *IF*?: **142**	13
Gall. (55)	1	–	4	1	J?: **161**, **182**	47
Brit. (256)	–	–	–	74	E?: **353**. J?: **339**. *IF*?: **212**, **243**, **248**, **264**, **285-286**, **336**, **339**, **417**, **437**. Against perjury: **299**.	169
Ger. (59)	2	–	10	7		40
Raet. (6)	1	–	2	1	–	2
Nor. (1)	–	–	–	–	E?: **526**.	–
Pan. (9)	1	–	4	1		3
Total (623)	23	39	47	92		390

the victims to the deities invoked. Indeed, we can even find phrases like *ut hu(n)c (h)ostiam acceptum (h)abiatis*, with which the practitioner turns his enemy into a sacrificial victim.[368] In such instances, *defigentes* were plainly requesting that their enemies be killed (Watson 2019: 75f.).

But simply ending a victim's life was not always the desired outcome. In fact, there is also a more common and imaginative group of curses in which deities are invoked so that they can punish victims in different ways. Such punishments are generally directed against a victim's body but can also extend to other areas such as the victim's financial ruin.[369] Some practitioners ask that their enemies suffer from various physical and/or psychological illnesses, such as leprosy (*lepra*), cancer (*cancer*), fevers

(*febris*),[370] madness (*amentia*) or anxiety (*angustiae*).[371] More commonly, however, *defigentes* directly demand capital punishment. The target's death is usually conceived of as the culmination of a slow and painful process during which the victim ought to suffer from other torments, such as fainting,[372] torture,[373] dismemberment,[374] madness,[375]

---

[368] According to **490** (A, ll. 5–6). Likewise, cf. the phrases found in **1** (ll. 2–4: *... 'h'anc (h)ostiam acceptam habeas et consumas...*) and **121** (A, ll. 3–5: *...accipias corpus eius qui meas sarcinias supstulit...*).

[369] Like in **157** (A, ll. 1–4: *quomodo hoc plumbu(m) non paret et decadet sic decadat aetas membra vita bos grano(m) mer(x)...*) and **498** (A, ll. 2–5: *qu[omo]di hoc liquescet se[-c.3- sic co]llum membra me[du]lla peculiụm d[e]l[i]ques[ca]nt*).

[370] For fevers, cf. **5** (l. 9: *patiatur febris*); for leprosy, cf. **57** (ll. 1–2: *qui s[ubbertis]ti libra puerum Elissei ita subber[te] domum Ber[-c.2-]atis...*'); for cancer, cf. **483** (ll. 9–10: *ut illius manus caput pedes vermes cancer...*).

[371] For this topic and madness in particular, see **484**, ll. 6–7: *amentita surgat amentita suas res agat*; for anxiety, see **16** (col. I, ll. 2–3 and 5–6: *... quomodo (ha)ec anima intus inçlusa tenetur et angustiatur (…) sịç ụt anima mẹntẹṣ çọrpos Collecticii quem pepeṛeṭ Agneḷḷa*).

[372] **96** (A, l. 5 and B, ll. 1–2: *Quintus Agrippini s(ervus) ụteṛ salṭuẹnṣịṣ languiat aigrotêt ex omologi(s) fẹṛị(s) igni(s) (...) devincit (...) et sic moriatur*) and **115** (l. 3: *...[persequa]ris eum ut male contabescat usque dum morị[et]ur*). For the death of victims in general, see López Jimeno 1997: 34 and Marco Simón 2009.

[373] Cf. *DT* 292, B, ll. 2–4: *...demando tibi ex [hoc die] ex <h>ac ora ex <h>oc momento ut crucietur*.

[374] Like in **117** (ll. 16–18: *corpus omnịs menbra (...) bisc[e]d[a] Porcelli qui (...) [cada]t langụ<e>ạt et ru[at?]*) and **118** (ll. 17–19: *disulvite omnị[a] membra omnis viscida ipsius*).

[375] Cf. the *defixio* from Cirta/Constantine (*CIL* VIII, 19525, A, ll. 9–11: *ut facia[s] il[l]um sine sensum sine memoria*) and **486** (A, l. 6: *des ei malam mentem*).

the liquefaction or combustion of the victim's body[376] or the paralysis of the body's vital functions.[377] Indeed, the extreme cruelty of the some *defigentes* can be shocking: one from Mogontiacum/Mainz asks that the victim be the witness of his own death,[378] while another *defigens* asks to listen as her victim perishes (this, of course, would also offer irrefutable proof that *defixio* was successfully carried out).[379]

7.3. Erotic *defixiones*

Although there is literary evidence for erotic magic already in Archaic Greece,[380] it was not until the fourth century BCE that we have the earliest examples of erotic curses.[381] Traditionally, scholars have distinguished between two types of erotic curses[382] depending on the desired outcome: the first category consists of the so-called *diakopoi* that seek to break up or at least interrupt an amorous relationship (this type is attested from the fourth century BCE to the third century CE).[383] The second group is made of the so-called *agōgai*, which are meant to attract the amorous attention of the beloved (these curses are attested between the second and fourth centuries CE).[384] The *PGM* provide evidence for both types of curses (though more attention is given to the *agōgai*), to the extent that the vast majority of spells and *defixiones* described in these handbooks are concerned with erotic magic.[385]

In marked contrast to the Greek world, where some authors have argued that as much as one quarter of all *defixiones* are erotic,[386] only a small percentage of the curse tablets from the Roman West (23 of 623) belong to this category. Over half of these curses hail from North Africa (especially from Hadrumetum) and were certainly

Figure 7.1. Erotic *defixio* of attraction, in which *charaktêres* and various individuals can be seen (two of which appear to be kissing; from Martin 1928: 59, fig. 2).

written by professional practitioners. The remaining curses have been found scattered throughout the western Roman provinces. Most of these tablets date to the Empire, though there are two erotic curses that date to the Republic.

If we analyse the desired outcomes of these erotic curses, seven of the tablets can be classified as *diakopoi*: the earliest two examples (**2** and **71**) date to the second and first centuries BCE, while the other five date the High Empire.[387] As is later recommended in the *PGM*,[388] these texts frequently request that hatred arise between the two lovers, which would then lead to the end of their romantic relationship.[389] Occasionally, such a request is accompanied by references to the victims' physical appearance[390] or sex life, which the curse seeks to interrupt (see Figure 7.1).[391]

When compared to the *diakopoi*, the group of Latin *agōgai* is much more substantial: there are 16 tablets, which date between the first and third centuries CE. Besides the two curses from Germania and Raetia (**472** and **524**), the rest of these erotic curses of attraction come from Hadrumetum, Carthage or Thysdrus/El Jem and were written by professional practitioners. Hence the similarities between the North African curses and the recipes found in the *PGM*: in both corpora, falling in love is treated as a sort of disease,[392] which causes the victim (usually a woman)[393] to suffer from various conditions, including insomnia,[394] the paralysis of the body's vital functions[395] or the inability to

---

[376] The liquefaction of the victim's limbs ...*quatmodum hoc plumbum liquescet* (**488** B, ll. 4–5) is a common request in the collection from Mogontiacum/Mainz. Accordingly, see **493** (ll. 14– 15: ...*a[d qu]em modum sal in [aqua liques]cet sic et illi membra m[ed]ullae extabescant*), **498** (cf. n. 369) and probably **499** (B, ll. 4–5: ...*d[i]liquescant quat{m} modi hoc liquescet*). On occasions, the way of disintegrating the victim's limbs is through combustion, which appears to be alluded to in **16** (col. II, l. 1, where the practitioner asks that the body and soul of Collecticius *ardęąt*) and perhaps also in **30** (l. 2: ...*in foco (...) ut p(er)eat*).

[377] Cf. **68**, ll. 6–8. The phrase *neip putiiad*, which Mancini (2006: 78) has identified as analogous to Latin *ne possit*, precedes a list of the vital functions that are to be paralysed.

[378] Concretely, **486** (A, ll. 6–10): ...*des ei malam mentem malum exitum quandius vita vixerit ut omni corpore videat se emori praeter oculos*.

[379] See **499**, B, ll. 2–3: ...*ut eorum ixsitum audiam*.

[380] In general, see Gager 1992: 78–83; Faraone 1991a: 13–15 and 2001 (where he looks back to work published in 1990, 1992, 1993 and 1994); Ogden 1999: 35–37; Kropp 2008: 184–86; Martin 2010: 113–32.

[381] Faraone 1991a: 13, n. 59.

[382] For other further classifications, see Gager (1992: 80, n. 8 and 9) and Dickie (2000: 565). Likewise, Faraone (1999 and 2001: VIII) proposes a new distinction: 'rituals used mainly by men to instill erotic passion in women (*êros*) and those used primarily by women to maintain or increase affection (*philia*) in men' (on this differentiation, also see Dickie 2000: 582–83).

[383] Cf. Homer, *Il.* XIV, 216ff. In this passage, Hera asks Aphrodite to lend her a girdle 'in which are fashioned all manner of allurements; in it is love, in it desire, in it dalliance—persuasion that steals the senses even of the wise' (translated by A.T. Murray).

[384] For the dates, see Faraone 1991a: 15 with n. 66.

[385] Cf. Petropoulos 1988 and Dickie 2000: 565–73.

[386] As Gager 1992: 78 and Ogden 1999: 35 assert.

[387] **140** dates to 70 CE, while **15** and **173** have been dated to the second century CE.

[388] Cf. *PGM* XII, 370–75; LXI, 39–47, 60ff. and O2, 25ff.

[389] Cf. **71** (IA, l. 6: *ut il(l)ic il(l)a(n)c odiat*) and **2** (A, ll. 1–6: ...*quomodo mortuos qui istic sepultus est nec loqui nec sermonare potest seic Rhodine apud M(arcum) Licinium Faustum mortua sit nec loqui nec sermonare possit*).

[390] Cf. **71**, IA, ll. 2–3: ...*facia(m) capi(l)u(m)*.

[391] Thus, in a curse from Rome (cf. **15**), a persuasive analogy is established between the victims and the medium in which it was inscribed (a small sculptural group depicting two adults flanking a child) so that the victims ...*non qumbere inter s[e]* (A, l. 14); that is, so they could not maintain sexual relations. Likewise, the mention of a penis in the curse from Aquinum/Aquino (cf. **73**, l. 10; although the reading seems problematic) and of a *fututor* ('copulator') in the curse from Maar (cf. **173**, ll. 1–2) could be connected to a possible request for a man's impotence, like that that Ovid describes at *Am.*, III, 7.27–36 and 73–84).

[392] Cf. Winkler 1991: 222–24.

[393] Among the tablets studied here, the only exceptions are **472** and a curse from Hadrumetum (*DT* 270). Likewise, of the 35 erotic recipes found in the *PGM* only 5 have male victims.

[394] Insomnia plagues the victims of *DT* 230 (A, l. 2), 265 (A, ll. 8–9), 266 (l. 7), etc.

[395] This includes being unable to eat (*DT* 266, ll. 7–8), sit down (*DT* 270, l. 7) or speak (*DT* 270, l. 8). For a discussion, see Martinez 1995.

remember her loved ones.[396] These conditions are supposed to continue until a burning[397] and uncontrollable[398] passion drives the beloved into the *defigens'* arms. The aggressive and profoundly symbolic[399] language used in the *PGM* and the North African curses contrasts with that found in the two curses from Europe, which are milder and only ask that their victims love the respective *defigentes*.

Finally, we must mention other curse tablets that perhaps should be grouped together with the erotic *defixiones* (in Table 7.1 these curses are marked with 'E?'), though their texts are not as explicit as those just discussed. Amongst these, a curse from Faviana/Mautern (cf. **526**), which should perhaps be classified as a *diakopos*, targets a woman named Silvia and asks that *inversu(m) maritu(m) c{e}ernis* (**526** B, ll. 1–2; perhaps an attempt to break up a couple?). A curse from Rome (cf. **48**), which for its part could be possibly included among the *agōgai*, targets Caecilia Prima and asks (among other torments) that various parts of her body burst into flames.[400] Furthermore, the text repeats the word *turpidines* (cf. **48** B, ll. 3 and 5, for *turpitudines*), a term that is synonymous with *obscenitas*, that is 'obscenity, lewdness' (Lewis and Short, s.v. II). In addition, the *defigens*, probably a man (cf. **48** B, l. 33), invokes Aurora, who was considered to be a 'hunter of young lovers and a destroyer of romantic relationships' (Bevilacqua 2006–07: 327). Another curse, which comes from Old Harlow (cf. **353**), may have been written because of an amorous rivalry, since there seems to be reference to an affair ('*negotium Ettern(a)e*', **353** A, ll. 2–3). Finally, it is worth noting that scholars have generally interpreted the anatomical curses, in which a victim's body and vital organs are directly cursed, as erotic *defixiones*, even if there is no direct evidence for this in the texts themselves.[401]

7.4. Agonistic *defixiones*

Provoked by the extreme intensity that characterized theatrical and athletic competitions in Antiquity, agonistic *defixiones* first arose in the fifth century BCE.[402] This date is based on Pelops' famous prayer to Poseidon in Pindar's *Olympian* 1.[403] That said, the earliest archaeological evidence from the Greek world dates to the third century BCE and consists of curses directed against actors and athletes. In contrast, agonistic curses from the Roman West concern the games from amphitheatres and circuses, spectacles whose popularity soared during the High Empire. Despite differences in exact context, Gager is certainly right to stress, 'what Greek and Roman performances shared was a keen sense of competition, copious rewards and enormous popularity' (1992: 43).

For their part, the *PGM* contain two recipes for agonistic curses: the first (*PGM* III, 1–164) calls for the drowning of a cat in whose body the practitioner is told to place three tablets and then wrap the cat's body in a fourth *defixio* written on a sheet of papyrus on which chariots, charioters, chariot boards and racehorses have been drawn.[404] Next, the *defigens* is told to place the animal in a grave or in the stadium[405] and then sprinkle the area with the water used to drown the cat. The second *PGM* recipe (IV 2210–17), which is less elaborate, urges the practitioner to burn garlic and a snake's slough before inscribing a cursing formula on a tin tablet, which should then be deposited in the grave of someone who had died prematurely.

Although the archaeological record has not turned up physical evidence for the rituals described in the *PGM*, there are 39 agonistic curses written in Latin, almost all of which hail from North Africa. Among the exceptions that come from elsewhere, the earliest is a curse from Astigi/Écija (cf. **132**) dated to the first century CE) that targets the *grex Antoniani*, 2 *factiones*, 8 *agitatores* and 13 *quadrigae*. So far, this is the only agonistic tablet from Hispania, and the only one of this genre from the whole Roman West that has been written by an amateur practitioner. In support of this hypothesis, we note its very simple structure: a list of names both in the nominative and the accusative. In addition to this *defixio*, we must also add a curse from Rome (cf. **5**) belonging to the 'Sethian' collection and dated to either the fourth or fifth century CE. This curse, which was written by a professional practitioner, only tangentially belongs to the group of agonistic curses, since it targets Praeseticius, the miller who worked for one of the stables belonging to rival *factiones*.[406]

Of the remaining curses belonging to this group, most were deposited in the necropoleis of Hadrumetum and Carthage, though there are two series of curses that were discovered in Carthage's circus and amphitheatre. The

---

[396] Cf. *DT* 230 (A, l. 9–11), 266 (ll. 15–17: ...*ut obliviscatur patris et matris et [propinquor]um suorum et amicorum omnium [et aliorum] virorum*), 268 (l. 3), etc.

[397] The 'heat' of passion is clearly communicated through the use of verbs like *uro, comburo* and *aduro*, which are found in *DT* 227 (ll. 1–3), 270 (ll. 6, 9–11, 18 and 19) and in those curse tablets published by Audollent in 1908 (frag. 1, l. 7 and frag. 2, l. 5) and 1930 (l. 4).

[398] See *DT* 266 (l. 19: ...*solum me in mente habeat*), 270 (ll. 8–9) and Audollent 1930, l. 9.

[399] Cf. Gager 1992: 81f. and Versnel 1998: 252–58.

[400] With verbs like *uro, peruro* and *aduro*. Cf. **48** A, ll. 17–19 and B, l. 17.

[401] This is the case with **56**, **129** and **535**, all of which target women. To these, we could add **51**, which, according to Audollent (1906: 367) was written by 'un amoureux dedaigné [qui] voue au malheur la femme qu'il aime et son rival'. In this text, the author, who curses his victims limb by limb, asks that their bodies be dissected; after being inscribed, the *defigens* pierced the tablet so that the hole coincided with the word *pectus* (between A, ll. 4–5 and B, ll. 3–4), which hardly seems to be accidental. For the piercing of the tablet coinciding with specific words or formulae, see section I.5.4.

[402] Faraone 1991a: 11–13 and Ogden 1999: 32–33. For agonistic curse tablets in general, see Gager 1992: 42–49; Kropp 2008: 181–84; Martin 2010: 93–98; Tremel 2004 on curses and sporting events; Gordon 2005 and 2012b. For an extended version of this section, which includes Greek and Latin *defixiones* in the Roman West, see Sánchez Natalías 2020c: 72–74.

[403] Cf. Pind., *Ol.* 1, 75–78, where the hero urges the god to stay his rival's spear.

[404] *PGM* III, 19–20: τὰ ἅρμα<τα> καὶ τοὺ[ς] ἡνιόχους καὶ [τοὺς δί]φρους καὶ τοὺς μονάτορας.

[405] This is following the proposal of Heintz 1998: 342, n. 34, where the reconstruction [τῷ σ]ταδ[ίῳ] is offered.

[406] According to the interpretation of Solin (1976: 90 and 1995: 118). Twenty Greek tablets from the same collection belong to the group of agonistic *defixiones* (see Tremel 2004: 70–90).

spatial and temporal proximity of these curses (all date to the High Empire) help explain the various shared formulae, which originated in a small number of models. Furthermore, tablets can occasionally be grouped together based on the use of the same *charaktêres*, *onómata* or even iconography.[407] Direct analysis of some of the series has revealed that the curses were in fact written by the same hand.[408] Within the group of North African agonistic *defixiones*, the different objectives that *defigentes* pursued allow us to distinguish between two subcategories: curses pertaining to the amphitheatre and those related to the circus.

The former, discovered at the close of the nineteenth century in what could very well be the *spoliarium* from Carthage's amphitheatre, consists of 55 tablets (only 9 of which have been published).[409] Most of these texts target *venatores*, also known as *bestiarii*, who were the stars of the *venationes*, a type of spectacle dedicated to hunting of wild animals. These games were first held in the circus and then later in the amphitheatres between the second century BCE and the sixth century CE.[410] Generally, Carthaginian practitioners hoped that the *venatores* would be publicly vanquished in the amphitheatre.[411] At times, the *defigens* asks that a *venator* suffer from insomnia the night before entering the arena.[412] As a result, he would be too weak and sluggish to catch[413] or kill[414] his prey and, finally, the hunted would end up killing the hunter (see Figure 7.2).[415]

The majority of agonistic curses from North Africa, however, are oriented toward the circus, a fact that attests to the great popularity of these games and the emotions that they provoked in Imperial Carthage and Hadrumetum. Indeed, the passion and excitement that is reflected in the *defixiones* is also attested in the literary record. Thus, Ammianus Marcellinus (*Historia* XXVIII, 4) states that for the die-hard fans of chariot races, the Circus Maximus was 'their temple, their dwelling, their assembly and the height of all their hopes'.[416] Other authors lament the

Figure 7.2. *DT* 246: a servant characterized as Mercury Psychopomp checks the death of another gladiator in the arena (From Peyras 1996: 131).

importance given to the *factiones* (for Procopius, these rivalries could divide a city)[417] and *aurigae*. According to Brown (1970), charioteers, as clients of the local aristocracy, represented certain political and social interests, which made them into 'undefined mediators' between these aristocrats and the lower classes. Given the extraordinary nature of the rivalries between different *factiones* and *aurigae*, daily life was spiced up with fistfights, gambling and, of course, *defixiones*, which were considered an indispensable tool for determining the outcome of a given race.

These tablets were mostly deposited in the city necropolis[418] and date to the High Empire. Written in both Greek and Latin, the bulk of Latin texts hail from Hadrumetum, whereas the majority of Greek texts come from Carthage (where only four such Latin *defixiones* have been found).[419] Whatever language used for writing these circus curses, the objective was always the same: destroy the other *factiones*. With this aim in mind, practitioners would write the names of *aurigae* as well as their horses

---

[407] See Gordon 2005: 69–76 and Németh 2011.

[408] As I was able to confirm during the autopsies of the tablets *DT* 276–84. These are part of my current research project, 'The Latin *defixiones* from North Africa Revisited' (DeLAR).

[409] Specifically, there are *DT* 246–54. Of these tablets, only *DT* 252 and 246 were written in Greek. For the archaeological context, see section I.6.5.3.

[410] According to Mancioli 1987: 66–68. This spectacle was brought to Rome by M. Fulvius Nobilior to celebrate his triumph over Aetolia and Cephallenia (187 BCE; cf. Livy XXXIX 22, 2). The practice was banished from Italy by Totila in the sixth century CE.

[411] Cf. *DT* 247, ll. 1–6: ...*[occi]dite exterminate vulnere Gallicu quen peperit Prima in ista oṛa in ampiteatri*; *DT* 248 B, ll. 1–4; *DT* 250 B, l. 6, among others.

[412] Cf. *DT* 250 A, ll. 4–5: ...ιεκρι *auferas somnum, non dormiat Maurussus quem peperit F[e]licitas.*

[413] Cf. *DT* 247, l. 10: ...*non liget ur[su]*; *DT* 250, B, l. 10: ...*nec laç[ueos] possit super ursum mittere* and *DT* 253, ll. 12–13 and 19–20.

[414] Cf. *DT* 247, ll. 15–18: ...*uṭ neque ursu neque tauru singulis plagis oçcida[t n]eque binis plagis occid<a>t neque ternis plagiṣ oc[ci]dat tauru ursu*; *DT* 253, l. 20.

[415] Cf. *DT* 247, l. 20: ...*allidat illu ursus et vulneret illu*; *DT* 250 B, l. 18: ẹt remiṣe ferarum morsus.

[416] Translated by J.C. Rolfe. Cf. also Tac., *Dial.* 29.

---

[417] Cf. Procop., *Wars* I, 24. And so it happened in 532, when the greens and the blues united against Justinian in the Nika riots. The uprising was brought to an end after six days of unrest thanks to the decisive intervention of Theodora, who reminded the emperor 'purple makes for a lovely shroud'. Thus, she interrupted the plan to flee that was being organized.

[418] Except for a group of 13 tablets discovered inside the circus of Carthage, which were specifically found across from the *carceres* and near the *spina*. For a discussion, see section I.6.5.3 n. 336.

[419] Ogden, for his part, maintains, 'it is curious that even in the Latin west circus curses tend to have been written in Greek: perhaps because most charioteers came from the Greek east' (1999: 33).

and ask that the animals' feet be tied together,[420] that they would be unable to move[421] and hence fall to the ground[422] and lose the race.[423] *Defigentes* also sought to impair the *aurigae*, asking that they be unable to steer their chariots and control their horses,[424] or to see their opponents;[425] all of this would prevent them from ultimately winning the race. For some *defigentes*, however, such requests did not go far enough, and in several tablets we find much more drastic demands: the famous series of curses invoking Baitmo Arbitto, for example, ask that the *aurigae* and their horses be dismembered[426] and tortured[427] before dying.[428]

7.5. Juridical *defixiones*

While the previous section addressed agonistic curses centred on the sporting events held in the amphitheatre and the circus, we can also identify strong agonistic elements in curses dealing with the law courts. In these spaces, rhetorical and legal competitions took place and would be settled only after the (im)partial decision of the *iudex* was delivered.[429] In this setting, *defixiones* proved to be an important resource that was undoubtedly thought to improve one's chances in court, since they sought to silence the accusations and testimony that could implicate or harm a *defigens*. These texts, which were written before a verdict was reached,[430] reveal a complex range of emotions, such as fear, guilt and shame, provoked by the prospect of public humiliation.[431] The potential use and influence of *defixiones* in the legal realm was well known in Antiquity and could even be bandied about as a justification for a lawyer losing train of thought while speaking. In this regard, Cicero mentions Curio, 'who all of a sudden forgot his entire case and said that this had been caused by Titinia's spells and incantations'.[432] Also well known is the case of the orator Marcus Aquillius Regulus, who used to paint a

circle around one of his eyes (the exact one depended on whether he was representing the plaintiff or the defendant) to protect himself from the evil eye (Pliny, *Ep.* VI, 2.2). Pliny the Elder, for his part, explains that carrying part of a hyena's intestinal tube during a trial could lead to success in law-courts and help a speaker win certain types of cases (among other risky situations), by it (cf. *HN* XXVIII, 106).

The *PGM*, for their part, contain two references to the use of amulets in courtrooms[433] as well as a recipe for a juridical curse tablet.[434] In the latter, the *defigens* is instructed to use the lead from a yoke to make a tablet on which he or she would write the following formula: 'restrain the wrath of him, (...) and the anger and tongues of everybody, in order that they might not be able to speak to him'.[435] Next, the practitioner is to fumigate the tablet with incense and then put it under the sole of his or her left foot.[436]

The use of juridical *defixiones* is first attested in Selinunte in the sixth century BCE.[437] Indeed, such curses played an important role in the Greek world, from which we have 67 identified items.[438] Interestingly enough, the formulae found in these Greek curses were later taken up and employed in the Roman world.

So far, we know of 47 juridical *defixiones* from the Roman West, which mostly hail from Italia, Africa, Hispania and Germania.[439] The earliest examples, which date to the Republic and were found in Italia and Hispania, were clearly influenced by Greek curses.[440] That said, we must remember that most of the non-Greek juridical *defixiones* from the Roman West date to the High Empire. In this group of *defixiones*, it is commonplace to brand the victim as an *inimicus*[441] or *adversarius*,[442] though occasionally more precise lexemes are used to specify someone's particular role in a legal proceeding. Such

[420] Cf. Jordan 1988: no. 3, col. C.

[421] For one of many examples, see *DT* 233, ll. 29–32: *...trado tibi os equos ut deteneas illos et inplice[ntur] [n]ec se movere posse[nt]'* and *DT* 275, ll. 29–30: *...ne currere possint nec frenis audire possint nec se mo<v>ere possint.*

[422] A good example would be *DT* 272 A, ll. 11–12: *...cadan<t> frangan<t> disiungantur male guren<t>*, among many others.

[423] Cf. *DT* 272, A ll. 12–13: *...palma<m> vincere [n]on possin<t>*; *DT* 280, l. 14; *DT* 281, ll. 13–14, etc.

[424] A good example is *DT* 275, ll. 32–33: *...nec lora teneant nec retinere equos possint*, among many others.

[425] Cf. *DT* 275, ll. 33–34: *...nec adversarios suos videant*, among others.

[426] Such as in *DT* 288 B, ll. 5–7: *...auferas ab eis nervia vires medullas impetos victorias*; *DT* 289 B, ll. 6–7.

[427] Cf. *DT* 292 B, l. 4; *DT* 293, ll. 5–6 and *DT* 294, ll. 9–10.

[428] Cf. *DT* 286 B, ll. 4–10; *DT* 287 A, l. 12 and *DT* 295, l. 25.

[429] For a similar assessment, see Bablitz 2007: 199, who affirms, 'the Roman courtroom was an arena where parties entered into combat'. For juridical *defixiones* generally, see Faraone 1991a: 15–16; Gager 1992 116–24; Kropp 2008: 180–81; Martin 2010: 47–62; Scholz 2011a. For an extended version of this section, which includes Greek and Latin *defixiones* in the Roman West, see Sánchez Natalías 2020c: 70–72.

[430] See Faraone 1991a: 15 and especially n. 67.

[431] See Gager 1992: 116–17.

[432] Cicero, *Brutus*, 217: *subito totam causam oblitus est idque veneficiis et cantionibus Titiniae factum esse dicebat* (translated by D. Ogden 2001: no. 172). In addition, we should mention Aristophanes *Vespae* 946–48, where we read of an orator whose jaw froze up during a speech before the jury (see Faraone 1989).

[433] See *PGM* XXXVI, 65–68 and IV, 2145–240.

[434] See *PGM* VII, 925–39.

[435] *PGM* VII, 934–39: κάτεχε τὴν ὀργὴν τοῦ δεῖνα καὶ πάντων τὸν θυμὸν καὶ τὰς γλώσσας ἵνα μὴ δυνηθῶσιν λαλεῖν τῷ δεῖνα, translated by R.R. Hock (*apud* Betz 1992²).

[436] This final performance has been related to the representations of captives in royal sandals, through which the Pharaoh constantly commemorates past victories and encourages future ones. Cf. Faraone 1991b: 173–74.

[437] That is *SGD* 95.

[438] According to Faraone 1991a: 16, whose data has also been used by Gager (1992: 117) and Ogden (1999: 31).

[439] To a lesser degree, these tablets are also found in Gallia, Pannonia and Raetia. See Table 7.1.

[440] This influence is especially clear in the tablet from Marsala (cf. **109**) which dates to the third century BCE and was written in a mixture of Latin and Greek. The curse targets a group of individuals whom the *defigens* would like to silence. The remaining tablets from the Republic (dated to the first century BCE) are **63–64**, **66**, **103**, **49–50**, **125–26** and **137**. To these, we should probably add a curse tablet from Corduba (on this, see García Dils de la Vega and Rubio Valverde 2018: 278–81).

[441] Cf. **103** (Col. II, ll. 5–6: *...si quis [i]nimicus inimi[ca] adve[r]sariu hostis*), **17** (B, l. 1), **137** (l. 10), **182** (l. 1), **160** (Tab. 1, l. 10), **468** (A and B, l. 1), **470** (ll. 1, 2 and 9), etc.

[442] Cf. **103** (Col. II, l. 6; see the previous note), **49** (A, ll. 5–6: *...si qui aryosarius aut aṛvosaria*), **17** (B, l. 6), **135** (B, l. 4–5), **478** (A, ll. 3–4), **528** (l. 9), **529** (A, l. 1 and B, l. 5), *DT* 221 (l. 10), among others.

terms include *advocatus*,[443] *testes*,[444] *iudices*[445] as well as '*et omnes qui illi ass[unt] et doc[e]n[t illu]m…*'.[446] Since they were well aware of the danger that damning testimony provided, *defigentes* are pre-eminently concerned with silencing opponents and witnesses:[447] if a *defigens* could immobilize their tongues[448] and impair their mental faculties,[449] their opponents would be unable to respond to questions in court,[450] testify and, ultimately, win a suit.[451]

7.6. *Defixiones* against thieves

At the time when Audollent put forth his taxonomy of curse tablets in 1904, the category of *defixiones in fures, calumniatores et maledicos conversae* was the smallest, with only five examples from the Latin West. Today, this is no longer the case: the important archaeological discoveries of the final third of the twentieth century have turned this once small group into the most fully attested type of curse from the Roman West.[452] Indeed, this type of curse tablet now constitutes almost a sixth of the entire corpus.[453] This increase in the number of instances has piqued scholars' interest in this type of text so much so that certain authors have argued that the category does not really exist.

7.6.1. *A different approach: prayers for justice?*

As alluded to above, Versnel has proffered a new definition of this category of inscriptions and has questioned whether or not they should truly be classified as *defixiones*.[454] Instead, he has defended a new category that he calls 'prayers for justice' and defined as 'pleas addressed to a god or gods to punish a (mostly unknown) person who has wronged the author (by theft, slander, false accusations or magical action), often with the additional request to redress the harm suffered by the author'.[455]

Some of the defining characteristics of the 'prayers for justice' include the use of epithets and honorific titles to name the deities and the humble and respectful tone used by the authors. They normally justify their action and, on certain occasions, give their own names to the deity invoked. While these characteristics have been used by Versnel to distinguish 'pure' prayers for justice from curse tablets, the scholar is also aware of the vast area left in between these two categories. In fact, he labels an important number of texts as 'border-area cases', in other words, texts whose characteristics combine aspects of curse tablets and 'prayers for justice'. The acknowledgment of such a notable grey zone demonstrates just how difficult it is to establish hard lines between categories.

The debate over and interest in Versnel's proposal has nearly divided the scholarly community into those who embrace the category of prayer for justice (e.g., Faraone, Jordan, Tomlin and Urbanová), those who are sceptical of it (e.g., Gager, Ogden, Kropp, Martin and Gordon) and those who have rejected it outright. Among the last group, M. Dreher has been the adamant in the recent years, arguing that these texts would be better defined as *defixiones criminales*. For this scholar, this new typology has nothing new when compared with the old Audollent's label *defixiones in fures*. In fact, the high number of 'border-area cases' should preclude us from making any neat distinction between curses and prayers for justice (Dreher 2012: 30), just as the authors of these texts themselves probably did not think in such terms.[456]

But, as I said, other experts in the field have only rejected certain aspects of the so-called 'prayers for justice'. Scholars like Ogden (1999: 38–39) have pushed back against Versnel's idea according to which 'gods other than the usual chthonic deities are often invoked' (2010:

---

[443] Cf. **63** (frag. C, ll. 10–11), **134** (A, l. 5), **135** (A, ll. 6–7), **160** (Tab. I, ll. 8–9), etc.

[444] Cf. **63** (frag. C, ll. 10–11).

[445] Cf. **22**, ll. 13–14: *…arbitri Surae.*

[446] Cf. **471**, ll. 3–5. Furthermore, in **520** A, ll. 4–5, any overlooked adversary is included with the expression *…et quisquis adversus il(l)am loqut<us est>.*

[447] The desire to render a victim mute is expressed with the verb *obmutesco* (Cf. **160**, Tab. II, ll. 6–8: *…quomodi in hoc m[o]nimont<o> animalia ommutuerun(t) nec surgere possun<t> nec illi*; **529**, B, l. 6, etc.) or more exceptionally, *taceo* (Cf., perhaps, **277**, l. 3: *…tacituri…*). Many curse tablets employ phrases with *mutus* (e.g., **131**, ll. 1 and 4: *…mutus tacitus siet*; **522**, A, ll. 1–2: *…mutus sit Quartus* and l. 4: *…ut e[i]us os mutu(m) sit Mutae*; *DT* 219, A, ll. 2 and 8–9: *…facias ilos muttos*). Reference is made to robbing a victim of the power of speech with the lexeme λαλια, found in **109** (A, l. 7); also see the phrases in **478** (A, ll. 5–6 and B, ll. 3–5: *…neque loqui pos[s]it*); **529** (B, ll. 6–7: *…ne contra nos lucuia(nt)*); *DT* 217 (A, ll. 2–3: *…nec dicere nec facere*); etc. Finally, note the Oscan curse **66**, which reads *…nep fatíum nep deíkum pútian`s´* (ll. 6 and 8), which Vetter (1953: no. 4) has interpreted as equivalent to Latin *nec fari nec dicere possint.*

[448] Such as the Oscan **64** (ll. 6–7: *…olu solu fancua recta sint*, interpreted by Vetter (1953: no. 7) as *…ut illorum lingua rigidae sint*), the Latin **532** (ll. 7–9: *…eo modo hoc ego averso graphio scribo sic linguas illorum aversas ne pos(s)int facere contra (h)os…*) and *DT* 218 (ll. 6–7: *…adligate linguas*); among many other cases. Additionally, perhaps we should add the Oscan **65**, an anatomical curse that targets the tongue (*fanguam*, l. 3).

[449] Cf. **109** (A, l. 6: *…καὶ ψυχὴν αὐτοῦ ὡς μὴ δύνα[ται]*, repeated on A, l. 8 and B, l. 2), **522** (A, l. 7: *[Qu]a[rt]us ut insaniat*), etc.

[450] Cf. **467** (B, ll. 1–3: *…sic non possit respo[nde]re qua(e)s[tionibus]*), **470** (ll. 8–9: *…nusquam contra nos [inve]nisse respo̦ns[io]nis cum loquantur inimici*); *DT* 218 (ll. 8–9: *…ne adversus nos responderae*), etc.

[451] Cf. **160**, Tab. I, ll. 5–6: *…nec illi hanc litem vincere possint.*

[452] Mostly in Britannia, where the sanctuaries dedicated to Sulis Minerva (Aquae Sulis, Bath) and Mercury (Uley), together with scattered findings, have provided an impressive collection of evidence.

[453] Authors like Gager (1992: 177) and Ogden (1999: 38), nevertheless, include in this category all of the *defixiones* found in Aquae Sulis/Bath and Uley. This is suspect since many of the texts are illegible or too fragmentary to be securely classified as curses against thieves. For this type of curse in general, see Kropp 2008: 186–89; Martin 2010: 67–79; Scholz 2011b; Urbanová 2018: 24–30 and 180–203. An extended version of this section has appeared in Sánchez Natalías 2022.

[454] Versnel 1987 and especially 1991, 2010 and 2012.

[455] Versnel 2010: 279, where he adds, 'The other typical features are: 1. the principal states his or her name; 2. some grounds for the appeal are offered; this statement may be reduced to a single word, or may be enlarged upon; 3. the principal requests that the act be excused or that he be spared the possible adverse effects; 4. gods other than the usual chthonic deities are often invoked; 5. these gods (…) may be awarded a flattering epithet (…) or a superior title (…); 6. words expressing supplication (…) are employed as well as direct, personal invocations of the deity; 7. use of terms and names referring to (in)justice and punishment' (also see Versnel 1991: 68). For a contrary view, see Gager 1992: 179, n. 2.

[456] Cf. Gordon 2013: 267f.; Faraone and Gordon 2019: 322f.

279). Ogden has rightly pointed out that among the deities mentioned in these curses there still seems to be a preference for those who have chthonic connections, like Mercury,[457] Demeter[458] and certain infernal demons.[459] Indeed, we could easily expand this list to include Proserpina (cf. **120**), Dis Pater, Cerberus and Veracura (cf. **530**), Hades (cf. **121**), Nemesis (cf. **337**) and Diana (cf. **343**). Finally, we ought to add that even if available evidence allows us to form general ideas about deities like Sulis, Metunus and Niskus, the fact remains that little is known about these figures and questions about whether they are chthonic or not still have to be resolved.[460]

Scholars have also been wary of Versnel's claims about the humble language and respectful tone found in these tablets (e.g., the use of epithets and honorific titles). Thus, Kropp has analysed these features as a 'protective strategy' through which the author (i.e., the *defigens*) finds a way to communicate with a supernatural audience, which in the author's eyes is at once mighty and possibly dangerous.[461] In Kropp's own words, 'the *defigens* articulates his awareness of the status difference between him and the god invoked, insofar as he gives his request a non-peremptory character and, at the same time, qualifies his own position as dependent and inferior' (2010: 366).

Finally, let's address the question of an author identifying him- or herself in the text. While it is true that in the bulk of known curse tablets *defigentes* do not normally name themselves (though, for obvious reasons, we find exceptions in certain erotic curses),[462] in the present group of texts some writers share their own names with the deity invoked. This has been taken as evidence for the absence of fear before the deity, since they are asking for justice.[463] But, at the same time, such reasoning would imply that all the authors who did not specify their names were, in turn, afraid of the deity.

In my opinion, this conscious decision can be understood in a different manner: as the result of the varying perceptions that practitioners had about divine omniscience. For some of them, gods were omniscient and able to find the stolen property with almost no information at all. For others, giving the gods more information about a case would be helpful and increase the chance of a successful resolution. In this scenario, where (obviously) the authors of the texts did not know the identity of the wrongdoers, the only name that could possibly be provided was his or

her own.[464] Generally, the practitioner gives his/her name in the nominative, sometimes followed by a patronym and, exceptionally, by a matronym. A curse tablet from Aquae Sulis/Bath, **303**, provides a good example of this: in reporting the theft of six silver coins, the practitioner not only identifies himself as Annianus, but also provides his mother's name (Mantutina). The addition of this final piece of information is certainly extraordinary and reflects the author's desire to be clearly identified by the deity (as usually happens with erotic curse tablets).

Even if Versnel has moved the debate forward more than any other scholar to date, no consensus has been reached and the validity of the category 'prayer for justices' remains an open and important question within the larger field.[465] As a scholar, I am aware of how useful taxonomies can be for understanding any phenomenon from Antiquity. That said, the debate in this case has gone too far, and the rigidity of these taxonomies is no longer helpful. Given that curse tablets worked as a magico-religious technology that was adapted by the different societies that employed them, it is much more useful to understand these artefacts from a more *emic* perspective (*contra* Versnel 2010: 326). To establish a hard border between 'prayers for justice' and curse tablets seems not only artificial but also unnecessary. Doing so just brings back to the great dichotomy between 'magic' and 'religion' that scholarship has sought to abolish for the last decades. As Gordon has pointed out, curse tablets are better understood in terms of instrumental religion, that is, as a tool that served individuals to solve their specific, personal crises. As is always the case, the way we categorize something largely depends on our own point of view: in Gordon's words (2013: 269), 'the instrumental religion of one party is the malign magic of the other party. It is entirely a matter of perspective'.[466] The fact that a certain practice was not institutionalized or sanctioned by the Roman authorities does not mean that it was not normalized within specific social contexts and communities.[467]

To conclude, Versnel has identified important differences among the so-called 'prayers for justice' and the larger corpus of *defixiones*. Despite these differences, all these tablets are fundamentally a private and direct means of communicating with the divine. After considering the supposed differences between the two groups, there remains, in my view, more fundamental commonalities,

---

[457] Cf. **346**, **355–56**, **358**, **361**, **459**, **523**, etc.

[458] Cf. *DT* 2–3, 6, 11–12 and *SGD* no. 60.

[459] Cf. *DT* 74–75, *SGD* no. 21.

[460] Ogden maintains, 'while Minerva had no chthonic associations, Sulis' sacred spring was a body of underground water' (1999: 38–39).

[461] Cf. Kropp 2010: 366, where she notes that the 'interaction between human-beings and supernatural powers, especially infernal ones, invites such strategies–we may recall that prayers to the gods of the underworld were not spoken aloud.'

[462] Except in the case of erotic *defixiones*, where the *PGM* recommend that the practitioner include his own name, a practice which, as is well know, is found in the curses themselves.

[463] As Tomlin puts it, 'the writer is asking for justice, and is not afraid to give his name' (2002: 16).

[464] Nevertheless, within Britannia, the practitioner identifies him- or herself in less than half of the *defixiones in fures* (for some examples, see **205**, **210**, **237**, **346**, **350**, **356**, **451**, etc.). Outside of Britannia, this sort of self-identification is securely documented in four further curses (**479**, **483**, **492**, where the *defigens* identifies herself with her husband's name, and **523**). For a cognitive approach to the self-identification of practitioners in British curse tablets against thieves, see Sánchez Natalías (forthcoming).

[465] See Gager 1992: 175–78; Graf 1995: 155f.; Ogden 1999: 37–39; Martin 2010: 67–68; Dreher 2010 and 2012; Gordon 2013: 266–69 and 2014: 783–84; Faraone and Gordon 2019: 321–23. Versnel (2010: 277–78, 324–27 and 2012) has answered some of these critiques.

[466] On this, see also McKie and Parker 2018: 2f. and McKie 2019: 445.

[467] Such as the sanctuary of Isis and Mater Magna in Mainz, for which see Veale 2017.

including formal characteristics (types of materials used, deposit contexts, manipulation, etc.) and intent. Indeed, these tablets reveal the same emotions (e.g., anger, wrath and desperation) that underlie the larger group of *defixiones*.[468] As should be clear at this point, I prefer Audollent's denomination '*defixiones in fures*', which I use throughout the rest of this volume.

7.6.2. Defixiones against thieves (or in fures)

Written in a response to a theft, curses against thieves seek to recover a stolen object and/or punish the wrongdoer. So far, the earliest examples of such curses come from the Greek world, and more specifically from Cnidus in Asia Minor. There, excavations carried in the nineteenth century by C.T. Newton uncovered the temple of Demeter, in whose temenos they 'found in several places portions of thin sheets of lead, broken and doubled up. On being unrolled, these sheets proved to be tablets inscribed with imprecations' (Newton: 1863: 382).[469] In six of these texts,[470] dated between the second and the first centuries BCE,[471] the *defigentes* denounce the theft that they have suffered and ask that the culprit publicly admit to his or her wrongdoing while being wracked with fevers and other torments.

The desired confession attested in the curses from Cnidus has often been compared to certain Lydian and Phrygian stelae,[472] dated in between the second and the third centuries CE, in which the guilty party publicly confess their crime while asking for reconciliation with the gods. But, in addition to these stelae, there are also interesting parallels in *PGM* V, where we find two recipes for catching a thief. The first recipe (*PGM* V, 70–96) gives the following instructions: first paint an eye on the wall and make a hammer from a piece of wood taken from the gallows; next, strike the painted eye with the hammer while reciting the formula: 'Hand over the thief who stole it. As long as I strike the eye with this hammer, let the eye of the thief be struck and let it swell up until it betrays him'.[473] The second recipe (*PGM* V, 182–212) is preceded by an invocation to Hermes (which makes perfect sense, given his own experience as a thief). It recommends gathering up the usual suspects and offering them some wheat and cheese, while saying 'Master IAO, light-bearer,

I hand over the thief whom I see'. At this point the papyrus adds: 'If one of them does not swallow what was given to him, he is the thief.'[474]

The *PGM* recipes as well as the texts from Asia Minor share a common feature: the public confession of the guilty party. Such a confession, however, is not attested among the curses against thieves from the Roman West (regardless of the language in which they were written). Thus, it is worth wondering whether these types of confessions were local solutions to a similar problem: how to catch a thief.

When it comes to the Roman West, and besides 20 tablets mostly hailing from Hispania and Germania,[475] the overwhelming majority of the *defixiones in fures* come from Britannia and date between the second and fourth centuries CE. There, most of the evidence has been found in the sanctuaries of Sulis Minerva (Aquae Sulis, Bath) and Mercury (Uley). That said, it is worth stressing that there are also over 20 tablets that come from different parts of the island. This would mean that, so far, and without counting the dense concentrations of the main sanctuaries,[476] the number of curses against thieves is still higher in Britannia than in any other province from the Roman West. In addition, there is also another important point to consider: of the whole corpus of British curses, the only tablets that explicitly record the reason for which they were written are the ones in response to a theft. The rest of the texts are either too fragmentary or too sparse for us to determine the *causa defigendi*. Was the technology of curse tablets being adapted in Britannia for an acutely felt need?

Whatever the case may be, it is worth stressing that the close temporal and geographical proximity of these British curses have allowed us to define them as a compact group (as is the case with the agonistic curses from North Africa). While this collection does use phrases and expressions found in some 'continental' curse tablets, they also contain an important series of idiosyncratic formulae of great interest.

A fundamental feature of many of these curses is the transfer of part or all of the stolen property to the deities invoked. According to Roman law, transferring something that you no longer possessed remained possible, since a stolen object still legally belonged to the owner, even if (s)he did not physically have the item. This transference of ownership has the effect of turning a normal theft into a sacrilegious act and hence branding the thief as impious.[477] This type of transference could consist of a full donation of the stolen property to the deities invoked (such as in

---

[468] On the negative emotions at display in the Greek examples (which served as a socially accepted outlet), see Salvo 2012.

[469] *Contra* Versnel 2010: 280–81 and Urbanová 2018: 25–26, n. 59, who think that the tablets were on display. Newton himself proposed that hypothesis, arguing that the curses 'were *probably* suspended on walls, as they are pierced with holes at the corners' (1863: 724, emphasis added). Nevertheless, of the known curses, only *DT* 2 has a hole in the middle of the upper edge. Therefore, and even if this tablet was displayed at one point, it was eventually folded or rolled up (as the rest were so) before being deposited in the sanctuary.

[470] See *DT* 2–4, 6 and 11–12.

[471] According to Versnel (1991: 72). Gager 1992: no. 89 dates them to the first centuries BCE.

[472] Known as 'confession stelae'. For a discussion, see Versnel 1991: 75ff. and, more recently, Gordon 2016.

[473] *PGM* V, 91–95: παράδος τὸν κλέπτην τὸν κλέψαντά τι. ὅσον κρούω τὸ οὐ<τ>άτιον σφύρῃ ταύτῃ, ὁ τοῦ κλέπτου ὀφθαλμὸς κρουέσθω καὶ φλεγμαινέσθω, ἄχρι οὗ αὐτὸν μηνύσῃ (translated by W.C. Greese *apud* Betz 1992²).

[474] *PGM* V, 211–12: ἐὰν δέ τις αὐτῶν μὴ καταπίῃ τὸ δοθὲν αὐτῷ, αὐτός ἐστιν ὁ κλέψας (translated by W.C. Greese *apud* Betz 1992²).

[475] There are other isolated examples from Italia, Gallia, Raetia and Pannonia.

[476] On the problems derived from dense concentrations of data and subsequent interpretation, see Faraone 2012.

[477] Faraone *et al.* claim, 'by ceding the stolen goods to the god, the curse retroactively turns a common thief into a blasphemous temple robber' (2005: 170).

127, **237**, **265**, **337**, etc.). Nevertheless, this is not always the case: at times, only a half of the value of a stolen object is given to the gods (cf. **205** and **443**); in other cases, the amount is a third (cf. **356**) or a tenth of the stolen object (cf. **349**). In these occasions, which so far have only been attested in the British corpus, the deity would be paid back with a fraction of the stolen property's value only after its recovery. In such situations, the author of the text establishes a sort of agreement with the gods in a way that is almost contractual.[478]

Traditionally, defining such an agreement has proven quite controversial. For some scholars, it can be labelled as a sort of *votum*.[479] Nevertheless, and as Versnel has rightly pointed out, this does not quite work, since the object is 'ceded, not vowed' (2010: 342–434) to the god or goddess. Even if we cannot define this agreement exactly as a *votum*, it remains likely that the practitioners who wrote these tablets were influenced by this concept, given its presence in the sanctuaries where the curses were deposited (Tomlin 1988a: 70 and McKie 2019: 444f.).

As mentioned above before, Britannia is the only province where there is evidence for giving the deity a fraction of the total value of the stolen object. Thus, it seems appropriate to wonder whether we are dealing with a local and somewhat idiosyncratic adaptation of an existing magical-religious technology. Perhaps the practitioners were adjusting the traditional *votum* to address a new problem. In these texts, the authors present a unilateral agreement with the deities, which has a contractual nature. Once they have handed over the property of the stolen object to the gods, the practitioners had also passed over a sense of *obligatio*, which is inherent to the *votum*. In other words, the gods became the ones who —if they so wished— would be responsible for finding the object. At this point, the issue would be solved only when both the deity and the practitioner received their portion of the stolen object, as stipulated in the text itself. Through this mechanism, practitioners were not only encouraging divine action, but also establishing a mechanism to see whether the gods followed through on their side of the bargain, if you will.

The culprit, who for obvious reasons is rarely named in the *defixiones in fures*,[480] can be referred to with phrases like '*qui involaverit*'.[481] Most frequently, however, the thief is referred to through an all inclusive formula comprised of opposing pairs, such as '*si vir si femina, si servus si liber...*'.[482] When it comes to punishment, the practitioners

could be, at times, somewhat impatient, vehemently asking the deities invoked[483] to act as soon as possible (*quantocius*: cf. **259** and **367**), or before seven (*ante dies septem*: cf. **457**) or nine days (*ante dies novem*: cf. **267**, **340**, etc.).[484] While the simplest scenario in this kind of text is handing the thief over to the deities invoked (cf. **220**, **359**, **451**, etc.), the most common punishments include the paralysis of the wrongdoer's vital functions[485] or the repayment of the stolen object with the thief's own blood.[486] Sometimes the practitioner wants a punishment to last until the culprit returns the stolen goods to the temple,[487] while at other times a *defigens* will ask that the curse hounds the thief for the rest of his or her life.[488]

---

femina is found instead or the phrase is completed with the addition of *puer/puella* and/or *baro-mascel/mulier*, like in **249** (A, ll. 3–4 and B, ll. 1–3), **364** (l. 3, where we find *vel* instead of *si*), **451** (ll. 6–8), among many others. These formulae were so popular that they could even appear in abbreviated form, like in **386** ('*sbsmspsp*'= *si baro si mulier si puer si puella*) and **351** (ll. 3–4, '*simausib*' =*si m(ulier) au[t] si b(aro)*). To these we must add the Hispanic curse from Italica **127**, which reads ...*si quis puel(l)a si mulier sive [ho]mo involavit* (ll. 7–9). Besides the pair *servus/ liber*, there are others that refer to legal status, like *libertinus* (cf. **236**, ll. 10–11), *si ancilla* (cf. **257**, l. 7) and *si ingenuus* (cf. **459** l. 5). An isolated, but extremely interesting, pair is found in **303** A, ll. 1–2: ...*seu gen(tili)s seu Ch(r)istianus*; also note ...*si paga[n]us si mil[e]s* (cf. **450**, B, ll. 2–4). Finally, we ought to mention the formulae which refer to anyone who may have important information about the theft, like in **302** (A, ll. 3–4: ...*qui medius fuerit*) or **342** (l. 4: ...*et si qui afuere*), among others.

[483] Cf. **215** (A, ll. 10–12: ...*dea Sulis maximo letum [a]digat*; compare with **361**, ll. 7–8); **259** (B, l. 9: ...*cum quantiocius consumas*); **350** (l. 8: ...*quicumque illam involasit a devo moriotur*; **451** (ll. 16–19: ...*qui hoc involavit sanguem eiius consumas et decipias domin[e] Ne[p]tune*).

[484] For this magical deadline, see Marco Simón 2010b; for magical time frames in general, see Sánchez Natalías 2019a.

[485] This punishment is usually found in a *non permittas* formula, which can be followed by the phrase *nec somnum* and/or *nec sanitatem* (cf. **205**, **237**, **361**, etc.). There are multiple versions of this formula, which keeps the victim from eating, drinking, talking, procreating, sitting, lying down, defecating, etc. For a few examples, see **358** (ll. 4–9 and 12–14: ... *ne meiat ne cacet ne loquatur ne dormiat ne vigilet nec salutem nec sanitatem... ne co(n)scientiam de perferat*); **365** (ll. 8–10: ...*sanitatem ei non permittas nec iacere nec sedere nec bibere nec manducare*); **443** (ll. 7–9: ...*sanit[atem] nec bibere nec ma[n]d[u]care nec dormi[re] [nec nat]os sanos habe[a]nt*).

[486] E.g., **249** (A, ll. 5–7: ...*sangu(in)em suum in ips'um` aen'um` fundat*); **299** (ll. 8–9: ...*facias illum sanguine suo illud satisfacere*); **304** (ll. 5–6: ... *sanguine et vitae suae illud redemat*); **337** (ll. 5–8: ...*non redimat ni vita sanguine suo*); **346** (l. 3: ...*sangu(i)no suo solvat*); **451** (ll. 10–11: ... *sanguem eiuş qui conscius fueris* and ll. 16–18: ...*sanguem eiius consumas et decipias*).

[487] E.g., **205** (ll. 9–11: ...*donec perfera(t) usque templum [No]dentis*); **215** (B, ll. 2–6: ...*do[ne]c caracallam meam ad templum sui numinis per[t] ulerit*); **443** (ll. 9–10: ...*nessi hanc rem [meam] ad fanum tuum [at-] tulerint*); **356** (A, ll. 6–8: ...*nissi quand[o] res s(upra) dictas ad fanum s(upra) d[ic]tum attulerit*).

[488] See **250** (B, l. 4: ...*quoad vixerit*); **350** (ll. 3–4: ...*usque die`m´ quo moriatur*); **459** (ll. 6–7: ...*diem mortis*); perhaps **257** (ll. 3–5: ...*tandiu (...) quandiu hoc [ill]ud*, which in Tomlin's words 'may have the sense of "so long as he shall live"... or "so long as he shall retrain the stolen property"' (*apud Tab. Sulis* 52); **305** ([B, ll. 2–5] where the victim is asked to do something impossible: ...*nisi ut Euticia modium nebulae modium veniat fumi*).

---

[478] Cf. Sánchez Natalías forthcoming 1.

[479] Lambert 2004. Kiernan 2004, for his part, has connected the formulae attested in these curse tablets with the ones attested in other votives.

[480] Except for **259**, **355**, **441**, **443**, **456** and **457**, where the name of the thief (or a suspect) is given.

[481] E.g., **220** (ll. 2–4: ...*qui destrale involaverit*); **349** (A, l. 9 and B, l. 1: ...*qui<sq>uis involavit*); **451** (l. 2: ...*d<o>no (h)ominem qui <so>l<i>d'um` involav[it]*); **454** (l. 5: ...*eu(m) qui involaverit*).

[482] One of the most commonly repeated is *si vir si femina si servus si liber*, which is found (in whole or in part) in **215** (A, ll. 7–9), **268** (l. 4), **310** (A, ll. 3–4), just to mention a few examples. Sometimes the pair *vir/*

8

The Pantheon of Deities Invoked

8.1. Introduction

Undoubtedly *defixiones* provided one of the most direct and private ways to communicate with the divine in Antiquity. As a result, these texts provide a valuable source of information about various divinities and supernatural beings that are underrepresented in —if not totally absent from— other types of sources. It is only in curse tablets that we can learn about such deities and see the kinds of schemes in which practitioners sought their assistance.[489]

As can be deduced from Table 8.1, only 180 of the 623 *defixiones* from the Roman West contain theonyms or explicit references to any gods who were tasked with enforcing the contents of a curse.[490] However, we ought to add an additional 228 curses to this number which were deposited in sanctuaries or other sacred spaces: even though these texts do not mention the sanctuary's titular divinity explicitly, it is only logical to deduce that such curses were addressed to that god.[491] The same logic applies with graves and necropolis: even though 112 *defixiones* do not explicitly mention the Di Inferi or the Di Manes to which these spaces were consecrated, these curse tablets were likely conceived of as messages to these gods (*contra* Cubrera 1999a: 160). Accordingly, the number of curse tablets that mentioned or can be linked to a deity rises to 520 curses or 84 per cent of the entire corpus. Furthermore, of the remaining tablets many are damaged or fragmentary; hence, they could certainly have invoked a god. In other cases, however, it seems likely that a practitioner would have orally invoked a deity while reciting specific formulae like those preserved in certain recipes from the *PGM*.[492]

Among the 167 curses that contain a theonym or direct references to a god, we find a wide range of deities, demigods, demons and other supernatural beings of Graeco-Roman, indigenous or eastern origins. Many of these supernatural beings are only attested once in the corpus of *defixiones* from the Roman West. Table 8.2 only includes those that are mentioned on more than one occasion, many of whom are attested in various provinces.

8.2. Graeco-Roman gods and supernatural entities

Given the so-called process of 'Romanization',[493] it is hardly surprising that Graeco-Roman *numina* appear in tablets from every province from the Roman West, though at a lesser frequency in North Africa, where a very different sort of divine being predominates.

In this collection of divinities from the Graeco-Roman pantheon, there is a fairly compact and consistent group made up of chthonic deities, which are occasionally referred to with the fixed phrase *Dis Inferis*.[494] That said, we also frequently find Pluto and Proserpina, the lords of the underworld,[495] who are sometimes accompanied by their monstrous dogs.[496] Within this group, special attention ought to be paid to a Roman curse tablet dated to the first century CE (cf. **48**, Bevilacqua 2009 and 2010b), in which we encounter a large group of mythical beings in conjunction with the king and queen of the underworld. In addition to well-known beings (e.g., Aurora, the Sphinx, the Giants, the Furiae, the Maniae or the Chimera), we also find a series of predatory birds (*aves Nocturnae*, *aves Harpyiae*), the *Ustores inferi* (body burners) and the *Ossifragae* (the bone breakers). Leaving aside this tablet, we should also include Ceres,[497] Mercury,[498] the Manes,[499] the monstrous Lamia[500] as well as people who died prematurely among the underworld beings invoked within the curse tablets from the Roman West.[501]

---

[489] For this issue, cf. Ogden 1999: 44–46; Kropp 2008: 94–103 and Abb. 3; Bailliot 2010: 83–93 and Marco Simón 2010d. For the Greek *defixiones*, see Kagarow 1929: 59–75. This section is an updated version of a Spanish publication (cf. Sánchez Natalías 2013b).

[490] The 180 curse tablets comprise almost a third of the total. In this group, we find generic terms to refer to gods, such as *deus* (cf. **157**, **162**, **185**, etc.), *domina* (cf. **128**, *DT* 269, etc.) and *daemon* (cf. **114**, *DT* 229, 233, etc.).

[491] There are, however, some quite interesting exceptions: in the sanctuary of Sulis Minerva, for example, there is a curse that addresses Mercury (cf. **258**) and others that evoke Mars (cf. **238** and **302**). The latter deity is also named in several tablets from the temple of Mercury in Uley: cf. **357** (where he is mentioned alongside Mercury) and **356** (where the author wrote Mercury's name over an original invocation of Mars-Silvanus, which may suggest that there was a mistake in the original invocation), **373** and **431**.

[492] For the importance of orality in the *actio magica*, see section I.4.1 above. For the recipes in the papyri, see *PGM* III, 29–40, 43–53, 71–94 and 98–161; IV, 335–406; IV 1748–812; IV, 2235–36; V, 335–43; VII, 431–32; etc.

[493] On this controversial term, see Beltrán Lloris 2017 with further bibliography.

[494] For just several examples, see **56**, **70**, **105**, **122** and **129**.

[495] Cf. **10–14**, **103**, **160**, **526** (where they are called *Iupiter Infernus* and *Iuno Inferna*), **533** (where he is called *Dito Pater*), among others. Pluto is invoked as *Dominus Megarus* in the tablet from Salacia/Alcácer do Sal (cf. **121**; for a discussion, see Marco Simón 2004: 86). Persephone/Proserpina appears in **109** and **120** (where she is called *Ataecina Turibrigensis Proserpina*; see Marco Simón 2011b: 49–55) as well as the North African tablets *DT* 268 and (perhaps) *DT* 213, among others. Furthermore, the references to the *regina tenebrarum* in *DT* 288–89 could also allude to the same goddess.

[496] Both *Tricipites et bicipites*, cf. **103** and **48**.

[497] Cf. the Oscan curse **68**, where she is invoked as Keres Arentika.

[498] Cf. **81**, **258**, **346** (invoked alongside *Virtus*), **353**, **355–58**, **459** and **523** (alongside Moltinus) as well as the North African curses *DT* 251 (called *sangtus deus Mercurius infę[rnu]ṣ*) and *DT* 253, among others.

[499] Cf. **17**, **469** (where the *larvae* are also mentioned), **526** (together with Pluto and Aeracura), **530** (where they are called the *ministeria infernorum*), *DT* 222, etc.

[500] Cf. **82**. So far, this is the only known instance of such an invocation.

[501] E.g., the *atélestoi* found in the tablet from Lilybaeum/Marsala (**109**) and perhaps the *biaothánatoi* in *DT* 295 (ll. 27–28).

Table 8.1. *Defixiones* invoking a deity according to provenance (It.= Italia, Afr.= Africa, Hisp.= Hispania, Gall.= Gallia, Brit.= Britannia, Ger.= Germania, Raet.= Raetia, Nor.= Noricum, Pan.= Pannonia)

	Explicit mention of a deity	No explicit mention of a deity, but deposited in a consecrated space	Total	Remaining curses
It.	32	22 (sanctuaries of Rome and Roccagloriosa) 41 (necropolis *vel sim.*)	95/119	24
Afr.	39	2 (other sacred spaces) 40 (necropolis *vel sim.*)	81/88	7
Hisp.	9	7 (necropolis *vel sim.*)	16/30	14
Gall.	15	10 (sacred spaces) 8 (necropolis *vel sim.*)	33/55	22
Brit.	66	103 (Aquae Sulis/Bath, Sulis Minerva) 61 (Uley, Mercury) 1 (other sacred spaces) 1 (necropolis *vel sim.*)	232/256	24
Germ.	13	27 (Mogontiacum/Mainz, Attis and Magna Mater) 13 (necropolis *vel sim.*)	53/56	3
Raet.	3	1 (necropolis *vel sim.*)	4/6	2
Nor.	1		1/1	–
Pan.	2	1 (Savaria/Szombathely, Iseum) 1 (other sacred spaces) 2 (necropolis *vel sim.*)	6/9	3

Table 8.2. Table containing the supernatural beings that are invoked on more than one occasion in the curses from the Roman West, classified by provenance (It.= Italia, Afr.= Africa, Hisp.= Hispania, Gall.= Gallia, Brit.= Britannia, Ger.= Germania, Raet.= Raetia, Nor.= Noricum, Pan.= Pannonia). For the supernatural beings invoked only once, see index.

Supernatural beings	It.	Afr.	Hisp.	Gall.	Brit.	Ger.	Raet.	Nor.	Pan.
Ablanathanalba	5								
Abraxas	1			1					
Angels	2	1							
Attis			1			3			
Cerberus	8								2
Christ	6								
Demons/Daemones	1	19							
Diana/Nemesis				2	2				
Di Inferi	5		2						
Dis Pater/Pluto/Hades/Orcus	7		3	1			1	1	3
Hermes/Mercury	1	2			30		1		2
Iao		6	1 (?)						
Jupiter				1	1				
Magna Mater/Cybele						8			
Manes	1	1				2		1	2
Mars				2	9				
Muta Tacita							1		1
Neptune (/Metunus)					4				
Nymphs (Anna Perenna) (Niskas/Niskus)	3			3	1				
Proserpina/Persephone Aeracura/Veracura	8	2	1	1				1	3
Sulis Minerva					21				

As a result of Greek influence, the first curses to invoke chthonic divinities are Oscan and appeared in southern Italy, specifically in Petelia/Strongoli (cf. **81**) and Capua (cf. **68**). Dated to the fourth or third century BCE, these texts invoke Hermes and Keres Arentika (together with the supernatural beings that are members of her 'crew'), respectively. Other early examples, dated to the third century BCE, come from Carthage and Lilybaeum/ Marsala and summon Persephone (who appears together with the Titans and *atélestoi* in **109**).[502] Beginning in the first century BCE, we can note a diversification of the gods mentioned in the corpus: Pluto, Cerberus, the Manes and the Dei Inferi all enter the record. Furthermore, beginning in the first century the geographical regions in which chthonic deities are mentioned in *defixiones* began to expand, until including all corners of the Roman West.

With the group of Graeco-Roman deities found in the curse tablets, we must also mention those that are chthonic and who tend to appear in texts dating to the High Empire. Such gods include Jupiter,[503] Gea,[504] Diana/Nemesis[505] and Mars.[506] In some curses, it is clear that the gods (or other supernatural beings) are invoked since they were particularly well suited to carry out the *defigens*' requests. This is certainly the case with Muta Tacita, who was summoned to silence those who may have testified against a *defigens* in the law court (cf. **522, 529**, etc.), and Cacus, who was invoked together with Mercury and the Celtic Moltinus in order to catch a thief (cf. **523**). Graeco-Roman deities presided over local cults, as we see in Neapolis/ Terralba (cf. **113**), where Marsyas was worshiped or in Italica/Santiponce (cf. **127**), where we find Domina Fons, who has been the subject of some debate.[507] Besides Domina Fons, there are other aquatic deities, like Neptune (invoked in four British curses found near rivers)[508] or the Nymphs,[509] among whom the best attested is the ancient goddess Anna Perenna, in whose sanctuary there is evidence for an intriguing religious syncretism during Late Antiquity.[510]

8.3. Indigenous divinities

As is well known, the process of 'Romanization' was not simply a one-way street: in the religious context not only were certain Roman cults taken up by provincial societies, but indigenous religion was also recognized and protected under the Roman Imperial rule.[511] In addition to the numerous official examples of this bidirectional process and maintenance of local practices, we must also look towards the illicit and subaltern ways in which local traditions came to influence the practice of writing *defixiones*. Although these tablets began as foreign technology in indigenous provincial communities, they nevertheless were taken up and used as a means to communicate with indigenous deities, who appear to have been thought of as more 'reliable' in the eyes of certain practitioners. The consequences of this act of adapting a Roman practice to the indigenous pantheon are far from trivial: as Marco Simón has pointed out, in some cases the mention of these deities in *defixiones* provides us with the only evidence for the existence of their cult (2010d: 293–97). To date, we know of examples of this phenomenon from Hispania, Gallia, Britannia, Raetia and Pannonia, which all date to the High Empire. Among the attested invocations, we can distinguish two types: *interpretationes* and those directed to indigenous divinities (either alone or in conjunction with other Graeco-Roman divinities).

To start with the former case, there are rare but interesting instances in which Graeco-Roman deities are assimilated to indigenous gods, which is the result of an *interpretatio* carried out by the local community. A good example of this is seen in the goddess Ataecina-Proserpina, who is mentioned in a curse from Emerita Augusta/Merida inscribed on a marble plaque (cf. **120**). The indigenous theonym Ataecina has been linked to Proto-Celtic **adaki* (>*adaig*, 'night'), which would certainly suit a chthonic goddess.[512] Another nice example of *interpretatio* is found in the British goddess Sulis Minerva, who was worshiped at the sanctuary in Aquae Sulis/Bath. In nearly half of the curses from this sanctuary which contain an invocation of the goddess, we find the indigenous theonym Sulis, which may reflect a local preference that endured for centuries after Roman conquest.[513]

There is only a small group of seven *defixiones* in which an indigenous deity is exclusively invoked. Such texts have, to date, only been found in Gallia and Britannia. The *defixiones* from Gaul contain three tantalizing theonyms: Niskas, Maponos and Adsagsona.[514] The first

---

[502] For the Carthaginian curse, I follow the interpretation of Amadasi Guzzo 2003 who proposes that Persephone-Elat is invoked (esp. 28, n. 17 and 30). For a different point of view, see Faraone *et al.* 2005.

[503] Securely invoked in **349** and perhaps in **168**.

[504] Referred to as *Domina Terra* in *DT* 220.

[505] Diana/Nemesis is invoked in two British curses against thieves that were deposited in the amphitheatres of London and Isca Silurum/ Caerleon (cf. **343** and **337**) as well as in another two curses from Augusta Treverorum/Trier, where she appears alongside Mars (cf. **182–83**).

[506] Cf. **238, 302, 452, 356** (together with Silvanus), **357** (together with Mercury), etc.

[507] The editors of the *defixio* (Gil and Luzón 1975: 126–27) have proposed *Fonsfor* or *Fons Fori[nae]* as the reconstruction of the theonym, whereas Canto (1985: 161) has proposed *Fons Fovens* and Tomlin (2010: 254) has suggested *Fons Font[i]*, which seems more convincing given the palaeographical features of the text.

[508] Cf. **441, 449** and **451**.

[509] Cf. **92**, where they are invoked with the formula *uti vos Aqu`a´e ferventes siv[e] ̣ṿọs Nimfas [si]ve quo alio nomine voltis adpe[l]lari*. On this formula, which is typical of Roman priests, see the interesting remarks by Gordon 2019b: 429.

[510] The nymphs are named directly in **23**. A reflection of this syncretism is evidenced by the simultaneous invocation of Christ and the *deas vest[ra]s* found on **31**.

[511] Cf. Marco Simón 1996: 236–38.

[512] Cf. Marco Simón 2011b: 49–55 (esp. n. 48 on the theonym's etymology).

[513] The goddess is called Sulis in 16 tablets (**213, 215, 224–26, 249–50, 254, 259, 267–68, 270–71, 274, 299** and **311**), Sulis Minerva in 5 curses (**237, 239-240, 251** and **265**) and Minerva in one (**275**). Note that Sulis Minerva is the most common way of naming the goddess in the seven inscribed *paterae* that were deposited in the sacred spring.

[514] If we accept Schwinden's reconstruction for the curse from Arlon (cf. **204**, Schwinden 1988: 29–30), we can add the theonym *Cam[ulus]*.

name is attested in three tablets that were discovered at the spring in Amélie-les-Bains in 1845 and were written in a language that has defied certain identification (cf. **150–51** and **154**). The theonym Niskas, which Lizop has connected to the Basque word *neskas* ('young women'), may refer to the nymphs who watched over the spring. Niskas, we will see, may even have a homologue in Britannia. With respect to Maponos, Fleuriot (1977: 178f.) has analysed the theonym as **ma(k)kʷo-* ('young man') with the suffix *-ono-*; he appears to be a god who was linked to Apollo. Although Maponos is attested in the Gaulish *defixio* from Arverni/Chamalières (cf. **163**, deposited in a sanctuary of which he may have been the patron deity), this god was also worshiped in Britannia, where several intriguing inscriptions mentioning his cult have been found.[515] Finally, Adsagsona is invoked in the Gaulish curse from L'Hospitalet-du-Larzac (cf. **158**), which was discovered in a grave and targets a group of women (we do not know why the *defigens* wrote the curse). According to the text's editors, Adsagsona could possibly be the theonym of a chthonic deity, on the grounds that the curse contains the Gaulish word *autumnos* ('underworld').[516]

The British examples, which come from Ratae Corieltauvorum/Leicester and Lydney, mention Nodens and Maglus, respectively. The first, Nodens ('cloud-maker'), is a well-attested indigenous divinity of healing, whose sanctuary was built in Lydney Park in the third century CE.[517] Maglus, for his part, is invoked as a god (*deo*) in **456**; according to Tomlin (2008a: 208), this could be a theonym only attested here in the British Isles, which is derived from the Celtic root **maglos* ('prince').

Finally, we must turn to the four cases in which there is a joint invocation of indigenous and Graeco-Roman gods who are not connected through an *interpretatio*. So far, these instances hail from Britannia, Raetia and Pannonia.[518] The curse from Hamble (Britannia, cf. **451**), which was discovered in an estuary, invokes Neptune and Niskus. The latter appears to be an aquatic deity that has been connected to the Niskas mentioned in the curses from Amélie-les-Bains (cf. **150–51** and **154**). Unfortunately, so far there is no further evidence that has shed more light on this tantalizing parallel.

The curse from Siscia/Sisak (Pannonia, cf. **529**), which was found near a river, is a juridical *defixio*. The curse invokes the Roman goddess Muta Tacita together with the indigenous Savus. This was, no doubt, an effective pairing, since the first was meant to silence the victims,

while the second, who is the personification of the river in which the tablet was deposited, was meant to drown them. Lastly, the two remaining curses come from Raetia and contain the Celtic theonyms Ogmius and Moltinus. The first deity is found in a *defixio* from Brigantium/Bregenz (cf. **521**) alongside Dis Pater[519] and is analogous to the Graeco-Roman Hercules. Moltinus, for his part, is a Celtic god of cattle. He is invoked in the curse from Veldidena/Wilten (cf. **523**) together with Mercury and Cacus in order to catch a thief and recover the *defigens*' lost property, that is, a sum of money and several steers. Given the *defigens*' purposes, the invocation of Moltinus and Cacus seems apt.

8.4. Oriental powers

The third group of *numina* that are invoked in the *defixiones* consists of oriental deities like Cybele, Attis, Isis, Christ and the demon Abraxas (among others).[520] Such eastern cults began to arrive to Rome at the end of the third century BCE. The spread of these cults is well documented in a conspicuous group of curse tablets from all over the Roman West, which mostly date to the Imperial period.

Cybele, the first of the oriental deities to arrive to Rome around the year 205 BCE, is often found paired with Attis in the corpus of *defixiones*. She is, in fact, one of the most invoked deities, as can be seen in curses from Salacia/Alcácer do Sal (cf. **121**), Groß Gerau (cf. **482**), Centum Prata/Kempraten (cf. **518–19**) and Mogontiacum/Mainz, where 2 of the 34 *defixiones* explicitly mention the pair of Cybele and Attis (cf. **490** and **494**). As Gordon (2012a) has pointed out, these gods are invoked as avengers not so much because of their mythological background but rather due to their respective iconographies, which must have had a powerful impact on practitioners. Thus, the representations of Cybele in her chariot drawn by lions and of Attis with his Phrygian cap surrounded by stars were highly evocative. In the case of Magna Mater, her iconography was thought to represent her untiring ability to hunt down a curse's victims; in Attis' case, his cap was taken as a reference to his extraordinarily effective cosmic powers.

In contrast to Cybele and Attis, the rest of the above-mentioned oriental deities appear with much lesser frequency in the corpus of *defixiones* from the Roman West. Of these deities, the Egyptian Isis enjoyed a flourishing cult in Hispania during the High Empire. Nevertheless, there is only a single curse tablet from her sanctuary in Baelo Claudia/Bolonia (cf. **128**), in which the goddess is invoked with the epithet *muromem*.[521]

---

[515] Cf. Green 1997, *s.v.* 'Maponos'.

[516] For a concise discussion, cf. Lambert *apud RIG* II.2: L-98, p. 266.

[517] For an overview of this deity, see Green 1997, *s.v.* 'Nodens'. On certain occasions, Nodens is linked to Mars and Silvanus.

[518] In the Spanish version of this section (cf. Sánchez Natalías 2013b), I mistakenly added Hispania to this list, assuming that Salpina was a deity invoked in a curse tablet from Cordoba (cf. **122**). This had always been assumed since the *editio princeps* of the text (for the latest instance of this assumption, see Marco Simón 2013, with previous references). Nevertheless, as I realized shortly after, Salpina ought to be taken as the personal name of the curse's victim (cf. **122** and Sánchez Natalías 2014).

[519] Following the reconstruction proposed by Egger 1943.

[520] In the Spanish version of this section (cf. Sánchez Natalías 2013b), I wrongly added the Egyptian Seth, who was supposedly invoked in **24**, a container from the sanctuary of Anna Perenna in Rome. However, a re-examination of this short text (Sánchez Natalías 2020b) led to a stronger interpretation of the curse, in which the victims' name (and not the deities') can be read (cf. **24**).

[521] Which would be for *muronem*, derived from the epithet *Myronyma* (for a discussion, see Bonneville *et al.* 1988: 22, n. 4). In addition to the curse from Baelo Claudia/Bolonia, we must add the one found in the

In addition to Isis, we also find Abraxas, the cock-headed anguipede whose name (equivalent to the number 365) evoked cosmic totality. The earliest invocation to this deity comes in a second-century CE curse tablet from Autun (cf. **166**, Gallia Lugdunensis). The text, written in a mixture of Greek and Latin, contains a list of names together with a series of *voces magicae* and the name of Abraxas between two *charaktêres*. This curse's sophistication strongly suggests that it was written by a professional practitioner. This is also the case with a Late-Antique curse tablet from the sanctuary of Anna Perenna in Rome (cf. **30**), where Abraxas is invoked as a mediator between the practitioner and the deity who was supposed to harm the victim. In this same fountain, a series of containers have also been thought to contain a representation of Abraxas.[522] Nevertheless, and as argued above (cf. section I.4.2.2.1), this identification ought to be revised, given the absence of some characteristic iconographic features of Abraxas and the presence (on his abdomen) of the abbreviated Christian formula Ἰησοῦς Χριστός Ναζωραῖος, Ἰησοῦς Χριστός Ναζωραῖος, καὶ Θεός, Θεός, Θεός (cf. Németh 2012b and 2015). This formula, attested with slight variations on several containers (cf. **25–27** and **35–36**), is quite plausibly a way to identify or 'name' the figure, as happens in other instances (cf. Baitmo Arbitto, Figure 4.7). In other words, I think this could be a new and (doubtlessly surprising) representation of Christ. Whatever the case may be, Christ also seems to be invoked in a different curse tablet from this same findspot (cf. **31**, ll. 4–5), whose text reads: *deas vest[ra]s (...) et Christum nostrum*. Although the reading has proven difficult to decipher (see the different versions published by the editor) and I have been unable to confirm it from the published drawings, the sentence would point towards two different (but related) religious spheres: your (pagan) deities and our Christian ones. Therefore, whatever practitioners were active at the Fountain of Anna Perenna identify themselves as Christians, a characteristic which would certainly job with some other aspects of the artefacts that they produced.[523]

Last, but certainly not least, we must mention the North African curses from the High Empire, where there is a marked preference for invoking demons rather than deities. This tendency could be explained by the fact that the texts were mostly written by professional magical practitioners, who were trained (or at least influenced) by Graeco-Egyptian magical practices. In this magical tradition, such supernatural beings played a fundamental role, as is clearly attested in the *PGM*.

Among the most frequent invocations to demons, we find '*adiuro te demon*'[524] and '*demon quicumque est*',[525] which often appear alongside the formulae '*adiuro te demon quicumque est te demando*'.[526] Through these invocations, the practitioners directly addressed the deceased who occupied the spaces which would be used to deposit curses, either in the necropolis or in what might be the *spoliarium* of Carthage's amphitheatre.[527] In both of these contexts, we find examples of tablets in which the origin of these powers is linked to the underworld, which is hardly surprising.[528] However, in two Carthaginian curses, the texts specify that those demons who ought to execute the curse came from Egypt-Campania and Hispania-Africa, perhaps in an attempt to imbue the demons invoked with greater 'exoticism' (and power).[529] In an attempt to encourage the demons to act, these professionals could name them alongside certain divinities, such as *deus pelagicus* ('the god of the sea'), who is invoked in the well-known Baitmo Arbitto series.[530] Such a choice makes perfect sense, given that Baitmo is represented on top of a boat (cf. section I.4.2.2.1, Figure 4.7). In addition to the *deus pelagicus*, some tablets also invoke a *deus vivus omnipotens* (which could well be an early reference to Christianity)[531] or even the Jewish god Ιαω Σαβαωθ.[532]

---

sanctuary of Isis in Savaria/Szombathely (cf. **531**); although there is no written invocation in the curse, it seems probable that the goddess was invoked orally during its deposition.

[522] See section I.4.2.2.1 and n. 175. For his relationship with Anna Perenna, see Piranomonte and Marco Simón 2010: 11–13.

[523] To the already mentioned invocation of Christ on the containers (cf. **25–27** and **35–36**), we could also add the suggestive analogy between light and life pointed by Mastrocinque 2007 for the lamps whose wick was made of a curse tablet (cf. **19–20**, **30–31**).

[524] Cf. *DT* 248 (A, ll. 1–2), 250 (A, ll. 27–29), 290 (B, l. 1), etc. A variation on this formula is found in *DT* 233 (ll. 27–29): ...*excito [t]e demon qui <h>ic conversans*.

[525] Cf. *DT* 265 (B, ll. 5–7).

[526] Cf. *DT* 286 (B, ll. 1–2), 291 (A, ll. 3–7 and B, ll. 1–2), Audollent 1910 (B, ll. 1–2), etc.

[527] Cf. *DT* 251, col. I, l. 4, where the practitioner invokes the *anim(a)e (h)uius loci* (for this context, see section I. 6.5.3).

[528] Cf. *DT* 250 (A, ll. 28–29), 266 (ll. 2–3) and 295 (l. 11).

[529] Specifically, cf. *DT* 230 (an erotic curse found in a grave and dated to the second or third century CE, in which Καταξιν, Νοχθιριφ, Τραβαξιαν, Βιβιριξι and Ρικουπιθ are invoked) and *DT* 250 (an agonistic curse from the amphitheatre dated to the fourth century CE, in which the demons Βαχαχυχ, Ιεκρι, Νοκτουκιτ, Βυτυβαχκ as well as the *deus omnipotens* Παρπαξιν are invoked).

[530] Cf. *DT* 286, 290–91, 293 and Audollent 1910.

[531] Cf. *DT* 247, ll. 18-19, *DT* 248 (A, ll. 2–3, where we find mention of *deum vivum*) and 268, l. 4 (where *Persefina*, for Persefona, is invoked together with *de[um] me[um] vivum*).

[532] Cf. *DT* 286, 291, 293 and Audollent 1910. Ιαω is invoked on his own in *DT* 264. If we accept Corell's far from certain reading, this deity may also be attested in **143**.

Distribution of *Defixiones* in the Roman West[533]

9.1. Introduction

In Antiquity, curse tablets were a transferable magico-religious technology. As such, and together with other cultural innovations from the Graeco-Roman world, they travelled throughout the area that would come to be 'the Roman West'. Reconstructing exactly how this process unfolded has proven a rather difficult question, since the geographical diffusion and cultural adaptation of cursing rituals not only depend on individuals (both the professional 'magicians', whom Plato already mentioned, and individual practitioners who possessed enough know-how to make curse tablets),[534] but also on larger, more complex phenomena (e.g., Greek colonization or what scholars have traditionally called 'Romanization').[535]

To date, the oldest curse tablets from any part of the Mediterranean are the Greek texts from Sicily (largely from Morgantina and Selinunte). Leaving aside the thorny question of whether writing curse tablets was a Sicilian innovation or whether the practice came from the metropolis,[536] we say with certainty that the permeable practice of writing curses spread along Greek colonization routes to end up reaching other areas of the Mediterranean basin (such as the Italian and the Iberian peninsulas, and perhaps even to North Africa) and the Black Sea. Once taken up by the local communities, curse tablets were adopted and adapted to better serve the specific idiosyncrasies of each community. In certain cases, it was these very local populations that transmitted this magical-religious technology to the Romans.[537] Once entrenched within Roman social and religious culture, the habit of writing curse tablets slowly continued to be disseminated via the Roman army. In fact, military conquest and the establishment of new trade and communication routes unavoidably gave rise to new intercultural contact between various populations. The practice of writing curse tablets spread alongside other technological and cultural innovations between these communities. Here it is worth stressing how even a legally sanctioned practice like writing curses could spread slowly but relentlessly through areas that were in contact with Rome. Indeed, this is one of the more illicit and surreptitious facets of 'Romanization'.

In an attempt to depict the diffusion of this cultural practice throughout the Roman West, this section provides a geographical analysis of this cultural phenomenon.[538] With this purpose in mind, I rely on a series of maps which respect the provincial division and the *limes* from the High Empire.[539] Obviously, such divisions did not have the same importance or relevance in earlier historical periods. Nevertheless, I have decided to use them as a means of better organizing and guiding the following discussion. The corpus of curses has been divided into three different periods, each of which has its own map. These respect standard periodizations used in Roman History (Republic, High Empire and Late Antiquity).[540] In addition, there is a fourth map that contains an overall picture of the phenomenon across all periods. If there is only a single item from a site, the map includes the curse's number in the following sylloge. For sites that have yielded various tablets, it was often impossible to include all catalogue numbers; therefore, in those cases the map simply contains the site's name. More information about the number of curses from these sites can be found in the following pages and in the sylloge proper.

In the following pages, the dates used for curses are based on three different factors: the archaeological context, palaeography and linguistic features of each tablet. Given that *defixiones* were often 'intrusively' introduced in a particular site after other artefacts had already been deposited, archaeological context can often only provide a *terminus post quem*. Therefore, the 'internal characteristics' of each text (i.e., palaeography,[541] linguistics or, rarely, prosopography)[542] can provide a more concrete date, though it must be stressed that there has not always been scholarly consensus of the dating

---

[533] For a preliminary version of this section, see Sánchez Natalías 2012c. Urbanová 2018: 398–412 provides a series of maps whose aim is to underscore the differences and similarities between curses and 'prayer for justice' and their spread in the Roman West (both chronologically and in the case of curses, according also to content).

[534] On this, see section I.2.

[535] On the controversial term of 'Romanization', see Beltrán Lloris 2017.

[536] Cf. Curbera 1999a: 158f. and Vitellozzi 2019: 342.

[537] See section I.9.2.

[538] Greek curse tablets have not been included in this analysis. For their spread throughout the Roman West, see Sánchez Natalías 2019c.

[539] It must be stressed that the maps for Late Antiquity as well as the global one use provincial divisions from the reign of Diocletian with the Mauritaniae (Tingitana, Caesarense and Tabia), the Numidiae (Cirtensis and Militiana), Proconsularis Zeugitana and Byzacena.

[540] This is irrespective of the problems related to standard periodizations, as rightly pointed out by Flower (2008: 5–9).

[541] For an overarching analysis of the palaeography of the Latin *defixiones*, see Bartoletti 1990; additionally, see the studies of corpora from Aquae Sulis/Bath (cf. Tomlin 1988a: 84–94), Mogontiacum/Mainz (cf. Blänsdorf 2012a: 41–47) as well as the so-called 'Sethian' *defixiones* from Rome (cf. Wünsch 1898: 53–56). There are other important studies of smaller groups of *defixiones*, such as 10–14 (cf. Fox 1912a: 51–55, plate VIII), or even single tablets, such as 16 (cf. Muzzioli 1939: 47f., Tav. II) or 132 (cf. García Dils de la Vega *et al.* 2013: 247–48), among others.

[542] The appearance of specific formulae as well as the (very rare) mention of well-known victims allow us to determine a curse's date more securely; a small group of curses from Emporion (cf. 134–36), in which the local authorities are cursed, provide the best example of this. For the use of formulae to date texts from the sanctuary of Sulis Minerva, see Tomlin 1988a: 73f.; for further references, see section I.4.3.

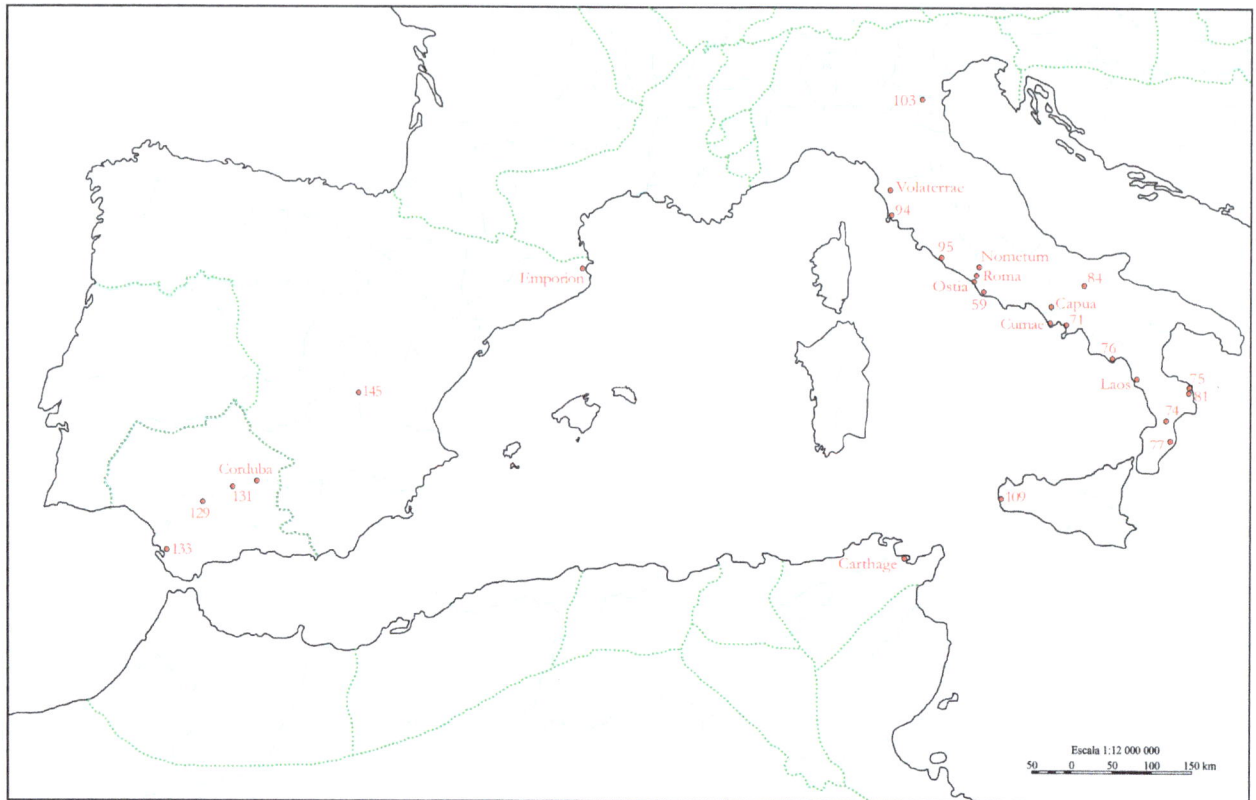

Figure 9.1. Defixiones dating to the Republican period.

of certain palaeographical features. Given the scarce evidence and unavoidable role of (at times subjective) scholarly judgement, in many cases proposed dates fall within a rather wide range that cannot always be limited to a single century (e.g., 'from the High Empire between the first and third centuries CE'). The limitations concerning what we can say in good faith about a *defixio*'s date, of course, greatly complicate the present task.

Finally, curse tablets with an unknown provenance have not been included in the maps, though they are included in the overall numbers used throughout this section.[543] In addition, all of the *defixiones* that cannot be dated have been included in a final map which seeks to give a full picture of the spread and distribution of cursing practices throughout the Roman West.

9.2. Distribution of *defixiones* during the Republic

The oldest evidence for cursing in Latin comes from Rome's first legal code, the *XII Tables*, which were written in the mid-fifth century BCE. Tablet VIII threatens to punish *qui malum carmen incantassit*, that is, 'whoever casts a magic spell'.[544] This legal prohibition undoubtedly provides evidence for cursing practices that have not been

preserved in the archaeological record, since, as the verb *incantassit* implies, these appear to have been oral curses. In addition, two additional laws from Tablet VIII further suggest that magical-religious practices primarily took the form of oral speech acts in the fifth-century Rome. The first one reads, *si quis occentavisset sive carmen condidisset, quod infamiam faceret flagitiumue alteri* ('if anyone had "sung in enmity", that is, composed a song which would bring infamy or disgrace on someone else') and alludes to the slandering of a rival.[545] The second law reads *qui fruges excantassit* ('whoever has bewitched fruits')[546] and alludes to a magical damage to the harvest and hence by extension to the owner's wealth. In short, the lexemes employed in the law (*carmen, incantassit, occentavisset* and *excantassit*) stress orality. Importantly, this contrasts with contemporary Greek tablets discovered in Sicily in which the cursing verbs refer to writing (γράφω and its compounds: καταγράφω, ἐνγράφω, ἐγκαταγράφω) and not speaking, as Poccetti has shown (2005 and 2015: 378–82).[547]

If we turn to the archaeological record, the earliest curses were written in Greek and were found in Sicily, though, as said before, these curses will not be discussed here. The map clearly shows that the first non-Greek curse tablets were Oscan and found on the Italian Peninsula, dating to the fourth century BCE (see Figure 9.1). These artefacts, which must be understood as arising from the

---

[543] These curses hail from Italy (cf. **16** [all we know is that it was donated to the Museo Nazionale Romano in the 1930s (see Muzzioli 1939: 42)], **112** and **116–19**), Hispania (cf. **149**), Britannia (cf. **459–60**) and Pannonia (cf. **535**).

[544] *XII Tables* VIII, 1a. Translation by Crawford 1996. On this (and the two following references), see Rives 2002 and 2003.

[545] *XII Tables* VIII, 1c. Translation by Crawford 1996.
[546] *XII Tables* VIII, 4. Translation by Crawford 1996.
[547] Cf. also Chiarini 2019.

cultural interaction between Greeks and Oscans, hail from the sites of Roccagloriosa (cf. **76**), Castiglione di Paludi (cf. **77**), Crimisa/Cirò Marina (cf. **75**) and Tiriolo (cf. **74**). To this list of tablets, we must add a curse tablet from Capua (cf. **68**), three from Laos/Marcellina (cf. **78–80**) and another from Petelia/Strongoli (cf. **81**), all of which date to the fourth or third century BCE. Interestingly, all these settlements are located near the sea (either the Ionian or Tyrrhenian), which meant that they were easily accessible to Greek traders. In fact, Eubeans, Phocaeans, Aecheans and Dorians all turned the area stretching from the Gulf of Naples to Calabria into a zone of Greek influence and colonization (Poccetti 2015: 384f.).

Thus, the concentration of curses in the above-mentioned settlements must be understood in light of their deep connections to the Hellenic world: Greek colonization in Magna Graecia left its imprint on magical practices throughout southern Italy.[548] Indeed, this imprint is especially discernible in a curse from Petelia/Strongoli (cf. **81**) which contains a rather peculiar mix of Greek and Oscan. The text, which was written in both languages, contains a list of names in which the nominative forms reflect Oscan morphology, while the genitive forms use Doric Greek endings. In addition, the cursing formula placed at the end of the text was written in both languages (although it is not a translation *sensu stricto*).

By the third century BCE, at least four new curses can be added to the earliest *defixiones* from the Italian Peninsula. In fact, we not only find curses in a broader geographic area, but also in new cultural contexts, such as Samnium, Sicily (where, of course, there were already Greek curse tablets), Etruria and North Africa. More specifically, these third-century tablets include an Oscan tablet from Aquilonia/ Monte Vairano (cf. **84**), a curse written in both Latin and Greek from Lilybaeum/Marsala (cf. **109**), an Etruscan text from Aquae Populoniae/Campiglia Marittima (cf. **94**) and two Phoenician curses from Carthage. The Phoenician curses were discovered in the necropoleis of Bir ez-Zeitun and Douïmes (cf. *DT* 213–14, both found at the end of the nineteenth century). Unfortunately, the poor condition of the first tablet has prevented scholars from offering a reading or a date of the text.[549] The second curse, however, is in much better shape and has given way to a stimulating discussion about the origin of cursing rituals in North Africa. Indeed, recent studies have proffered a series of competing theories: while Faraone and other scholars have argued that this tablet is an instance of a 'prayer for

justice', a genre that has its origins in the Near East,[550] Amadasi has claimed that the tablet actually betrays Hellenic influences on the grounds that there is a probable invocation of Persephone and the presence of formulae that are paralleled in the Attic corpus of *defixiones*.[551] The latter hypothesis strikes me as the more probable, given that Amadasi's argument reflects the spreading of curse tablets from Sicily to other territories, such as the Iberian or the Italian peninsulae, mapping onto larger patterns of commerce and colonization.

If we return to Italy, the oldest lead curse tablet written in Latin dates to the second century BCE and does not come from Rome, but rather Pompeii (cf. **71**). Accordingly, this find spot brings us back to the gulf of Naples, a zone that was obviously under Greek influence. Due to the well attested use of *defixiones* and the similarities between certain formulae, Poccetti has argued that the early Latin-language curses should be closely linked to the Oscan world.[552] During the second century BCE, however, we begin to find new Latin curses further north in Ostia (cf. **52**) and Caere/Cerveteri (cf. **95**). Both of these curses were found in a necropolis, and they share the same structure: a simple list of the victims' names.[553] To these Latin texts we should add three Etruscan curse tablets from Volaterrae/ Volterra (cf. **88–90**), which were found at the entrance of a hypogeum. According to Massarelli (2014: 185 and 195, n. 5), the texts were written in the type II alphabet from Maggiani's typology, which, together with certain prosopographical features, allows us to date the texts in the second century BCE.

Together with these examples of rather abbreviated and curt curses, there are eight known *defixiones* from Rome that date to the first century BCE (cf. **1–3** and **10–14**). These texts differ markedly from the earlier Latin curses: not only are the texts longer, but they also contain complex formulae and invoke a different set of deities. A good example of this is found in the famous five curses that are now housed at Johns Hopkins University (cf. **10–14**): written, in all likelihood, by a single practitioner, these texts share extremely similar formulae and all invoke Proserpina, Pluto and Cerberus. But Rome is not the only site that evidences an increased use of *defixiones*: also from Latium, there is a set of three curses that were found

[548] On this, see Poccetti 2015: 383–86 (with previous references) and more recently Vitellozzi 2019. Both authors explore the similarities between the Oscan and the Greek texts. In addition to these, see also McDonald (2015: 137–49), who elucidated the influence of Greek speakers from Sicily (and abroad) on the Oscan texts. For an in-depth analysis of the Oscan texts, see Murano 2013.
[549] Cf. *DT* 214. On this tablet, Clermont-Ganneau has claimed (*apud DT* 214): 'Le P. Delattre a aussi découvert récemment, à Carthage, une tabella devotionis avec inscription phénicienne; mais elle est dans un tel état de mutilation que l'étude n'en a pas encore été possible, les fragments s'effritant au moindre contact.'
[550] Cf. Faraone, Garnand and López-Ruiz 2005: 169 and 180ff.
[551] Amadasi Guzzo 2003: 25–31, esp. 31, where the author concludes 'il formulario di questa tavoletta si discosta dalle maledizioni note in ambito semitico di nord-ovest, per avvicinarsi invece ai formulari greci. L'iscrizione è stata messa in rapporto con le tabelle attiche (…) Se davvero la dea invocata è Persefone, il cui culto è stato introdotto a Cartagine dalla Sicilia, si potrebbe proporre che anche l'uso di deporre scongiuri in piombo nelle tombe (...) sia entrato a Cartagine —come il culto di Demetra e Kore— dal territorio siciliano di cultura greca'.
[552] Cf. Poccetti 1993d: 73–96, esp. p. 80; Poccetti 1999: 545–61, esp. p. 555, where he stresses, 'La diffusione della scrittura di maledizioni su lamine plumbee nel mondo romano non avviene prima della fine dell'età repubblicana e probabilmente per mediazione osca: non casualmente le prime *tabellae defixionis* latine appaiono in ambienti di stretto rapporto con gli italici (Campania e Delo) e riportano formulari comuni a quelle osche.' On the earliest Latin curses from the Italian peninsula, see Bevilacqua 2017 and Vitellozzi 2019: 354–56.
[553] For a discussion, see section I.4.3.

within a cinerary urn in Nomentum/Mentana (cf. **49–51**); further south in Campania, there is also a collection from Cumae (cf. **62–65**), which were written either in Latin or Oscan and are largely judicial in nature. To this list of first century texts, we should also add another tablet from Capua (cf. **66**). Finally, further north in Ateste/Este (cf. **103**) another Latin-language curse containing an invocation to Proserpina, Pluto, Cerberus and his two-headed brother Orthus has been found in a necropolis (probably a judicial *defixio*).

During the first century BCE, we also see that the practice of writing curses spread outside Italy. In the Iberian Peninsula, important cities like Emporion, Carmo/Carmona and Corduba/Cordoba have turned up important evidence.[554] In ancient Emporion, which was founded by colonists from Phocaea around 600 BCE and served as Rome's entrance to the peninsula (Gn. Scipio disembarked there in 218 BCE and began his conquest), we find the largest collection of *defixiones* from Hispania: of the eight curse tablets from this site,[555] one dates from the first century BCE (cf. **137**). In the Republican period, ancient Carmo was one of the principal cities of Ulterior Baetica, of which Corduba became the capital when the province was created. There is one tablet from the former site (cf. **129**) and two from the latter (cf. **125–26**). Like the tablet from Emporion, these two are juridical in nature. To these texts, we should also add the one from El Portal (cf. **133**), discovered under unknown circumstances and the text of which consists of a list of names. Although the curse's editor has dated the tablet between the second half of the second century BCE and the beginning of the first century BCE (which would make of this *defixio* the oldest Latin curse tablet from the Iberian Peninsula), the palaeographical features of the text (similar to **129** or **131**) more likely point to a first-century BCE date.

Of the seven curses dated to either to first century BCE or CE, six of them come from Hispania.[556] Three of these texts were found in Corduba/Cordoba (cf. **122–24**) and one in Emporion (cf. **139**). The Corduba/Cordoba curses, all of which were found in the same necropolis, were written for unknown purposes (two of them consists of mere lists of names [cf. **123–24**] while the third [cf. **122**] consigns its victim to the underworld deities). Another tablet comes from Celti/Peñaflor (cf. **131**) and seeks to silence its victim. The sixth curse from Hispania is a unique bilingual lead tablet written in Greek and Latin that was deposited in an abandoned Iberian settlement near Barchín del Hoyo (cf. **145**). Finally, from Italy there is a text discovered in the

remains of a necropolis at Antium/Anzio (cf. **59**), which merely contains the victim's name.

By way of conclusion, and irrespective of the questions about where the practice of writing curse tablets first originated (i.e., probably in Sicily, as the archaeological record has demonstrated so far), it seems clear that the spread of the practice of inscribing curses is best explained as the result Greek cultural influence. In an initial stage, this practice clustered in southern Italy amongst the Oscan settlements and subsequently spread to other Latin and Etruscan communities in the Peninsula. In the second and first centuries BCE, the practice of writing *defixiones* spread beyond the Italian Peninsula, reaching not only the principal cities of the Iberian Peninsula but also Carthage in North Africa.

9.3. *Defixiones* from the High Empire

As part of the hidden side of the 'Roman epigraphic habit',[557] the practice of inscribing curse tablets exploded during the High Empire. The numbers speak for themselves: of the whole corpus, more than a half of known curse tablets have been dated between the first and third centuries CE. Even if curse tablets have nothing to do with the monumentalization of writing or with the growing interests in self-representation, the proliferation of these 'testi privatissimi'[558] provides a window onto practitioners' innermost worries and concerns. The processes of 'Romanization' coupled with the greater diffusion of writing led to a sharp rise in creation of curses. In fact, and as the following map demonstrates, this tendency is attested in all of the empire's provinces (see Figure 9.2).

In the first century CE, we see two main nuclei for the production of *defixiones*: Italy and North Africa. In the Italian Peninsula, the largest concentration of texts comes from the areas located between Picenum and Bruttium et Lucania: two-thirds of the known curses were found between Urbs Salvia/Urbisaglia (cf. **86**) and Copia Thurii/Sybaris (cf. **82**).[559] Further north, there is a tablet from Altinum/Altino (cf. **104**) and another from Verona (cf. **107**), while outside of the peninsula other texts were found on Sardinia (Orosei, cf. **110–11**) and Corsica (Mariana/Lucciana, cf. **115**). If we turn to North Africa, Carthage emerges as the focal point with over 30 tablets,[560] though there is also a curse from Hadrumetum (*DT* 304). Turning to the Iberian peninsula, in Hispania Citerior there are four tablets from Emporion (cf. **134–36** and **138**) and another

---

[554] See Marco Simón 2019 for a discussion of the spread of curse tablets in the Iberian Peninsula. The author examines not only the first Greek and Latin texts, but also a dozen Iberian texts that (despite problems with the language) could be identified as *defixiones*.

[555] Two of the eight tablets are in Greek (dated to the end of the fourth or beginning of the third century BCE), while the other six are in Latin (cf. **134–39**). To these we must add two new *defixiones* still under study (see the notice for Emporion in the introduction to Hispania, cf. section II.2).

[556] Although these tablets could be included in either the Republican or High Empire map, I have chosen the former to make the maps more legible.

[557] On this concept, coined by MacMullen (1982), see Beltrán Lloris 2014b.

[558] Cf. Palumbo in Bettarini 2005: VI.

[559] Here I am referring to the curses from Rome (cf. **17** and **48**), Antium/Anzio (cf. **60**), Cumae (cf. **61** and **64**), Cales/Calvi Risorta (cf. **70**), Marsi Marruvium/San Benedetto (cf. **83**) and Septempeda/San Severino (cf. **85**). Also add two tablets from *loca incerta* (cf. **116** and **119**).

[560] For all African *defixiones*, I have followed the date given by each curse's editor. It is worth stressing that there has been debate over the dates and I have not been able to examine all the texts in person. See *DT* 215–30; 232; 233; 243; 244; 247–51; 253; 254; 258–61; 303.

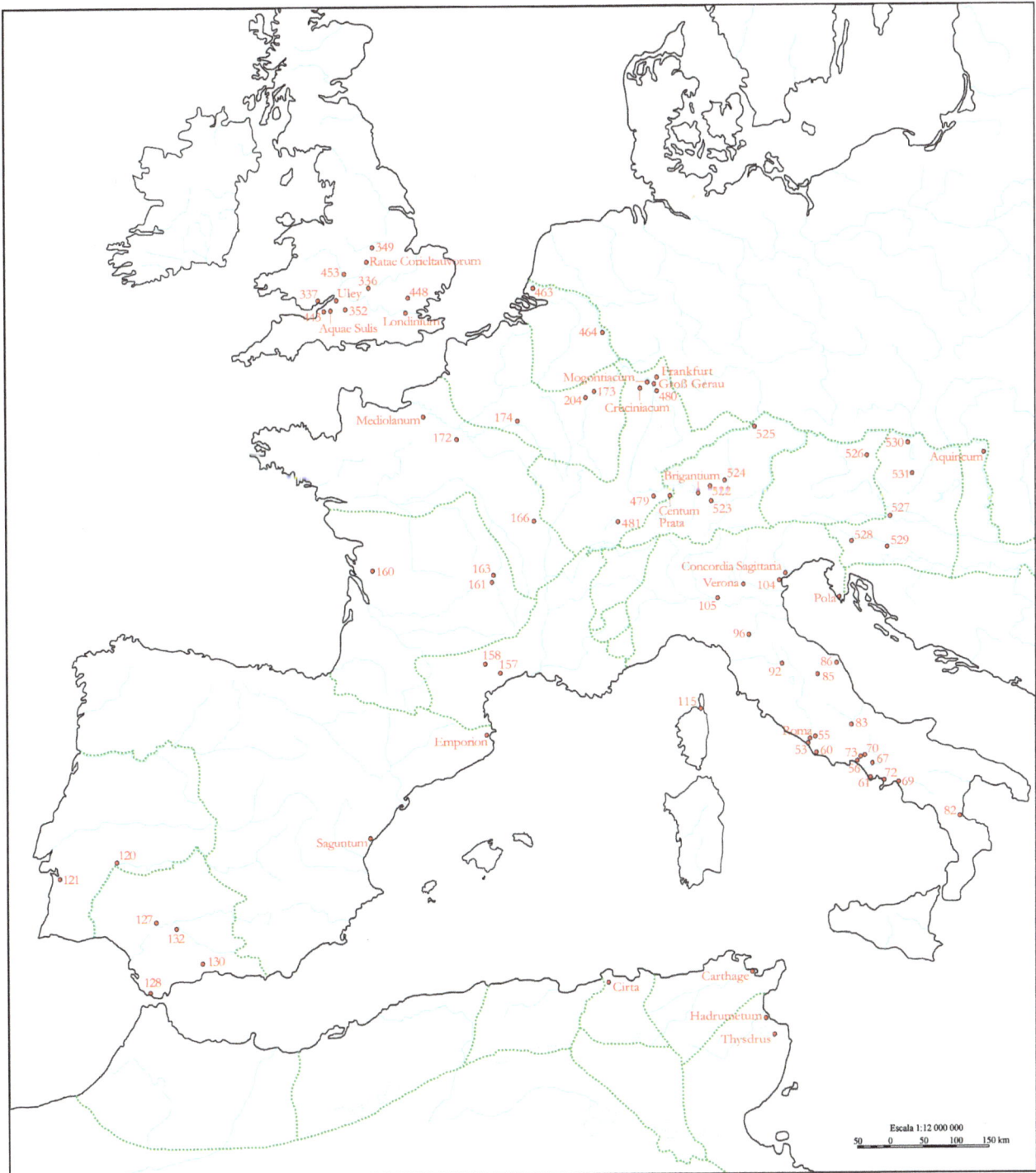

Figure 9.2. Distribution of defixiones during the High Empire.

from Saguntum/Sagunto (cf. **144**).[561] In Hispania Baetica, there is an interesting curse from Salacia/Alcácer do Sal (cf. **121**) which was written in response to a theft, and also an agonistic curse tablet from Astigi/Écija (cf. **132**).

In the same century, however, the practice of inscribing curses also moved north to Germania (Colonia/Cologne, cf. **464**; Cruciniacum/Bad Kreuznach, cf. **466–70**, **473–74**, **476** and Groß Gerau, cf. **483**), Gallia (Montfo, Arverni/

Chamalières and Autricum/Chartres, cf. **157**, **163** and **172** respectively), Britannia (London, cf. **338**) and Raetia (Brigantium/Bregenz, cf. **520**, Cambodunum/Kempten, cf. **522** and Veldidena/Wilten, cf. **523**). The majority of the tablets from this period should be classified as juridical.

Between the first and second centuries CE, Germania Superior stands out due to the impressive collection discovered at the sanctuary of Isis and Magna Mater (Mogontiacum/Mainz), where 34 *defixiones* dating to this period were found (cf. **487–517**). In connection with the Mainz collection, we should point again out Cruciniacum/

---

[561] To which we should add a *defixio* that was not inscribed (cf. the notice for Saguntum in the introduction to Hispania, section II.2).

Bad Kreuznach (cf. **471** and **475**), Groß Gerau (cf. **482**), Bodegraven (cf. **463**) and Waldmössingen (cf. **479**), where curses with a similar chronology have been discovered. If we turn to Britannia, there are four tablets that date to the first and second centuries CE that were discovered in London (cf. **342**), Isca Silurum/Caerleon (cf. **337**), Wanborough (cf. **352**) and Uley (cf. **369**). The last of these British texts deserves special mention, since it is the earliest representative of what would become the dominant trend in the province: depositing curses in sanctuaries. Finally, within this period, we have three tablets from Italy (from Tibur/Tivoli, cf. **55**; Pompeii, cf. **72** and Cremona, cf. **105**), five from Hispania (Aratispi/ Villanueva del Cauche, cf. **130**; Emporion, cf. **138** and Saguntum/Sagunto, cf. **140**, **142–43**),[562] two Gaulish examples from the Gallia (L'Hospitalet-du-Larzac, cf. **158** and Les Martres-de-Veyre, cf. **161**), one from Raetia (Brigantium/Bregenz, cf. **521**) and three from Pannonia (Emona/Ljubjlana, cf. **528**; Sisak, cf. **529** and Savaria/Szombathely, cf. **531**).

In the second century, we see an uptick in number of *defixiones* found in the provinces bordering the Mediterranean, especially in Hadrumetum,[563] the site from which nearly half of the known second-century CE curses come. Furthermore, the manufacture of curses is widely attested in Italy, from Regio X (Venetia et Histria) to Campania.[564] In Hispania, the four tablets dated to the second century share two main characteristics: they are all juridical and all hail from the southern half of the peninsula.[565] In addition, there are sporadic finds in the Gallia,[566] Germania,[567] Britannia[568] and Pannonia Superior,[569] most of which can also be classified as juridical.

Dating to the end of the second century through to the third century, there are two large caches of curses from Britannia, one from the sanctuary of Sulis Minerva (Aquae Sulis/Bath) and the other from the sanctuary of Mercury (Uley).[570] Between these two sites, there are over a hundred tablets dated to this period, the majority of which are *defixiones in fures*. So far, between the curses from

these sanctuaries and other isolated discoveries, Britannia quantitatively stands out as the most prolific province from the end of the second century through the third. Outside of Britain, the most noteworthy epicentre for the production of curses is found in Hadrumetum,[571] with 17 examples. The other North African sites that have yielded curses in this period are Thysdrus/El Jem,[572] Carthage[573] and Cirta/ Constantine.[574] Most of these curses are agonistic or erotic, and in contrast with the ones from Britain, were written by professional practitioners. In the rest of the Roman West during this period, there are only a few isolated *defixiones* with no discernible common characteristics. There are 5 tablets from Italy[575] as well as another 12 spread between the Gallia (Durocortorum/Reims and Wolberg, cf. **174** and **204** respectively), Germania (Aventicum/ Avenches, cf. **481** and Centum Prata/Kempraten, cf. **520**), Raetia (Peiting, cf. **524** and Abusina/Eining, cf. **525**), Noricum (Faviana/Mautern, cf. **526**) and Pannonia (from Carnuntum/Petronell, Aquincum/Budapest and *locus incertus*, cf. **530**, **532–34** and **535** respectively).

By way of conclusion, we can say that during the High Empire the increased production of curse tablets provides evidence for both a 'subaltern' facet of the 'Roman epigraphic habit' as well as demonstrating the geographical diffusion of this cultural practice through the process of 'Romanization'. Key factors in this phenomenon include the diffusion of literacy and the spread of basic knowledge about how to write a curse. To understand the extent to which locals took up and actively adopted the technology of cursing, we need look no further than onomastics, which reflects local epigraphy and provides substantial evidence for indigenous deities.[576] Even though this cultural practice expanded to every corner of the Roman world, we must acknowledge that five nuclei loom large in the existing evidence. Thus, we have the large collections from the sanctuaries in Aquae Sulis/Bath, Uley and Mogontiacum/ Mainz, where the practitioners wrote their own texts and seem to have been especially preoccupied with matters related to justice. In contrast, the collections from Carthage

---

[562] To these, we should add a curse of unknown provenance, cf. **149**.

[563] There are 18 *defixiones* from Hadrumetum: *DT* 266, 267, 270, 272–84; *AE*, 1907, 68–69.

[564] I am referring to the curses from Pola/Pula (cf. **101–02**), Verona (cf. **108**), Arretium/Arezzo (cf. **92**), Ostia (cf. **53**), Rome (cf. **15**), Minturnae/ Minturno (cf. **56**), Salernum/Salerno (cf. **69**) and Aquinum/Aquino (cf. **73**) which adds up to a total of nine tablets.

[565] Cf. Emerita Augusta/Merida (cf. **120**), Italica/Santiponce (cf. **127**), Baelo Claudia/Bolonia (cf. **128**) and Saguntum (cf. **141**).

[566] This is the case for the tablets from Mediolanum Santonum/ Villepouge-Chagnon (cf. **160**), Autun (cf. **166**), Mediolanum/Evreux (cf. **167–70**) and Maar (cf. **173**).

[567] Frankfurt (cf. **478**), Roßdorf (cf. **480**) and Centum Prata/Kempraten (cf. **519**).

[568] Specifically, a curse from London (cf. **339**), three from Aquae Sulis/ Bath (cf. **206**, **215** and **235**) and three from Uley (cf. **357–58** and **361**).

[569] Cf. **527**, from Poetovio/Ptuj.

[570] There are 52 *defixiones* from Aquae Sulis/Bath (**213–14**, **233–34**, **236–68** and **272–86**), while there are 56 from Uley (cf. **354–55**, **359**, **364–67**, **370**, **372–73** and **386–431**). To these, we must add the curses from Dodford (cf. **453**), London (cf. **343**), Chesterton-on-Fosse (cf. **336**), Ratae Corieltauvorum/Leicester (cf. **456–57**), Puckeridge-Braughing (cf. **448**) and two items from *loca incerta* (cf. **459–60**). Two more curses, from Ratcliffe-on-Soar (cf. **349**) and Pagans Hill (cf. **443**), date to the third century.

[571] There are 18 curses from Hadrumetum; for a discussion, see *DT* 263–65, 268, 269, 286–95, 297, Audollent 1910: 142–48 and Audollent 1930.

[572] See Foucher 2000.

[573] There are seven from Carthage (cf. *DT* 255; Audollent 1933b; Jordan 1996: 115–23 and Jordan 1988: 129ff.).

[574] *CIL* VIII, 19525. The date of this text ought to be reconsidered and placed in the fourth century CE given the palaeographical features of the text, which seems to be written in new Roman cursive. Such a proposal ought to be supported with an autopsy.

[575] Specifically, Concordia Sagittaria/Concordia (cf. **99–100**), Fontanaccia (cf. **96**), Verona (cf. **106**), Neapolis/Terralba (cf. **113**).

[576] There are many examples that are quite varied. Some texts betray linguistic syncretism, such as those in which there is a mixture of Celtic and Latin (cf. **219**, **223**, **453**) or Gaulish and Latin (cf. **159** and **163**). As far as onomastics go, in Britannia there are many examples of indigenous personal names as can be seen in tablets such as (cf. **235**, **258**, **266**, etc.; for a discussion, see Mullen 2007). A similar phenomenon can be detected in the Graeco-Oscan curses from south Italy (e.g., **76**, **78**, **81**). The invocation of indigenous deities, whom some practitioners may have considered more 'reliable', also merits mention. They include (but are not limited to) Maglus (cf. **456**), Nodens (cf. **205**), Ataecina Turibrigensis Proserpina (cf. **120**), Savus (cf. **529**) and Adsagsona (**158**). In my view, the evidence for such a wide array of local gods attests to local populations' willingness to take up the magical praxis of inscribing *defixiones* (for a discussion, see section I.8.3 and Marco Simón 2010d).

and Hadrumetum are largely agonistic and were written by local experts. Throughout the rest of the empire, there is a substantial number of curses spanning the Roman West from Salacia/Alcácer do Sal (cf. **121**) all the way to Agri decumates (cf. **477**, **482–83**, etc.). The wide geographical distribution of these tablets reflects the importance with which provincial societies invested the practice of writing *defixiones*. Furthermore, the different ways in which curses were used in particular local contexts attests to the flexibility of this religious-magical technology for addressing specific needs, concerns and anxieties.

9.4. *Defixiones* during Late Antiquity

As the following map clearly shows (see Figure 9.3), to date, the archaeological record has not provided widespread evidence for the use of *defixiones* in many provinces during Late Antiquity. This seems to be a continuation of a trend already initiated in the final decades of the third century BCE.

In general, the few examples that we do have for this period are either scattered throughout isolated sites

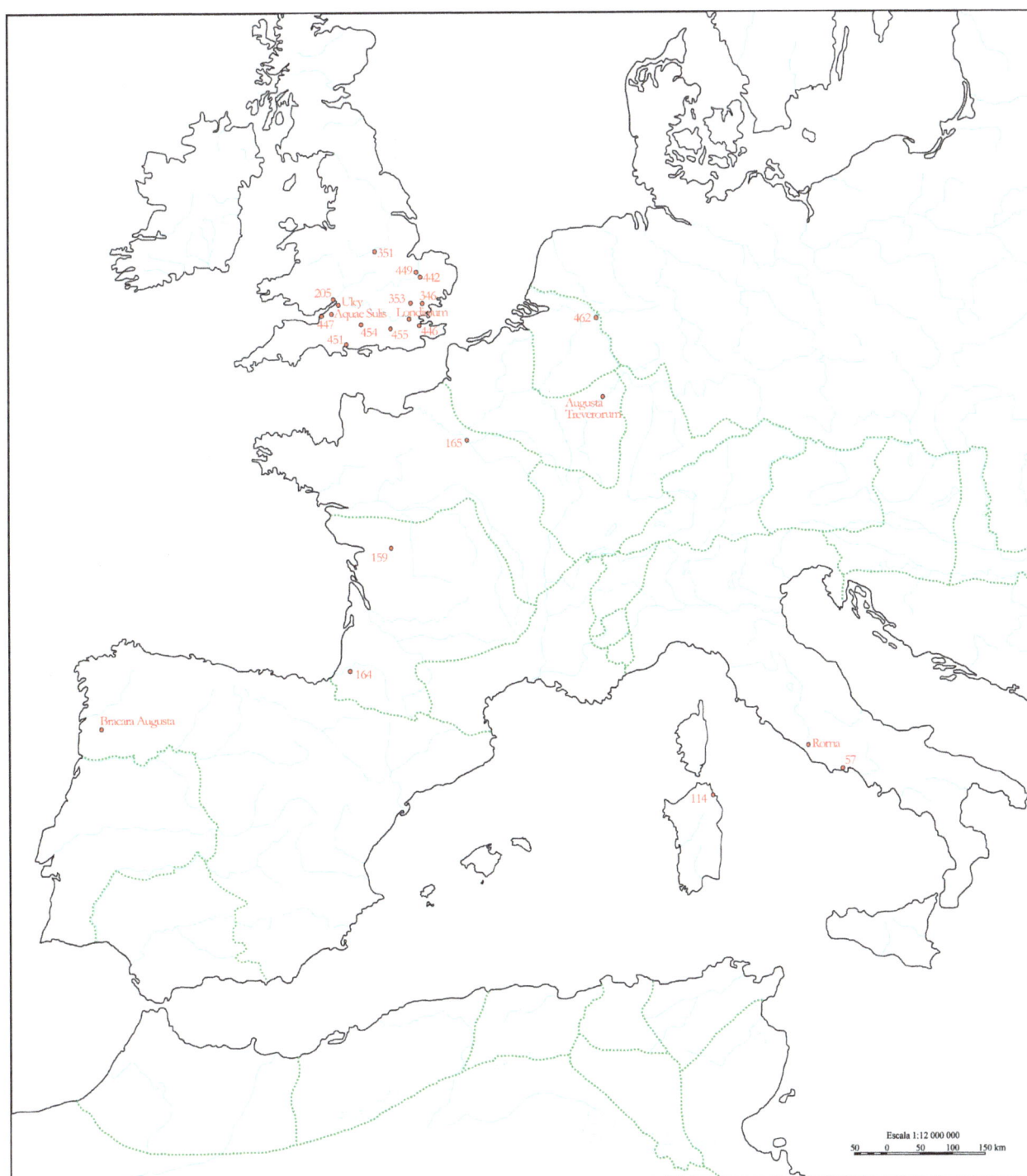

Figure 9.3. Distribution of defixiones during Late Antiquity.

or concentrated in important urban centres. While the evidence for the use of *defixiones* in Hispania, Germania, Raetia, Noricum and Pannonia is quite scarce, we do have good evidence for the continued popularity of this magical practice in other sites.

From the third to the fourth centuries CE, Britain provides a clear exception to the general trend due to the numerous finds from the sanctuaries of Sulis Minerva (Aquae Sulis/ Bath: cf. **210**, **269–71**, etc.) and Mercury (Uley: cf. **356**, **360**, **362**, etc.) as well as another 12 tablets in the southern third of Great Britain, which were discovered in the vicinity of the aforementioned sanctuaries and ancient Londinium.[577]

The Gaulish tablet from Rauranum/Rom (cf. **159**) also dates to between the end of the third century and the beginning of the fourth century CE. This curse was found in a well together with 40 tablets that apparently were not inscribed. As mentioned elsewhere, the fact that they were found together would suggest that these were also curse tablets and that other (possibly illiterate) practitioners were using the same space for conducting similar magical-religious practices.

One of the most important collections from Rome has been dated to the fourth century: the so-called 'Sethian' *defixiones*, which were discovered at the end of the nineteenth century in a columbarium near Porta San Sebastiano. This cache includes 5 Latin texts (cf. **5–9**) together with some 43 Greek tablets (cf. Wünsch 1898: *SV* 6-48). To this collection, which was written by several professional magical practitioners, we should also add another curse from the *urbs*: a tablet, which contains a list of *charaktêres*, was found together with an agonistic Greek curse tablet in a columbarium located at Villa Doria Pamphili (cf. **18**).

Another extraordinary collection (probably written by professional practitioners), dating from the beginning of the fourth century to the fifth century CE, has been unearthed in Rome. The cache was discovered in the fountain of Anna Perenna (cf. **19–47**), where curses were not only written on lead and copper sheets (sometimes inserted in lamps as if they were wicks) but also on small lead containers. In addition to this exceptional cache, we have to add the so-called 'Bologna' curse tablets, whose provenance is unknown and also appear to be the work of a professional magical practitioner (cf. **117–18**).

Outside of the Italian Peninsula, there is another important collection from Augusta Treverorum/Trier (Gallia Belgica, cf. **175–202**) that was discovered in the city's amphitheatre and contains 30 lead tablets dated to either the fourth or fifth century. From around the same time, Gaul has turned up two other isolated discoveries from

Aquae Tarbelliacae/Dax and Lutetia/Paris (cf. **164** and **165**, respectively). In addition to these, there are also two curses from Hispania (Bracara Augusta/Braga, cf. **146–47**) and one from Germania (Gelduba/Krefeld-Gellep, cf. **462**) that date to the fourth or fifth century. So far, there is only one *defixio* that has been securely dated to the fifth century, an extremely fragmentary tablet from Giuncalzu (Sardinia, cf. **114**). A curse from Fundi/Fondi (cf. **57**), which was discovered in the Grotto of Tiberius and was written by a practitioner who knew the Bible well, has been dated to the sixth century.

Despite some notable exceptions, we can generally say that the archaeological record shows the diminishing popularity of writing curses throughout Late Antiquity. Indeed, besides the fervent activity attested at the sanctuaries of Sulis Minerva, Mercury and Anna Perenna, as well as at Porta San Sebastiano and Trier's amphitheatre, finds from the rest of the Roman West are few and far between. These larger caches can be both multi- or single-authored. At the same time when individual practitioners who had baseline knowledge of cursing practices were writing their own texts (as can be clearly seen in Britannia), there were also professional practitioners offering their services in places like Rome, where tablets betray Graeco-Egyptian innovations (e.g., the use of iconography, *charaktêres* or *voces magicae*).

Although there is an argument to be made that the spread of Christianity and the persecution of magical practices were behind the waning use of *defixiones* in the Roman West (cf. Dickie 2001: 242–62), we should be careful not to generalize. Indeed, and even if cursing was prohibited by the law since (at least) the time of the *XII Tables*, yet these legal proscriptions were unable to halt the rising popularity of *defixiones* across the Roman West and their extreme success in specific cities, settlements and sanctuaries. Given the fragmentary state of our knowledge, it is hard to identify other variables that could have led to this change: perhaps in certain areas of the Roman West, cursing became more of an institutionalized practice (rather than a DIY one)? Maybe practitioners continued cursing but stopped using lead and opted instead for perishable materials that left no trace in the archaeological record? Was there a shift in social perception of how these tablets worked or even if they were actually effective? In addition to these potential factors, 'chance' could be also a key factor. As the incredible discoveries of *defixiones* in Britannia, Germania and Italia have shown over the last decades, with a little 'luck' a single excavation can reveal a new trove of tablets from any period of time and radically shift our understanding of the waxing and waning of this cultural practice.[578]

9.5. Overall distribution of *defixiones* in the Roman West

In addition to the period-specific maps found in the previous section, we must take a more general view of

---

[577] Here I am referring to the curses from Brean Down (cf. **447**), Hamble (cf. **451**), Farley Heath (cf. **455**), Calleva Atrebatum/Silchester (cf. **454**), London (cf. **341**), Eccles (cf. **446**), Old Harlow (cf. **353**), Canonium/ Kelvedon (cf. **346**), Thetford (cf. **442**), Brandon (cf. **449**), Ratcliffe-on-Soar (cf. **351**) and Lydney (cf. **205**).

[578] On this, see Tomlin 2010: 270, where he compares the evolution of the discoveries from Britannia and Hispania.

Figure 9.4. Distribution of defixiones in the Roman West.

the distribution of the corpus throughout the Roman West. With this goal in mind, the following map (see Figure 9.4) brings together the curses discussed in the previous sections as well as the tablets that cannot be dated.[579] For a variety of reasons, these tablets constitute nearly 20 per

cent of the whole sylloge. Nevertheless, we can distinguish three clear phases.

In the first phase, which stretches from the Republic until the reign of Augustus, we can see that the origin of this praxis is closely linked to the Hellenic communities of Magna Graecia. Their contact with other populations through colonization and trade (first in Italy and later in Hispania and probably in North Africa) planted the seed that allowed for the initial spread of *defixiones* through the Mediterranean provinces. The influence of Hellenic practices is clearly seen in the use of certain formulae,

---

[579] For Italy, cf. **40, 42–47, 87, 91, 93, 97–98, 112**; for Africa Proconsularis, see Hadrumetum (*AE* 1905, 171; Audollent 1908: 290–96 and *AE* 1968, 620), Carthage (*AE* 1907, 165 and *AE* 1933, 56) and Naro/Hammam-Lif (Audollent 1910: 137–41, Pl. XXVIII); for Hispania, cf. **148**; for the Galliae, cf. **150–56, 158, 161–62, 171** and **203**; for Britannia, cf. **207–09, 211–12, 216–32, 287–98, 317–35, 340, 344–45, 347–48, 350, 374–88, 440–41, 444–45, 450, 452** and **458**; for Germania, cf. **461**.

layout and even the contexts in which the tablets were deposited. In the Italian Peninsula, the Oscan population seems to be largely responsible for transmitting the habit of writing curses to the Romans.

In a next phase, it was the Romans who spread this originally Greek practice. Thus, during the High Empire, the use of curse tablets reached its zenith, both numerically and also in terms of geographical distribution. The diffusion of this cultural practice has been traditionally and logically associated with Roman conquest and the process of 'Romanization': as Roman legions arrived at new areas, they brought with them the practice of inscribing *defixiones* as part of their cultural baggage. Indeed, curses from this period have been found in the majority of provinces. This praxis was then adopted and adapted by provincial societies, as can be reflected in the onomastic aspects of the texts, the invocation of indigenous deities and even certain linguistic syncretisms.

That said, the boom in the production of curse tablets also coincides with a different process, that is, the 'Roman epigraphic habit'. This should hardly be seen as coincidental: the widespread use of *defixiones* also evidences the diffusion of writing more generally or at least a rudimentary knowledge thereof. Together with the spread of writing, there was also a spread in the basic knowledge of the technology of cursing, a magical-religious *savoir faire* that was probably, in many instances, transmitted by word of mouth. Such a technology was indeed very useful for attempting to solve all kinds of personal crises and misfortunes, above all for those who could not appeal to Roman authorities. In such instances, 'necessity created ability', as Hanson has put it (1991: 181).[580] But, at the same time as individual practitioners decided to manufacture their own curse tablets mostly in the north-western provinces of the empire, there were also professional practitioners offering their 'services' in cities such as Carthage or Hadrumetum, where the texts clearly betray Graeco-Egyptian techniques.

So far, the archaeological record signals a marked decline in the use of *defixiones* in Late Antiquity. Overall, curses have been found at a much smaller number of sites, both individually and in larger caches, which do point to sustained activity in certain areas, whether on an individual level (such as in the sanctuaries of Sulis Minerva in Aquae Sulis/Bath or Mercury in Uley), or through the contracting of professional practitioners (such as in the Fountain of Anna Perenna in Rome). Despite these limited sites where the practice seems to have been sustained, the overall evidence shows that the writing of *defixiones* waned during Late Antiquity: barely a sixth part of the known tablets can be dated to this period.

Finally, let us turn to geographical distribution. In Italy we see that the peninsula is rich in archaeological sites that have turned up *defixiones*. During the Republic, there was a dense network of sites in the southern portion of the peninsula, above all in settlements located by the sea which were in close contact with Greek colonies. In the High Empire, Rome emerged as the epicentre of a broader pattern of distribution of curse tablets that stretched from Concordia Sagittaria/Concordia all the way to Copia Thurii/Sybaris, with some examples attested also on Corsica and Sardinia. Turning to North Africa, the earliest known curse dates to the third century BCE. That said, it was not until the High Empire that the praxis truly blossomed, principally in the most important cities, Carthage and Hadrumetum, where several magical practitioners (both Latin and Greek speakers) offered their services. Moving to the north-west, we find a similar pattern in Hispania, though on a much smaller scale. The first known Latin tablets date to the Republic and come from two of the leading settlements of the time: Emporion and Corduba/Cordoba. During the High Empire, the practice continued not only in those communities, but also in Saguntum/Sagunto. The rest of the curse tablets have mostly been found in the southern half of Baetica.

Further north, it was not until the High Empire that the praxis of inscribing *defixiones* was adopted; as mentioned several times above, this process should be linked to the process of 'Romanization' and the arrival of the Roman army. In Gaul, for instance, the earliest curses date to the first century CE and are found mostly from Aquitania and Narbonensis (provinces that have turned up many isolated finds). The practice is attested here and there throughout the Late Empire, the cache from the amphitheatre in Trier (Gallia Belgica) being an outstanding example.

The first tablets to appear in Roman Britain date between the first and second centuries CE. By the end of the second and during the third century, the popularity of the practice increased exponentially. While the sanctuaries in Aquae Sulis/Bath and Uley do provide the bulk of the evidence, it is nevertheless true that curses tablets also hail from many other sites located in the South of the island, in conjunction with temples, urban centres and rural communities in civilian areas.[581] While acknowledging that the archaeological record is far from complete, we must work with the evidence that we do have. Within this framework, the sheer number of tablets discovered at the British sanctuaries dwarfs the caches that (so far) we have found at any other sanctuary or temple. Is difficult to explain how this technology became so popular for communicating with the gods, especially in such a personal manner. To this end and in contrast with other provinces (in which there are professional practitioners offering their 'services'), Britannia gives evidence of individual *scriptores*, a fact

---

[580] To buttress the idea that there was at least a fairly widespread level of basic literacy, we must remember that of the 130 tablets from Bath only 2 were written by the same hand (cf. **300–01**).

[581] On their distribution, see Mattingly 2004: 18–21. In general, see Tomlin 2002.

that demonstrates how this practice came to be embraced by local populations.[582]

In Germania, the bulk of the *defixiones* hail from Germania Superior. Indeed, the most prolific sites are Mogontiacum/ Mainz (with the sanctuary of Isis and Magna Mater) as well as nearby Cruciniacum/Bad Kreuznach. The curses from the Agri Decumates are also of great interest since they attest to the importance of the Roman army for the diffusion of this praxis. To date, all curses from Germania date to the High Empire. The same chronology applies to the curses from Raetia, Noricum and Pannonia, which have collectively offered 16 tablets scattered across the three *provinciae*.

To conclude, let us briefly return to the content of these curses. Even if most of the texts do not mention the reasons why they were written, when they do so, matters of justice (whether related to the courts or in response to a theft) are the most widely attested motivation for writing a curse tablet. That said, there is certainly a wide range of motivating factors: anything perceived as an injustice, a misfortune or a personal crisis could lead a practitioner to write or commission a *defixio*. Although for some scholars, this fact provides evidence for an ancient Mediterranean belief,[583] I think that this connection can be more broadly defined as part of the human condition: when faced with adversity, it is common to ask for divine intervention.

---

[582] The large number of individual authors is evident in the cache from Bath (cf. n. 580). For the existence of magical practitioners in North Africa and Rome (sanctuary of Anna Perenna), see section I.2 and nn. 39–41, with further references.

[583] As Tomlin has put it, 'the British texts… express a much older belief which is not western and localised, but is common to the Mediterranean world —the idea that we can ask the gods for justice' (2010: 247).